Indian Migrant Organizations

Indian Migrant Organizations

Engagement in Education
and Healthcare

Md Mizanur Rahman
and
Rakesh Ranjan

OXFORD
UNIVERSITY PRESS

OXFORD
UNIVERSITY PRESS

Oxford University Press is a department of the University of Oxford.
It furthers the University's objective of excellence in research, scholarship,
and education by publishing worldwide. Oxford is a registered trademark of
Oxford University Press in the UK and in certain other countries.

Published in India by
Oxford University Press
22 Workspace, 2nd Floor, 1/22 Asaf Ali Road, New Delhi 110 002, India

© Oxford University Press 2020

The moral rights of the authors have been asserted.

First Edition published in 2020

ISBN-13 (print edition): 978-0-19-012134-1
ISBN-10 (print edition): 0-19-012134-3

ISBN-13 (eBook): 978-0-19-099023-7
ISBN-10 (eBook): 0-19-099023-6

Typeset in Arno Pro 11/13.5
by Tranistics Data Technologies, Kolkata 700 091
Printed in India by Rakmo Press, New Delhi 110 020

To Ambassador Gopinath Pillai and Professor Tan Tai Yong;
two great Singaporeans who have been promoting South Asian
research and analysis globally.

Contents

Tables

Abbreviations

AAPIO	American Association of Physicians of Indian Origin
ABCD	AIDS, Blindness, Child-Mother Health, Deafness, Diabetes Screening and Education
AB-NHPM	Ayushman Bharat National Health Protection Mission
AFH	Asian Foundation for Help
AFMI	American Foundation of Muslims of Indian Origin
AIA	Association of Indians in America
AID	Association for India's Development
AIDS	Acquired Immune Deficiency Syndrome
AIF	American India Foundation
AMA	American Medical Association
APIRO	Association of Parents of Indians Resident Overseas
APXA	American Professional Exchange Association
ASEAN	Association of Southeast Asian Nations
ASER	Annual Status of Education Report
ATA	American Telugu Association
AWB	Agya Wanti Bhalla

BEd	Bachelor of Education
BAPS	Bochasanwasi Akshar Purushottam Swaminarayan Sanstha
BIOS	British Indian Orthopaedic Society
BSS	Bharat Sevashram Sangha
BTE	Behind the ear
CII	Confederation of Indian Industry
CISCE	Council for Indian School Certificate Examinations
CRY	Child Rights and You
CYC	Community Youth Collective
DBCT	Dream and Beauty Charitable Trust
DSW	Domestic Service Worker
ECNR	Emigration Check Not Required
ECR	Emigration Check Required
FBI	Federal Bureau of Investigation
FDI	Foreign Direct Investment
FICCI	Federation of Indian Chambers of Commerce and Industry
GAP	Gujarat AIDS Awareness and Prevention
GDP	Gross Domestic Product
GEMS	George Educational, Medical, and Charitable Society
GHWA	Global Health Workforce Alliance
GMAT	Graduate Management Admission Test
GOPIO	Global Organization of People of Indian Origin
GRE	Graduate Record Examinations
GREAT	Guru Ravidass Educational Assistance Trust
GSK	Gramin Shiksha Kendra
HDI	Human Development Index
HDR	Human Development Report
HEF	Himalayan Education Foundation
HIV	Human Immunodeficiency Virus
HOPE	Helping Organization for People, Environment
IAFPE	Indian American Forum for Political Education
IAHHA	Indo-US Academy of Health and Hospital Administration

IBEF	India Brand Equity Foundation
ICRIER	Indian Council for Research on International Economic Relations
ICSE	Indian Certificate of Secondary Education
ICWF	Indian Community Welfare Fund
IdEA	International Diaspora Engagement Alliance
IDF-OI	India Development Foundation of Overseas Indians
IDRF	India Development and Relief Fund
IDS	India Development Service
IMG	International Medical Graduates
IMRC	Indian Muslim Relief and Charity
IOM	International Organization for Migration
IOSUK	Indian Orthopaedic Society UK
IPCA	Indian Pollution Control Association
ISAS	Institute of South Asian Studies
IVC	International Village Clinic
JSS	Jan Swasthya Sahyog
JBVS	Jagriti Bal Vikas Samiti
KIP	Know India Programme
KOA	Kashmiri Overseas Association
KSA	Kingdom of Saudi Arabia
KZCT	Karnataka Zakat and Charitable Trust
LAMP	Learning and Migration Approach Programme
LCUK	Lohana Community of United Kingdom
MANSI	Maternal and Newborn Survival Initiative
MAMSS	Mahila Abhivrudhi Mattu Samrakshana Samasthe
MBBS	Bachelor of Medicine and Bachelor of Surgery
MCH	Maternal and Child Health
MERDS	Muthamizh Education and Rural Development Society
MGNREGA	Mahatma Gandhi National Rural Employment Guarantee Act
MIF	Mission India Foundation
MMR	Measles, Mumps, and Rubella
MOIA	Ministry of Overseas Indian Affairs

MOSPI	Ministry of Statistics and Programme Implementation
MoU	Memorandum of Understanding
MPI	Migration Policy Institute
MSMF	Manjari Sankurathri Memorial Foundation
NASA	National Aeronautics and Space Administration
NATS	North American Telugu Society
NAVAM	Nav Maharashtra Community Foundation
NCAI	National Congress of American Indians
NDA	National Democratic Alliance
NEET	National Eligibility Entrance Test
NGF	Next Generation Foundation
NGO	Non-Governmental Organisation
NHM	National Health Mission
NIRC	National Integrity and Responsibility Complex
NRB	Non-Resident Bihari
NREGA	National Rural Employment Guarantee Act
NRHM	National Rural Health Mission
NRI	Non-Resident Indians
NRIPA	NRI Parents Association
NUHM	National Urban Health Mission
NUS	National University of Singapore
OCI	Overseas Citizens of India
OIFC	Overseas Indian Facilitation Centre
OTC	One-teacher school
PAPN	Peoples Action for People in Need
PBBY	Pravasi Bharatiya Bima Yojana
PBD	Pravasi Bhartiya Divas
PBK	Pravasi Bhartiya Kendra
PGE	Protector-General of Emigrants
PGIMER	Postgraduate Institute of Medical Education and Research
PIO	Persons of Indian Origin
POE	Protector of Emigrants
PUKAR	Partners for Urban Knowledge, Action and Research
PVRI	Pushpagiri Vitreo Retina Institute

R&D	Research and Development
RANA	Rajasthan Association of North America
RSBY	Rashtriya Swasthya Bima Yojna
RTA	Renal Tubular Acidosis
SATHI	Support for Advocacy and Training to Health Initiatives
SBT	Salaam Baalak Trust
SEA	Society for Education and Action
SEARCH	Society for Education, Action and Research in Community Health
SEC	Society for Education of the Crippled
SFRS	Society for Rural Scholars
SPDC	Scholarship Programme for Diaspora Children
STEM	Science, Technology, Engineering, and Maths
TANA	Telugu Association of North America
TB	Tuberculosis
TCF	Toronto–Calcutta Foundation
TiE	The Indus Entrepreneurs
TOEFL	Test of English as a Foreign Language
UAE	United Arab Emirates
UNDP	United Nations Development Programme
UNICEF	United Nations Children's Fund
UPA	United Progressive Alliance
VHAT	Voluntary Health Association of Tripura
WHO	World Health Organization

Preface

The idea for this book developed during a meeting with Tan Tai Yong and Ambassador Gopinath Pillai at the Institute of South Asian Studies (ISAS), National University of Singapore (NUS) in 2012. These two great Singaporeans made an important observation about the development potential of the global South Asian diaspora, which is over 50 million strong and continues to grow. Ambassador Gopinath Pillai discussed how the South Asian diaspora population has been increasingly influential on the global stage, and is capable of shaping the development landscape of South Asia. Ambassador Pillai envisioned the importance of the South Asian diaspora as a social and economic force which could bring about changes in South Asia, and decided to focus on the global South Asian diaspora as a research theme of the ISAS in 2012. To conduct academic research at the newly formed South Asian Diaspora Cluster at the ISAS, Tan and Mizanur Rahman secured an NUS-funded research project on Diaspora and Development in South Asia in 2013. This book stems from the research conducted under this rubric. We are deeply indebted to Tan for his research interest in South Asia, and his academic support in securing the research grant for South Asian diaspora research and analysis.

We would like to acknowledge the institutional support that Qatar University provided during the preparation of this manuscript. We are particularly indebted to Mahjoob Zweiri, Afyare Abdi Elmi, Hela Miniaoui, Farhan Mujahid Chak, Luciano Zaccara, and Nikolay Kozhanov of Gulf Studies, Qatar University. We are also thankful to Ahmed Ibrahim Abushouk and Bakeel Al-Zandani for their encouragement and moral support.

Several friends, colleagues, and mentors continued to push, encourage, and teach us, in our conversations. A.K.M. Ahsan Ullah, Nicola Piper, Thomas Faist, Chilamkuri Raja Mohan, Iftekhar Ahmed Chowdhury, Binod Khadria, Lian Kwen Fee, Tong Chee Kiong, Habibul Haque Khondker, James V. Jesudason, Brenda Yeoh, Rahul Mukherji, and Khurshed Alam in particular have always inspired us to maintain our work on this book as a priority. It will be unfair not to mention some other friends and colleagues such as Niaz Ahmed Khan, Thakur Subedi, Ishtiaq Hossain, Mallik Akram Hossain, Shahjahan Bhuiyan, Sadananda Sahoo, Gurram Srinivas, Sarmin Luna, Jolin Joseph, and Hasan Mahmud and we are very thankful to them.

We thank our publishers at Oxford University Press for being patient with us. We are also grateful to the OUP publication team for the quality check and final tidy-up.

We are also deeply indebted to two anonymous reviewers who provided detailed suggestions and comments to improve the quality of this book. Benedict Young, a UK-based copyeditor, helped edit the manuscript for final publication. We are thankful to Ben for his service.

On a personal note, Mizanur Rahman would like to remember his parents for allowing him to travel to deep into India when he was a tenth-grade student at a school at Bagerhat, Bangladesh. This visit to India had a long-lasting impact on his educational and spiritual life. He would like to thank his professors from Aligarh Muslim University—Abdul Waheed, Abdul Matin, S. Zainuddin, Noor Mohammad, Mohammad Jamal Siddiqui, and S.B. Ahmad—for providing unreserved support and nurturing his intellectual curiosity. He was offered his first Indian tourist visa when His Excellency I.S. Chadha was the High Commissioner of India to Bangladesh (1985–9). He was offered a student visa to study in India when His Excellency K. Srinivasan was High Commissioner of India to Bangladesh (1989–92). He would like to thank these two for giving him an opportunity to see and feel the Mother India.

Surviving such an extended research experience would have been impossible without the support of our family. First of all, Mizanur Rahman is indebted to his father, Abdul Hamid Talukder and mother, Monoara Hamid. He is deeply indebted to his spouse, Zabun Naher: all that he has accomplished he owes to her. His children, Manha Afrah, Manha Aferdita, and Ahyan Zelman, have been a source of sustained inspiration for him. As a father, he has not been able to give them adequate time; he has missed out on a great deal of fun and games, and he hopes to make up for this in full!

Rakesh Ranjan would like to thank his institute, the Centre for Development Practice and Research, Tata Institute of Social Sciences, for institutional support in the research process. Special thanks go to Pushpendra Kumar Singh, Chairperson of the Centre, for his support and encouragement in the research process, and for providing him with an enabling work environment.

He would also like to express his sincere thanks to his PhD supervisor Gurram Srinivas for his continuous support and research training. He also offers sincere thanks to Sadananda Sahoo, Indira Gandhi National Open University, for cultivating his interest in migration and diaspora studies.

On a personal note, Rakesh Ranjan acknowledges that he could not possibly have progressed in his academic life without the unconditional support of his family. First, he would like to thank his parents, R.C.L. Das and Kamini Das. They invested in him all their emotions and earnings, as well as hopes for his better future. He also thanks his brothers Romesh Ranjan and Rajesh Ranjan, and sister Krishna Das. Last but not the least, he extends wholehearted thanks to his lovely wife Monika Bisht, his soulmate who always stood with him at crucial times. She has been a great source of positive energy in his life.

Migrant Organizations, Engagement, and Development

In terms of sheer size and global spread, the Indian overseas community is one of the most significant migrant groups in the world today, comparable in scale only to the Chinese diaspora. Given the extent and nature of Indian migration, and the complex way it has evolved over time, it is almost impossible to give a precise number for Indians overseas, and the individual growth dynamics of the Indian communities that takes root in other countries adds a further order of difficulty in determining the figure; yet based on a range of studies, it seems fair to say that the total Indian migrant population overseas is between 35 million and 40 million (Brown 2006; Burki 2015; Jain 2007; Kadekar, Sahoo, and Bhattacharya 2009; Khadria 2000, 2010; Koshy and Radhakrishnan 2008; Lal, Reeves, and Rai 2007; Rai and Reeves 2009). It is not its sheer size that makes the Indian migrant population distinctive, however, the Indian migrant population stands out among the many other emigrant countries due to the fact that a sizeable fraction lives permanently in the West, comprising skilled professionals who tend to be highly mobile and resourceful. All across the West, Indian migrants are to be found imbricated into the most elite institutions of their countries of settlement.

xxii   Indian Migrant Organizations

Realizing that the resources of its migrants can offer substantial benefits at home, India has made notable efforts to reach out to its emigrant population overseas. Policy measures have been undertaken to facilitate the movement of Indians internationally, to protect and promote their rights overseas, to organize events at home and in host countries, seeking out the well-off sections of emigrant population, and offering legal rights and privileges through the introduction of the Persons of Indian Origin (PIO), Non-Resident Indians (NRI), and Overseas Citizens of India (OCI) schemes. The Indian government also offers various tax incentives for emigrants, and endeavours to use their expertise, advice, and ideas to create opportunities for overseas Indian companies. A ministry for overseas Indians—the Ministry of Overseas Indian Affairs (MOIA)—was established in 2004 but was later, in 2016, merged with the Ministry of External Affairs as the Overseas Indian Division I and II—purely to look after and engage with Indian migrants abroad. These deliberate and sustained efforts to engage with the Indian emigrant population overseas, and to tap into their resources to stimulate development in India itself, set the context for the present research.

The Indian migrant population forms multiple patterns, which for analytical purposes we may divide roughly in terms of two classes of activity: individual-level and collective-level activities. On the individual level, migrants send remittances to their relatives, sometimes engage in business and politics, and transfer their skills and technical know-how to India. Much has been written on the remittances sent back to relatives in the country of origin (for a review, see Rahman, Tan, and Ullah 2014). Drawing on the category of individual activities, the impact of migration on families has also been widely reported by Chowdhury and Rajan (2018) and Rajan (2013, 2016) in their Kerala study. For instance, Zachariah, Mathew, and Rajan report that migration has resulted in nearly a million married women in Kerala with their husbands living away (Zachariah, Mathew, and Rajan 2001; Zachariah, Rajan, and Jolin 2014). They observe that the wives of emigrants thus gain autonomy, status, management skills, and experience in dealing with the world outside of their homes; these new capabilities, developed the 'hard way', remain with them for the rest of their lives, benefiting their families and society at large. The transformation of these women thus promises to contribute to the development of Keralite society in the long term[1] (Zachariah, Mathew, and Rajan 2001).

The focus of this book, however, rests not on the level of the individual or family, but rather on the collective. The Indian overseas population has formed a panoply of migrant organizations, whose activities include supporting social, economic, and political integration in the host societies, and arranging funding for certain individual and community purposes. And, these organizations not only assist migrants in the host country, but also provide material support to the communities in India—what is known as transnational Indian migrant organizations.[2] Often inspired and motivated by the spirit of 'paying back' to the motherland, Indian migrants have come together—within different social, cultural, regional, and professional organizations— to maintain solid transnational ties with India. These transnational migrant organizations are diverse in nature, and engage in a wide range of activities targeting different sectors of the economy of the origin country. This organized engagement has brought about remarkable changes in different sectors of the 'motherland' economy, including information technology (Chacko 2007; Chanda 2008; Hunger 2004; Kapur 2002; Khadria 2003, 2004; Tejada et al. 2014), trade (Karayil 2007; Levi 2002), tourism (Hannan 2004), and health (Levitt and Rajaram 2013; Roberts 2009).

Collective engagement thus constitutes an important area of research where the Indian migrant population in concerned. Research on migrant organizations tends to centre on the role of migrant organizations in host countries, yet migrant organizations exist also in the countries of origin as we have found in India, where they are formed and run by current or former migrants in collaboration with close family members,

---

[1] It is important to note that psychological separation, depression, lack of parenting, extramarital alliances, suicide, and so on are some side effects that erode the notion of development as well (for an overview, see Rahman, Tan, and Ullah 2014: 1–28).

[2] Organizations that are oriented toward the country of origin as well as the host country are specifically referred to as 'transnational' organizations (Akcapar 2009; Dumont 2008; Faist 2008; Portes et al. 2008; Zhou and Lee 2012).

and engage in various development initiatives. Perhaps reflecting the provenance of researchers themselves, the literature has had an undue focus on migrant organizations centred on the host countries; in search of a counterbalance. The present book also reports on migrant organizations established and run by current or former migrants in the origin country which are dedicated to serving the underprivileged sections of their own societies. Such migrant organizations generally address specific development goals, drawing upon resources and connections in both home and host countries to do so. The book thus looks at both types of organizations—local and transnational—and studies their engagement in development initiatives in India. Although an almost total absence of statistics makes it impossible to give an exact figure for the number of transnational Indian migration organizations, it is clear that sizeable numbers of such organizations are to be found in most major destination countries in the West, and that Indian migrants in many non-Western countries have also formed various types of migrant organizations.

Given the wide range of development areas in which migrant organizations are active, our focus of interest has been narrowed down on specifics. This book thus examines the engagement of Indian organizations in the education and healthcare sectors in India as well as explores selected transnational organizations in the West with a focus on the US, the UK, and Canada. It investigates what kinds of projects and activities such associations carry out, how associational initiatives are received and supported, and finally what bearing these associational engagements have on the development of educational and healthcare sectors in India.

The book, thus, stands within a rather new tradition in immigration studies, one which shifts the focus from questions concerning how immigrant groups adapt to their countries of settlement, to the ways in which immigrant communities engage with origin countries and contribute to these countries economically and socially through collective efforts. The focus of investigation lies at the intersection of three research areas: (a) migrant organizations in the origin country and in the countries of settlement; (b) engagement with the country of origin; and (c) developmental implications of such engagements on the origin country. A wide range of studies have been carried out from these three perspectives individually (for example, see Espinosa 2016; Johnson 2007; Kapur 2010; Merz, Chen, and Geithner 2007; Ketkar and Ratha 2010; Newland 2010; Newland and Tanaka 2010; Sahoo and Pattanaik 2014; Sidel 2007; Terrazas 2010a, 2010b), but not much research has been done in this particular intersection—migrant organization, engagement, and development—especially in the context of Indian organizations.

Our research concerns local and transnational migrant organizations of India which are engaged in healthcare and education, these two fields being selected because the needs of the healthcare and education sectors of India has remained largely unmet, despite noticeable developments in other sectors, and when it comes to collective initiatives it is these two areas that draw the main attention. We identified selected migrant organizations based in India and host countries and investigated how they have evolved, what kind of healthcare and educational projects and activities they are carrying out, and how such collective efforts are enabling change in the Indian healthcare and educational sectors. Despite the significant contributions of migrant collectives to the education and healthcare sectors, the literature has made little effort to determine the extent and level of engagement of migrant organizations and their contributions to these two sectors in India. This book attempts to narrow this gap in existing knowledge. In the following sections, the chapter reviews the state of knowledge about migrant organizations in general, and sets out in general terms how this research will approach them. The chapter goes on to review the history of Indian emigration and settlement, and closes by providing the overall research methods for this study.

The Emergence of Migrant Organizations

Immigrants have created organizations of many different forms in all their countries of settlement and throughout history (Fauser 2012; Halm and Sezgin 2013; Moya 2005; Park and Miller 1969 [1921]; Pries and Sezgin 2012b; Rex, Joly, and Wilpert 1987). Migrant organizations in the countries of settlement include professional organizations, nationalistic political associations, hometown associations, cultural societies, advocacy groups, mutual aid and benefit societies, trade unions, human rights groups, and religious organizations (Lacroix 2012; Moya 2005). Such organizations exist in great numbers—it has been found, for example, that there are over 3,000 Mexican migrant organizations in the US (Fitzgerald 2008). The growing presence of such organizations is a visible sign of the active engagement of migrants to improve their situation in the host country as well as to contribute to their country of origin.

Of these, many are transnational in nature, often raising funds from the diaspora in the host countries to undertake development projects in targeted sectors, communities, and regions of the origin countries. Their financial contributions are generally charitable donations that often support investments in local needs. In her study on transnational migrant organizations, Goldring (2004) reports some common themes among the development projects supported by migrants: (a) basic infrastructure and communication projects such as roads and bridges, and potable water, telephone, and internet cafes; (b) public service infrastructure and capitalization related to education, health, or social security; (c) recreation and other major status-related projects, such as sports fields; and (d) other community projects such as halls, public spaces, benches, and the preservation of cultural heritage and churches. Such functions vary according to the composition of the immigrant groups, the region of origin of the migrants, nature of the destination country (especially whether liberal or conservative), availability of resources, and the character of the transnational migrant organization itself.

Although such collective efforts have always existed among immi-grant groups, they are today intensifying and becoming more institu-tionalized, with the number of migrant organizations clearly on the rise. These migrant organizations constitute a growing sector of non-state actors, which has recently been shown to have significance for devel-opment in the origin countries (Faist 2008). They play a crucial role for individual migrants as well as for the immigrant community, by engaging with origin countries and contributing to development efforts in these countries in a sustained and meaningful way (Faist, Fauser, and Reisenauer 2013; Pirkkalainen, Mezzetti, and Guglielmo 2013; Portes et al. 2007; Portes and Zhou 2011; Pries and Sezgin 2012). Such transnational migrant organizations are an essentially grassroots and philanthropic phenomenon, and they build on ties and networks that connect them with their origin countries.

Immigrant organizations can be broadly seen as formal organizations which share the basic characteristics of the non-profit sector—being formal, private, non-profit-distributing, self-governing, and voluntary (Salamon and Anheier 1992). The organizations that concern us, then, are fundamentally non-profit organizations founded by immigrants themselves, with the purpose of serving the needs and interests of immigrants, and form part of the broader category of voluntary organizations.

Numerous theories have been put forward to explain the reasons for the emergence of such organizations.[3] Theories that look for macro-level explanations make reference to the migrants' need to counter phenomena such as market failure (Salamon 1995), or governmental failure (Weisbrod 1988); whereas explanations in terms of civil society (Putnam 1995) and interdependence theory (Salamon 1987) focus their analysis on society as a system. On the other hand, micro-level theories focus their analysis on individual needs and attitudes and make reference to such qualities as altruism (Rose-Ackerman 1997), voluntarism (Wilson 2000), and philanthropy (Schervish 2005) among the migrants themselves. Although these theories contribute to a broader understanding of the general phenomenon of voluntary organizations, they can be also applied to the subcategory of immigrant organizations.

Different scholars have given different categorizations of immigrant organizations. For instance, based on the range of their activities, Basch (1987) offers a ninefold categorization of migrant organizations: benevolent societies, sport and social clubs, welfare organizations, occupational associations, educational and cultural clubs, political clubs, performing cultural clubs, women's groups, and umbrella organizations. Moya (2005) distinguishes six types of organizations: secret societies, rotating credit associations, mutual aid societies, religious organizations, hometown associations, and political groups. Meanwhile, based on the orientation of immigrant organizations, Layton-Henry (1990) offers a threefold typology: organizations oriented toward the country of origin, organizations oriented toward the host country, and organizations oriented toward the country of origin as well as the host country, or the transnational organizations. This study considers the majority of Indian immigrant organizations to be transnational in character.

---

[3] For a review, see Babis 2016.

Local migrant organizations tend to be diverse in terms of formation and resource mobilization strategy, but have a common specific character in terms of needs, plans, and programmes. The engagement of such migrant organizations in the development process in the origin country is particularly important because such organizations can identify local needs and engage directly in order to make a difference in the areas of their interests and expertise. This is an emerging phenomenon—local migrant organizations and transnational migrant organizations emerging to serve the people in the origin country—but one that is scarcely looked in the literature. This book investigates the engagements of Indian migrant organizations in the health and education sector in India with respect to a number of questions: Why do migrant organizations form to work for the benefit of the origin country? How do they mobilize their resources? In what areas of the origin country do they usually engage? What implications does such engagement have for the sectors such as healthcare and education? This study attempts to provide a holistic understanding of the collective engagements of migrant organizations in the Indian context.

While the migration–development nexus has been addressed in many earlier studies, this book promises to add a new dimension to our knowledge by elaborating upon the migrant organization as a third actor, individual migrants and the migrant family being the other two actors (for details, see Zhou and Lee 2012) and illuminating the nexus from both within the migrant organizations themselves and across the jurisdictions in which they operate. Developing the organizational perspective upon the migration and development nexus promises to help us better understand the opportunities that migrant communities present for origin countries in today's increasingly interconnected world.

Approaching Migrant Organizations and Development

Studies on migrant organizations are usually organized according to three chronological periods:[4] In the first period, considered to begin after the Second World War, research on migrant organizations largely centred on the effects on assimilation and integration processes in host

---

[4]   For details, see Halm and Sezgin 2013: 1–15.

countries. It was believed in this period that successful integration into the country of settlement and interest in the country of origin were inversely related (Diehl and Schnell 2006). In the second period, beginning in the 1990s, research concentrated largely on the role of migrant organizations in terms of their political claims, social movements, and civic participation in relation to the host country. In the third period (year 2000 onwards), new studies began to emerge that focused on the transnational aims, activities, functions, motivations, and structures of the migrant organizations.[5] It is in this third period that increasing attention has been paid to the role of migrant organizations in the development process in origin countries.

Zeynep Sezgin and Dennis Dijkzeul (2014: 161–6) categorize existing research on migrant organizations into four major types: (a) migrant organizations in *migration research*; (b) migrant organizations in *humanitarian studies*; (c) migrant organizations in *organizational research*; and (d) migrant organizations in *development studies*. Each of these categories are discussed hereunder:

(i)   Migration studies tend to address the role of migrant organizations for host and home countries and for migrant communities within four research clusters: (a) effects of migrant organizations on the integration process; (b) the role of migrant organizations in the civic and political participation of migrants; (c) the emergence and development of migrant organizations; and (d) the embeddedness of migrant organizations in binational, supranational (for example, European Union), and global contexts in the West (for example, the promotion of human rights) (Halz and Sezgin 2012; Johnston 2009; Landolt and Goldring 2010; Pries and Sezgin 2012b; Sezgin 2008; Vermeulen 2007).

(ii) Interest in migrant organizations within humanitarian studies has grown rapidly. Studies have reported several types of humanitarian activities such as political, developmental, 'new donor', privatized, religious, and migrant humanitarianism (Avant 2005; Beneditti 2006; Collier 2003; Seybolt 2007; Stoddard 2002).

---

[5] For example, Bakewell 2008; Mercer, Page, and Evans 2009; Østergaard-Nielsen 2003; Portes et al. 2007; Pries and Sezgin 2010; Sökefeld 2008.

(iii)   Organizational research proposes four types of cross-border organizations: local, global, multinational, and transnational. They
propose a specific conception of transnational organizations with
decentralized distribution of their goals, resources, and internal
and external activities.[6]

(iv)   Studies of migrant organizations within development studies tend
to concentrate on the migration–development nexus, and especially the role of migrant organizations in attracting and channel-
ling remittances. American research on hometown associations
deals mainly with remittances (Levitt and Lamba-Nieves 2011;
Portes et al. 2007), while European research also dwells on the
important contributions that migrant organizations make to their
countries of origin (Galatowitsch 2009; Mercer, Page, and Evans
2009). However, as discussed earlier, the role of migrant organizations goes beyond remittances, engaging with broader aspects of
the origin country such as education and health sector. They set
goals, mobilize resources for the stated goals, and finally engage in
development activities directly.

Before we move on to discuss the relationship between migrant
organizations and development, we first need to clarify the term
'engagement'. Broadly speaking, the term is used to refer to various
transnational activities targeting home countries (Gamlen 2011:
267–8), and it was first widely used in migration studies by scholars and
policymakers associated with the US-based Migration Policy Institute
(MPI) in Washington, DC, and migration-focused international organizations such as the International Organization for Migration (IOM)
(Johnson 2007; Kapur 2010, Merz, Chen, and Geithner 2007; Newland
2010; Newland and Tanaka 2010; Terrazas 2010a). It is implicit in
any reference to the migration–development nexus that immigrants
and other related actors (for example, diasporas, their organizations,
migration-focused international organizations or agencies) in the destination country engage with origin countries in myriad ways, and that
the engagement of these actors is expected to stimulate development
in the originating state (Tan and Rahman 2013). But the engagement

---

[6]   For details, see Sezgin and Dijkzeul 2014: 166.

of migrants is not limited to any particular manner in which migrants, their organizations, or any international organization run on behalf of or by immigrants engage with the origin country (Johnson 2007; Kapur 2010; Ketkar and Ratha 2010; Merz, Chen, and Geithner 2007; Newland 2010; Newland and Tanaka 2010; Sidel 2007; Terrazas 2010a, 2010b). The International Diaspora Engagement Alliance (IdEA) promotes five core modes of engagement between immigrants and their country of origin around the world: volunteerism, entrepreneurship, philanthropy, social innovation, and diplomacy (Newland 2010; Newland and Tanaka 2010; Newland, Terrazas, and Munster 2010). Clearly, any form of such engagement by immigrants has the potential to advance growth and development in the origin country (Tan and Rahman 2003). However, the diaspora engagement literature still tends to focus mainly on migrants and diaspora engagements; it has not yet adequately looked closely at the engagement of immigrant organizations within the origin country itself.

Does Migration Bring About Development?

Since the 1950s, a key question that has concerned migration researchers is whether international migration actually does bring about development in the emigrant countries in the Global South. Although substantial literature has been produced on the topic, researchers have struggled to find a unanimous position on this question. This is because migration is a dynamic field: the patterns, composition, size, and nature of international migration change over time, often transmuting into a more intricate form by the time the earlier theoretical approaches and methods are about to bear fruit. What is interesting about the study of this nexus is that with the changes in international migration, new theoretical approaches and research methodologies have also been applied to explain the nature of the relationship between migration and development (Faist 2008). Thus, the study of the nexus remains a field of ongoing academic effort.

An earlier volume edited by Tan Tai Yong and Md Mizanur Rahman, elaborated the nexus between migration and development (Rahman and Tan 2015: 3–9), and the account presented therein is worth being referred to briefly. The relationship between migration and development has traditionally been explained from two contrasting theoretical approaches, formulated as early as the 1960s—the balanced growth approach and the asymmetrical growth approach (Fischer et al. 1997, Hermele 1997; Papademetriou and Martin 1991). Thomas Faist and his colleagues identified three phases of thinking on the migration–development nexus—(a) migration and development (the 1950s and the 1960s); (b) underdevelopment and migration (the 1970s and the 1980s); and (c) migration and (co)development (since the 1990s)—and explained how they have enriched our understanding (Faist and Fauser 2011: 2–11; Faist, Fauser, and Reisenauer 2013).

In the first phase, our understanding is dominated by the positive argument that migration has a positive impact on the sending society through remittances and return migration. The second phase is dominated by the argument that migration leads to underdevelopment in the periphery (developing countries/regions) due to the migration of both low-skilled and high-skilled professional individuals to the core countries. In the third phase, a more optimistic view emerges about the nexus between migration and development, in which the migrant is identified as the development agent par excellence and becomes seen as a key element in development cooperation (Faist and Fauser 2011: 7). New concepts emerged in this phase to formulate the benefits that developing countries derived from migration, such as 'return of human capital', 'brain gain', 'brain circulation', and 'reverse brain drain' (Boeri et al. 2012; Khadria 1999; Saxenian 2005; Zweig 2006).

Scholars, who are ardent advocates of transnationalism and a transnational approach to migration and development research, stress that migration is not a one-off process, but often entails repeated movements and continued transactions between migrants and non-migrants in the host and origin countries (Faist, Fauser, and Reisenauer 2013; Portes and Zhou 2011; Pries and Sezgin 2012b; Rex, Joly, and Wilpert 1987; Zhou and Lee 2012,). There is an almost unanimous view among migration scholars that the migration–development nexus should be approached from a transnational perspective which recognizes the emergence of new transnational agents in development discourse. These agents include transnational migrants and their extended kinship groups, migrant organizations, and the various national and international agencies (Faist, Fauser, and Reisenauer 2013; Khadria 2010).

Besides this, there is also a consensus that research needs to shed light on how these agents maintain their cross-border ties and activities, and what impacts do they have on the countries involved. There is a widespread acceptance of the idea of migration and (co)development, which Thomas Faist and Margit Fauser (2011: 7) called the 'celebration of transnational circulation'.

In line with this global thinking, this volume argues that the current enthusiasm about the migration–development nexus needs to adopt a transnational perspective that recognizes the emergence of new agents (such as the migrant organization) in the development discourse. Such migrant organizations are evident signs of the existence of transnational communities tying migrants and non-migrants across transnational social spaces. As we have already noted, immigrant organizations formed to provide specific services to the community members in the host country have long been a domain of considerable interest (Hooghe 2005; Ireland 1994; Kortmann and Rosenow-Williams 2013; Koopmans et al. 2005; Koopmans and Statham 2000; Pries and Sezgin 2012a; Rex and Moore 1967; Rex, Joly and Wilpert 1987; Schrover and Vermeulen 2005). By contrast, immigrant organizations that reach out to the people of the origin country are relatively new, yet their contributions are significant.

Research Perspective

This book proposes two methodological innovations which shape its research perspective: the unit of analysis and the dimension of development. Scanning through the literature on migration and development, one finds abundant literature on the impact of migration and the resultant remittances on local and regional economies in the origin country. The unit of analysis for such studies has usually been the individual migrant and/or the family. From the perspective of classical economics, the individual migrant is seen as the central decision-maker; whereas from the perspective of sociology and the 'new economics' of migration, it is the family which is identified as the real determinant of the decision to engage in migration (Stark 1991).

A burgeoning literature on the topic of immigrant transnationalism over recent decades has highlighted the growing contacts between immigrant communities and their origin countries, and case studies have proliferated on the diverse forms that these cross-border activities take (Portes and Zhou 2011). Yet Min Zhou and Rennie Lee (2012) argue that the exclusive emphasis on the individual and families has overlooked a third important actor—the *organization*. Concurring with them, in the present work we focus on transnational *collective engagement*, through case studies of migrant organizations formed and run by Indian migrants and the diaspora members overseas, rather than highlighting individuals' engagement or contribution to their own family members or their extended families (especially for the Indian joint family). Transnational collective engagement is often undertaken for public interest (community development projects) and is considered a powerful agent for social change or social transformation (Faist 2008). Introducing the migrant organization as the unit of analysis, we add a new dimension to the analysis of the migration—development nexus.

There is a growing belief that by developing the organizational perspective in migration studies in general, and the migration and development debate in particular, we can better cope with the challenges that the field experiences today (Pries 2008a). Migrant organizations constitute a meso-level unit of analysis, falling between micro-level research topics such as everyday life, identity, migrant families, and mobility on the one hand, and macro-level units such as regional migration systems, governance, and societal institutions on the other. In organizational studies we can identify different types of organizations based on the structure of their resource distribution and coordination mechanisms (Pries 2008b: 15–19). For instance, organizations with internationally decentralized resources and weak coordination features are usually referred to as 'multinational organizations'; organizations with centralized resources and strong coordination are generally referred to as 'global organizations'; and organizations with centralized resources and weak coordination patterns are frequently called 'international or focal organizations' (Pries 2008b: 15–16). Borrowing from Pries's conceptualization of transnational organizations, migrant organizations could be understood as transnationally active non-profit organizations with more or less decentralized resource structures and, at the same time, strong and effective coordination patterns.

In the study of migrant organizations, one of the most relevant issues is factors that influence the founding and sustaining of organizations and how these, in turn, influence functions. The questions of how and why migrant organizations originate, and how they manage to survive and to change over time, remain at the centre of organization studies. During the 1980s it was observed that no single theory has satisfactorily explained what conditions encourage the founding of immigrant organizations or what factors support or inhibit their continued existence (Olzak and West 1991: 459), and this observation is still valid although research on this point has progressed (Schrover and Vermeulen 2005: 825). As early as the 1960s, Breton suggested that three sets of factors stimulate the formation of immigrant or ethic organizations: cultural differences with the native population, the level of resources among the members of the immigrant group, and the pattern of migration (Breton 1964: 204). With the subsequent changes in composition, nature, and extent of immigration to the West, broader factors have been identified to better capture the growth of ethnic organizations. For instance, Schrover and Vermeulen suggest three factors that determine their growth: the migration process, the opportunity structure, and the characteristics of the immigrant community (Fauser 2012; Ireland 1994; Laubenthal 2007; Schrover and Vermeulen 2005: 825–6). These are more or less similar to Breton's threefold classification of cultural differences, level of resources, and pattern of migration.

The growth of immigrant organizations must be considered with an eye to the broader social, economic, and political context. Immigrant organizations form and mature under a favourable opportunity structure. Governments' attitudes toward immigrants and their organizations shape the opportunities that immigrants have for setting up organizations in a given society. Governments of receiving countries may forbid, condone, or stimulate immigrant organizations or their activities. The opportunity model predicts that the formation of organizations depends on the structure of political institutions and the configuration of political power in a given society (Schrover and Vermeulen 2005). The nature of government policies towards immigrant organizations thus shapes their formation and activities. The degree of support for immigrant organizations is also strongly related to the legal, social, and economic position of the immigrants in the host country.

Along with opportunity structure, group characteristics also play a critical role in the formation and continuation of immigrant organizations in a given society. The degree to which immigrant members identify with their immigrant group increases as the percentage of the population belonging to this immigrant group increases (Hechter 1978). However, large immigrant populations do not necessarily have many organizations (Schrover and Vermeulen 2005), although there is a propensity for more organizations when there are large immigrant populations scattered around different cities or states within a given country, especially large countries such as the US and Canada. A critical number of immigrants is needed to set up an organization. The character of immigrant organizations is determined by many factors related to the demographic and socioeconomic profile of the immigrant group: regional background, motivation, age, sex ratio, occupational structure, education, professional background, residential propinquity, political exposure, and so on. However, the reasons for the formation of immigration organizations for local causes in a given society may be expected to be different from those organizations that are formed to serve principally the country of origin. We focus on characteristics of migrant organizations, membership, and leaders, to shed light on the group characteristics in Chapter 2.

The second methodological innovation addressed in this book concerns the dimension of development. The notion of development employed in this book carries multiple meanings, corresponding to its socioeconomic, political, and human dimensions (Piper 2009). This book intends to go beyond the conventional economic conception of development by adding a broader institutional dimension to the debate on issues such as healthcare and education. To see this, we may take the common example of remittance payments. Migrant remittances occupy a central position in the debate on the relationship between migration and development. The spectacular rise of migrant remittances, which has recently crossed USD 400 billion mark, is often analysed and presented as hard evidence to either support or challenge the beneficial nature of the migration–development nexus. For India, the official estimate on remittance flows, including both private and collective remittances, was USD 78.5 billion in 2018 (World Bank 2019). India topped the list of remittance-receiving countries in 2019, surpassing the largest emigrant country in the world, China. The regional distribution of remittances in India is also very interesting, with Kerala, Punjab, and Goa accounting for over 40 per cent, putting them among the top remittance-dependent economies of the world (Kulkarni 2014: 199).

Yet many immigrants, especially immigrants who are settled in developed countries, want to contribute to their origin countries in a way that goes beyond financial remittances. They are often resourceful, concerned about the socioeconomic conditions of their countries of origin, and willing to make positive changes. They, therefore, organize to engage in transnational development activities within various associations and contribute to the particular sector of the economy which they deem appropriate, such as education, healthcare, transport and communication, or information technology. This may be in the form of technical know-how, medical equipment, contributions to building educational institutions, healthcare centres, or hospitals, launching exchange programmes linking educational and healthcare institutions in host countries with those of origin countries, endowing scholarships and awards, and so on. Such engagements by migrant organizations have a positive bearing on *institutions* as well as the *people* in the origin society. It is essential, then, to bear in mind the institutional benefits that may accrue from development initiatives, even where these are not directly manifest in well-being of individuals: the institutional development of today, provided conditions are favourable, should translate into the human well-being of tomorrow.

In the next section, we take a step back to review the history of Indian migration and the government's efforts to support it.

The Institutional Context of Migrant Engagement in India

Indians have a long history of emigration and settlement. The movement of migrants can be broadly differentiated into three phases: precolonial, colonial, and postcolonial. During the precolonial period, the movement of Indians overseas was mostly voluntary and took the form of traders (Levi 2002). During the colonial period, migration on a mass scale was largely directed towards plantation countries, governed by various contract systems (Sandhu 1969). Postcolonial migration was primarily towards highly developed economies, and comprised skilled workers including labour migration to gulf countries (Khadria 2006). Indian policies towards its overseas immigrant communities can be largely divided into two categories—the pre-1990s policies and the post-1990s policies (Abraham 2014).

The pre-1990s policies of the Indian Government towards Indians settled abroad were less than warm. After the independence, under the premiership of Jawaharlal Nehru, there were debates about the return of overseas Indians; on a number of occasions Nehru deprecated the argument for return and described overseas Indians as non-Indians, or used the term 'people of Indian descent' (Abraham 2014). This attitude was stark during the 1972 Ugandan Crisis. When Ugandan leader Idi Amin ordered the 400,000 Asians living in the country to leave within 90 days, the response of Indian government under the premiership of Indira Gandhi was relatively cold. Not more than 5,000 Indians were accepted by the Indian government, and there were calls for the visa policy to be reformed so that India did not become a 'dumping ground' for refugees (Abraham 2014).

The Fijian crisis in 1987 revealed that India's policy towards its overseas community had changed significantly. Faced with the military coup in Fiji, Prime Minister Rajiv Gandhi initially sought to impose commonwealth sanctions on Fiji. Thereafter, he also requested that regional powers such as Australia and New Zealand protect the Indo-Fijians. India's reaction during the Fiji crisis was significant also since the country at the time was suffering from an economic crisis and India had few resources to offer to its overseas community. Belying the previous governments' use of the economic inability argument to avoid attending to the problems of overseas Indians, Rajiv Gandhi took steps to make India's presence felt. While the attempt was fairly small and not particularly effective, this intervention can be seen as the first step towards recognizing overseas Indians as part of the country, and thus developing engagement policies with Indian migrants (Abraham 2014).

From independence to the end of the twentieth century, India's policy towards its overseas community was largely country-to-country based. India neither developed any dedicated policy to engage with its overseas community, nor made any political engagements. However, the new millennium saw a significant change in India's attitude to its population overseas. This became evident with the opening of the High Level Committee on the Indian Diaspora, formed under the leadership of L.M. Shinghvi. The committee's mandate was to 'review the status' of PIOs and NRIs with an eye to the economic, social, and technological contributions they might make in the future. The committee submitted its report in 2001 with number of recommendations to enhance state engagement with Indians living abroad. These included making provisions for overseas Indians to access dual citizenship or a form of living rights, so that they could more easily engage with the homeland. Following the recommendation, in 2002 the Government of India launched a special visa scheme for overseas Indians called the Persons of Indian Origin (PIO) Card. The card gave visa-free entry to overseas Indians, with exemption from the requirement for registration if their stay in India did not exceed six months. The cardholders were also given parity with NRIs in respect of the economic, financial, and educational facilities available to them. Yet while the PIO card gave opportunities for overseas Indians to engage with the homeland, the mandate remained limited. In order to provide more flexibility, in 2005 India made a Constitutional amendment and enacted the Overseas Citizenship of India (OCI) Scheme. Unlike the PIO, the OCI provides lifetime residence to the holder, as well as all the benefits of PIO. Overseas Indians were additionally given facilities such as registration exemption, freedom of movement (except in protected areas), and other citizenship rights (except political rights). In 2015, India stopped issuing the PIO card and merged all existing cards with the OCI scheme; all eligible overseas Indians upon registration were given the OCI card.

The OCI card, issued since 2005, presented an important opportunity for Indians living abroad to engage with the homeland. With its lack of restrictions and wide acceptability, the card conferred a real sense of belonging. Further, like any NRIs, the OCI cardholders were also permitted to open and maintain accounts in any Indian banks. The possession of an OCI card thus conferred a sense of connection, which lead naturally on to a sense of responsibility to serve the homeland. And since the scheme provided for free mobility, it also enabled the overseas community to visit and work for underprivileged people. As evident in the case of the Sahayata Trust, discussed in this book, overseas Indian doctors frequently visit the country to participate in medical camps, and many clinics host Indian-origin doctors; with their OCI cards, the doctors can come and go without any restriction. Clearly, then, the OCI card with its lifetime residence scheme, provides an opportunity for Indian residents in India, as well as the diaspora, to engage with each other.

Many other schemes were also recommended by the High Level Committee on Indian Diaspora to enhance the participation of overseas Indians. One of these recommendations was to establish a specialized institution in India to look after issues related to Indians living abroad. Following this recommendation, in May 2004, the Government established the MOIA exclusively to look after issues related to overseas Indians.

The Office of the Protector-General of Emigrants (PGE) was also merged with the MOIA. Earlier, the PGE office was with Ministry of Labour and Employment. In 2016, the organization was merged into the Ministry of External Affairs and renamed the Overseas Indian Affairs Division. The merger was implemented in order to scale up the activities and avoid inter-ministerial confusions—notably since embassies were part of the Ministry of External Affairs and many of the relevant matters called for the intervention of embassy officials.

Government of India Initiatives and Programmes for Overseas Indians

Alongside the establishment of a separate institution for Indians living abroad, the Government of India initiated a number of programmes to engage with them. Some of the specific policies are described in the following paragraphs.

Overseas Citizenship of India (OCI) Card

As already noted, the OCI card is a lifetime visa provided to foreigners with Indian origin, giving them freedom to travel and work flexibly in India. The OCI card is available to Indian citizens born after 26 January 1950, or persons belonging to a territory that became part of India after 15 August 1947. Facilities provided to cardholders include a multiple-entry, multi-purpose lifelong visa to visit India; exemption from foreigner registration requirements for a stay of any length in India; and parity with NRIs in financial, economic, and educational fields, except in the acquisition of agricultural or plantation properties. However, OCI cardholders are not entitled to participate in any political process, including voting, nor may they hold the offices of president, vice-president, judge of the Supreme Court and high courts, member of the Lok Sabha, Rajya Sabha, legislative assembly or council, or appointments to public service (government service).[7]

Pravasi Bhartiya Divas

The events known as the Pravasi Bhartiya Divas (PBD) are celebrations in India designed to strengthen government engagement with Indians living abroad. The events were inaugurated in 2003, with sponsorship from the Confederation of Indian Industry (CII), the Ministry of External Affairs, the Federation of Indian Chambers of Commerce and Industry (FICCI), and the Ministry of Development of the North Eastern Region of India. They are celebrated on 9 January (the date of the return of Mahatma Gandhi from South Africa). The broader objective of the PBD is to interact and network with the overseas Indian community. By 2019, India had organized 14 PBDs in different parts of India, the events being annual until 2015, and since then once in every two years.

During the PBD, awards are given to notable overseas Indians, 15 such awards being made in 2015.[8] Each PBD has a different theme, with a particular attention paid to Indian diaspora engagement in their selection. Indian nationals residing abroad use the PBD as a platform to interact with their government and the rest of the population, while diaspora Indians use the event to bring back knowledge and experience they have gained overseas. On average, every year 1,500 participants from more than 50 countries participate in PBDs. In 2017, the PBD

[7] See for instance the information on the OCI card described on the website of the Government of India, https://boi.gov.in/content/overseas-citizen-india-oci-cardholder, accessed on 16 October 2018.

[8] The website of the Pravasi Bhartiya Divas provides further information, http://www.pbd-india.com/the-event/10-interesting-things-you-should-know/, accessed on 12 October 2018.

that was organized in Bengaluru, Karnataka, had the theme 'Redefining Engagement with the Indian Diaspora'. The event was attended by delegates from 72 countries. There were over 6,300 members in attendance for PBD 2017 and over 1,500 NRIs as well as 150 PIOs.[9]

Alongside the PBDs in India, regional PBDs are also organized in different parts of world, intended to connect with overseas Indians in their country of settlement. In 2018, the regional PBD was organized in Singapore, celebrating 25 years of strategic partnership between India and Association of Southeast Asian Nations (ASEAN), and attended by 2,500 delegates. The theme of the convention was 'Ancient Route, New Journey: Diaspora in the Dynamic India–ASEAN Partnership'.

In addition to the PBD, the Indian Government has also constructed a centre named Pravasi Bhartiya Kendra (PBK) in New Delhi, to celebrate the diasporic history. The centre is 'expected to develop into a hub of activities for sustainable, symbiotic and mutually rewarding economic, social and cultural engagement between India and its Diaspora'.[10] The Kendra hosts a museum to depict the history of migration of the overseas Indian community, as well as their experiences and contributions.

Overseas Indian Facilitation Centre

The Overseas Indian Facilitation Centre (OIFC), a public–private partnership, was established in 2007 by the MOIA in association with the CII, with the objective of supporting the Indian diaspora to better connect with India, and assisting them in deepening their economic and intellectual engagement with India. The OIFC has organized several investment and interactive meets/roadshows in different countries, and also organized 'Market Places' during the PBDs in India. An electronic portal was launched by the MOIA to reply to queries by potential overseas investors and to promote and facilitate economic engagement

[9] http://www.pbd-india.com/2017/pravasi-bharatiya-divas-2017-in-bengaluru-india/, accessed on 10 July 2018.

[10] An information sheet is contained on the website for the Ministry of External Affairs, https://www.mea.gov.in/images/attach/pravasi_bhartiya_kendra_new_new.pdf, accessed on 6 October 2018.

by overseas Indians. The OIFC enabled NRIs to get information about investment opportunities in sectors such as education, healthcare, infrastructure, science and technology, and others. The organization was discontinued in 2017, however.[11]

Global INK

As part of the Government of India's strategic focus on the Indian diaspora, the MOIA used the OIFC to launch the Global Indian Network of Knowledge—Global INK, a secure portal for knowledge management and collaboration. The Ministry of Overseas Indian Affairs and OIFC envision engaging the institutions and individual experts in India and outside, persuading them to share knowledge among themselves. The key objective of this initiative is to draw upon the eclectic knowledge base of the Indian diaspora and unleash knowledge-sharing in the key focus areas where the Indian diaspora has made significant strides. The portal provides a framework of moderated online forums and features to harness knowledge, catering to different areas. It also aims to be an ideating platform, incubating valuable storehouse of knowledge. Global INK remains at 'arm's length from the government' and is managed by a professional team under the leadership of an independent moderator. It has the autonomy to catalyse knowledge exchange and to develop a wide network of overseas Indian physicists, scientists, technologists, and achievers residing across the world.[12]

India Development Foundation for Overseas Indians

The India Development Foundation of Overseas Indians (IDF-OI) was set up by the Government of India in 2008 as a not-for-profit trust to facilitate philanthropic engagements in social and development

---

[11]   News release, 12 December 2012, from the Ministry of Overseas Indian Affairs, http://pib.nic.in/newsite/PrintRelease.aspx?relid=90491, accessed on 6 October 2018. The information was collected from the Facebook site of the OICF, https://www.facebook.com/OIFC.IN/, accessed on 5 October 2019.

[12]   Information drawn from the website of the American Association of Physicians of Indian Origin (AAPIO), https://www.aapiusa.org/global-ink-indian-network-of-knowledge/, accessed on 15 October 2018.

projects in India by overseas Indians. The Trust was exempted from the provisions of the Foreign Contributions Regulation Act 2010 of the Ministry of Home Affairs, which enables IDF-OI to receive foreign contributions. Recognizing the emotional connect of overseas Indians with their place of origin, the IDF-OI has also partnered with state governments to highlight projects identified by them for contribution by overseas Indians. Fifteen states were working with IDF-OI, and received assistance from overseas Indians for projects in areas such as women's empowerment, sustainable livelihood, education, sanitation, and healthcare. The IDF-OI was discontinued in March 2018.[13]

MoUs and Bilateral Agreements

India has signed several memorandums of understanding (MoUs) and bilateral agreements with destination countries to provide support for Indians overseas, and decrease the incidence of human trafficking. One of the key initiatives include the signing of bilateral MoUs with destination countries 'to enlist the commitment of the host govern-ments to ensure better protection and welfare of Indian emigrants (*Annual Report*, MOIA 2014–15: 22). Over the years, India has signed labour MoUs with UAE (2006 and another in 2011), Qatar (2007), Kuwait (2007), Oman (2008), Malaysia (2009), and Bahrain (2009), as well as an additional protocol to the existing agreement with Qatar in 2007. Separately, India also signed an exclusive Agreement on Labour Co-operation for Domestic Service Workers (DSWs) with the Kingdom of Saudi Arabia (KSA) in 2014, along with signing a standard employment contract with KSA for DSWs. A joint working group was constituted 'to ensure implementation of the MoU and to meet regu-larly to find solutions to bilateral labour problems'.

Indian Community Welfare Fund

The Indian Community Welfare Fund (ICWF), set up in 2009, assists overseas Indian nationals in times of distress and emergency in the

---

[13] Website of the Ministry for Overseas Indian Affairs, https://www.mea.gov.in/idfoi.htm, accessed on 26 January 2019.

'most deserving cases' on a 'means-tested basis'. The ICWF has been a source of critical support in the emergency evacuation of Indian nationals from conflict zones, countries affected by natural disasters, and other challenging situations. In view of its immense utility, ICWF has been extended to all Indian missions and posts abroad. The ICWF guidelines have been revised further to make them more broad-based and to expand the scope of the welfare measures that can be extended through the fund.[14]

Overseas Indian Centres

Three overseas Indian centres are being set up, in Washington, Abu Dhabi, and Kuala Lumpur, as field organizations for the Overseas Indian Affairs Division of Ministry of External Affairs in those countries. The centres will have jurisdictions in all matters related to overseas Indians living and working in the country in question. The centres will be headed by a director-level officer along with supporting staff. The staff has already been sanctioned for three centres. Besides strengthening the grievance redressal mechanisms for overseas Indians, the centres will make necessary institutional arrangements to deliver a host of services to overseas Indians in economic, social, and cultural matters, directly, through outsourcing or through appropriate public–private partnerships.[15]

Know India Programmes

The Know India Programme (KIP) is a flagship initiative for diaspora engagement which familiarizes Indian-origin youth (18–30 years) with their Indian roots and contemporary India, through a three-week orientation programme organized by the Ministry. In 2016, the scheme was revamped to increase its duration from 21 to 25 days, with a 10-day visit to one or two states and preference given PIOs from Girmitiya

---

[14] Website of the Ministry for Overseas Indian Affairs, https://www.mea.gov.in/icwf.htm, accessed on 6 October 2018.

[15] See the information held on the Government of India website, http://www.mea.gov.in/overseas-indian-centres-abroad.htm, accessed on 29 December 2018.

countries.[16] Since 2016, six KIPs have been organized per year. Four KIP groups (37th to 40th editions) participated in the Youth Pravasi Bharatiya Divas and the 14th Pravasi Bharatiya Divas Convention, 7–9 January 2017 in Bengaluru. In the first 44 KIPs a total of 1460 PIO youths participated in this programme. An online portal (kip.gov.in) was launched in 2017, and Indian-origin youth now submit their online applications for participation in the KIP to the Indian Missions/Posts abroad. A maximum of 40 Indian diaspora youth are selected for each programme, and provided with full hospitality in India, 90 per cent of the total cost of international airfare being paid for by the Ministry.[17]

Scholarship Programme for Overseas Indians

The Scholarship Programme for Diaspora Children (SPDC) was introduced in 2006–7 to make higher education in Indian universities/institutes (in different fields except medical and related courses) in India accessible to the children of overseas Indians and NRI students, and to promote India as a centre for higher studies. Under the scheme, PIO/NRI students are awarded scholarship of up to USD 4,000 per annum towards payment of tuition fees, admission fees, and post-admission services for undergraduate courses in fields including engineering, technology, humanities, liberal arts, commerce, management, journalism, hotel management, agriculture, and animal husbandry. A revamped SPDC was launched in academic year 2016–17 with extension from 40 to 66 countries (including 17 countries with Emigration Check Required (ECR) status), enhancing the number of scholarships from 100 to 150 with 50 earmarked for children of Indian Workers in ECR counties. Of these 50 scholarships, one-third are reserved for children of Indian workers in ECR countries studying in India. The entire process of applying, processing, and so on is now through a portal (spdc.gov.in).

[16] 'Girmitiya' refers to the descendants of Indians migrated to other British territories with the agreement of the colonial governments, during the nineteenth century.

[17] See the information, Ministry of External Affairs, Government of India website, https://www.mea.gov.in/know-india-programme.htm, accessed on 3 October 2018.

Scholarships are offered for courses in Central Universities of India offering undergraduate courses especially those pertaining to information technology, nursing, pharmacy, and architecture. Applications are submitted and processed through a portal (spdcindia.gov.in). As of 2018, nearly 800 candidates have been awarded scholarships.[18]

Economic Policy Changes by the Government of India

Over time, the Government of India has initiated a number of economic policy changes to attract overseas Indians. In order to enhance the NRI and PIO investment and engagement, the Government of India made significant change in the investment policy. As per the revisions made in the Foreign Exchange Management Act in November 2017, investments by NRIs are treated as domestic investment to decrease the hassle faced by overseas Indians. Non-resident Indians are free to purchase any immovable property, other than agricultural property in India. Further, NRIs were also given authorization to acquire any immovable property, other than agricultural land, by way of gift resident in India or from an NRI or an OCI.[19]

While promoting investment from NRI Indians has been a primary motivation of the Indian Government since 2000, requisite banking reforms were also made in this regard. Non-resident Indians, including PIOs/OCIs, were given the option to maintain a bank account in India. These accounts are the non-resident external account, non-resident overseas account, non-resident (non-reportable) rupee deposit accounts, and foreign currency (non-resident) account. Although these accounts provide facilities to NRIs just like any domestic account, they also have particular functions. For example, the non-resident external accounts are used to remit earnings. The savings in this account are non-taxable and the amount transferred to these accounts automatically converts to Indian rupees. Upon transfer of money to this account, family members

[18] Website of the Ministry of External Affairs, https://www.mea.gov.in/spdc.htm, accessed on 6 October 2018.

[19] Information contained on the website of the Reserve Bank of India, rbi.org.in/scripts/NotificationUser.aspx?Mode=0&Id=11253, accessed on 17 January 2019.

or any nominated person can withdraw it. Further, money saved under this account can also be used as fixed deposit. Other three categories of accounts also serve their own specific purposes.[20]

Supplementary Initiatives by Diasporic Agencies

As discussed so far, over time, the Indian government has opened up the country for overseas Indians to visit and engage. Many diasporic agencies support and supplement these initiatives that are focused on motivating NRIs to support poor and needy people living in the homeland. These agencies also work towards the development of the homeland. One example is the role of Indian advocacy during the 'Y2K' crisis. Indians, especially from the US, shifted many of their businesses to India, which ultimately resulted in the outsourcing industry boom in India (Goldenberg 1998). During the 2003 H1-B visa cut in the US, the Indian lobby also worked to divert business to India (Clark and Wójcik 2018).

In the last two decades, a number of NRI organizations have also started participating directly in homeland-based activities. Organizations like the Global Organization of People of Indian Origin (GOPIO), The Indus Entrepreneurs (TiE), the American India Foundation (AIF), and others regularly organize events to connect Indians living abroad. The GOPIO organizes conventions in different parts of the world to network with the Indian diaspora. Further, the AIF and TiE, and other overseas Indian organizations also organize events to enhance the community relationship and to discuss issues related to the homeland. Many other third-party organizations also organize events to connect with overseas Indians. One of these organizations is the Institute of South Asian Studies (ISAS) of the National University of Singapore (NUS). The South Asian Diaspora Convention is an event organized by ISAS, NUS, held every two years. Although the event is not organized exclusively for Indians, a considerable number participate in it. The recent convention was attended by approximate 1,000 guests and more than 50 of the region's leading policymakers and business leaders, academics, and civil society leaders.

[20] Reserve Bank of India, https://www.rbi.org.in/scripts/FAQView. aspx?Id=52, accessed on 5 January 2019.

While the role of a favourable homeland policy does provide important support for the NRI community living in different parts of the world, the absence of such a policy was never, in fact, a bottleneck for overseas Indian engagement in development issues. Engagement by the Indian diaspora can be observed as early as the 1970s, when Pratap C. Reddy established the Apollo Hospital, and many of the organizations covered in the chapters of this book had engagement with India prior to any government attention. Further, many of the organizations had a volunteerist approach to dealing with Indian issues, which no absence of policy could hinder. Therefore, although the policy changes initiated by the Government of India have significant importance, the role for local or transnational migrant organizations should not be overlooked.

The Scope of the Research

Since independence, India has made a considerable progress on various aspects related to human life. Gross Domestic Product (GDP) per capita in India has increased from USD 304.20 in 1960 to USD 1963.55 in 2017.[21] At the time of independence, the life expectancy of an individual was 32 years (Rana and Sudgen 2013), but this has now increased to 68.3 years (Jāhāna 2016: 202). The literacy rate in India has increased from 18.33 per cent in 1951 to 74.04 per cent (Census of India 2011: 102). Yet, even where India has made progress on various issues pertaining to the life chances of common people, the condition has still not changed sufficiently. According to the *UN Human Development Report* 2016, India ranks 132, and falls within the 'medium' human development country category (Jāhāna 2016: 202). It is certainly true that human civilization calls for adequate and appropriate access to the facilities needed to enhance life chances. These factors include health, education, employment, income, and infrastructure; and while all these factors have an importance of their own, we consider education and health to be the most urgent and crucial requirements of human society. According to Sen (1999a: 39), education and health are fundamental to eradicating poverty and enhancing life chances for common people.

---

[21] 'India GDP per capita', database at *Trading Economics*, https://trading-economics.com/india/gdp-per-capita, accessed on 31 July 2018.

Sen considers that health and education are most crucial and essential components of 'social service' (Sen 1999b: 622). Therefore, considering health and education to be the two most important aspects of human development, the study specifically investigates the engagement of Indian immigrant organizations in these two sectors.

India is a country with significant healthcare challenges. According to a report, *Nutrition in India* published by Ministry of Health and Family Welfare, nearly half of the children under five years are chronically malnourished (Arnod et al. 2009: 6). And the condition is even more severe if overall illness is taken into consideration; according to Tavecchi and Rebecchi (2018: 14) nearly 50.8 million people in India have diabetes, comprising 17 per cent of the total population. India has a total of 1.93 million cases of tuberculosis (TB), 1.5 million cases of AIDS, as well as malaria, diarrhoea, and dengue which have become widespread. While the number of patients has seen a sharp increase, the status of the healthcare infrastructure is still not up to the mark. Compared with an average worldwide healthcare expenditure of around 6 per cent, India spends merely 1.4 per cent on public health. Considering that India has the second highest population, it is among the five countries with the lowest public health spending (Capolongo 2018: 11).

In line with the travails of healthcare, the condition of education in India is also clearly deficient. Admittedly, education in India has recently seen a considerable increase. Literacy has been boosted, as we saw above; yet while an increase in literacy does have a positive impact on life chances, the credentials constantly need to be rechecked. While school education is an important area of concern, employability after graduation is also a cause for concern. Less than 10 per cent of Indian management graduates are skilled enough to be employed (Rana and Sudgen 2013). In terms of public expenditure, India spends 2.6 per cent of the GDP on the education sector (*Economic Survey* 2018: 168), well below the global rate of 5 per cent of the GDP.

While healthcare and education in India remain sectors of critical need, the initiatives undertaken by federal or local governments cannot be considered as adequate to the scale of the challenge. Further, a clear rural/urban divide can also be observed: urban regions with higher concentrations of economic activity have more health and educational facilities compared to rural areas. According to Fan and Anand (2016), urban India has more trained medical professionals than rural India: there were 1,225,381 health workers in urban areas and 844,159 in rural areas, making availability of 145 per cent higher number of health workers in urban areas compare to rural areas. Of all health workers, 59.2 per cent were in urban areas, where 27.8 per cent of the population resides, and 40.8 per cent were in rural areas, where 72.2 per cent of the population resides. Broadly the same holds for the education sector, with most of the premier education institutions being located in urban areas.

The Indian immigrant population living in different parts of the world has a positive disposition towards the maintenance and restoration of the homeland (Safran 1991: 94), and shows sensitivity towards this rural–urban divide in essential services. Even where migrant organizations base their operations in urban centres, the activities are focused towards underprivileged areas such as slums or the countryside. Further, given their understanding of Indian infrastructure and the areas receiving lesser government attention, these organizations largely work for the weaker and underprivileged people living in rural areas. Since the gains from international migration are all too often confined to an analysis of economic growth, in this book we focus on healthcare and education, thus seeking to understand the effects of migrant organizations from a broader perspective that considers the implications for human development and quality of life.

Zooming in on the Indian migration and diaspora literature, one quickly remarks on the fact that the Indian migration and diaspora literature is relatively diverse and rich. The literature touches on various aspects of Indian migration, such as skilled migration (Bhagwati and Hamada 1974; Chanda and Mukharjee 2014; Ganguly 2003; Hazarika, Bhattacharyya, and Srivastava 2011; Kapur 2001; Khadria 2000, 2004; Tejada et al. 2014); diaspora identity (Dubey 2003); Indian diaspora in Singapore (Rai 2014); diaspora philanthropy and transnationalism (Agarwala 2015; Jain 2007; Kadekar, Sahoo, and Bhattacharya 2009; Kapur, Mehta and Dutt 2004; Osella 2018; Raghuram et al. 2008; Sahoo, Baas, and Faist 2012; Sidel 2004; Singh and Singh 2007; van der Veer 1995); migration and diaspora policy (Hercog and Siegel 2011; Najam 2007; Rajan 2010; Rajan and Kumar 2015; Sidel 2007; Soni and Soni 2006); social transformation (Osella and Gardner 2003); and diaspora, remittances, and development (Dhesi 2010; Kapur 2010;

Ketkar and Ratha 2010; Nayyar 1994; Pandey et al. 2006; Rajan 2012, 2014; Sahoo and Pattanaik 2014; Tan and Rahman 2013). Drawing inspiration from this body of recent research, the present study focuses on Indian overseas communities and their collective contributions to Indian development.

Research Methods

This project enabled us to travel to a number of developed countries, as well as origin countries in South Asia. In the process of fieldwork in the West and India, we noticed that many migrant organizations based abroad and in India are engaged in the healthcare and education sectors in India. While individual migrant engagement in the form of remittances to families and close relatives has been thoroughly studied, we did not know much about the collective engagements intended to serve the needy which often complement the development efforts of the origin country. Considering the extent and depth of the collective engagement and the novelty of such engagement in academic research, we decided to look at collective actors such as migrant organizations and their engagement in India's development efforts.

After surveying the migrant organization literature, we searched specific countries where there are large human-capital-rich Indian migrant populations, seeking transnational migrant organizations that straddle both the origin and host countries, and which are running development projects in India. This decision was informed by the assumption that new immigrants who are rich in human capital will have more opportunities as well as more resources to form organizations for collective engagement with India. For a variety of practical considerations, we chose organizations located mainly in North America and Europe. A thorough online search was made and a total of 934 organizations were reviewed, out of which 508 organizations were selected for closer analysis. In the second round of screening, we identified around 100 migrant organizations in the West that are regularly engaged in development programmes in India. We subsequently identified two key areas of engagement, namely healthcare and education, in which some migrant organizations are actively involved, with the sole purpose of improvement of the quality of life of people in India. We then identified

50 transnational migrant organizations that are engaged in health and education sectors in India. We should make it clear that these 50 migrant organizations are not the only organizations that are involved in health and education sectors in India; many other transnational organizations are also involved in that as well. We acknowledge that one of the limitations of this research is that we could not include more such organizations in our study.

It did not prove easy to identify or make contact with the local migrant organizations in India. We used different strategies to locate them, such as local vernacular newspapers, Facebook, individual websites, and our extensive network of personal connections with migration scholars in India. Although initially it was difficult to find such migrant organizations, once we engaged our network of personal contacts and broadened the online search, we found a good number of such organizations which are providing healthcare and educational services at the grassroots level. We finally selected 40 such local migrant organizations, spread over different states in India.

Our purpose is to shed light on three key components of the organizations we have selected: evolution, resource mobilization, and programmes related to healthcare and education. We thus aim to show how some migrant organizations engage in and contribute to healthcare and education provision in India. Established migrant organizations tend to use their websites to publish their history, membership, leaderships, resource mobilization strategies, nature of activities, events and future activities, yearly reports, and other related issues, and also share updates to the members by email. They also invite the media to report their events from time to time. In fact, their online presence is the primordial mode of communication with leaders, current and future members, and beneficiaries in home and host countries. Given the widespread of their membership across different countries, as well as the extensive range of their engagements in different states in India, this online presence presents itself to the managers of migrant organizations, not only as effective but also as fast, reliable, and transparent.

In the discussion with migrant organizations, we discovered that the organizations and their leaderships seek to reach out to the community through their online communication, and they also tend to attract new members online. Established organizations that persisted beyond the initial incubation period often survived and flourished because of their active online presence. When we discovered that established organizations also post most information online, including annual reports, we made the methodological decision to rely heavily on their websites, publications, and reports distributed online. Indeed, when we attempted to reach out to selected transnational migrant organizations for in-depth information, they referred us back to their websites for details. We went through the organizations' websites and found that they are by far the most comprehensive and detailed sources with regard to their evolution, resource mobilization, and activities. Therefore, for transnational organizations, we chose their websites and other secondary sources as the means to understand the role that such organizations play in healthcare and education in India. However, for local organizations, we travelled to over 15 states to interview and physically observe their activities in India.

Organization of the Book

Chapter 1, 'Nature, Formation, and Resources', provides an overview of both local and transnational migrant organizations, how they were formed at home and abroad, especially concerning the individual and group experiences in the early phase of formation, followed by a description of the different ways that these organizations mobilize resources. Chapter 2, 'Local Organizations and Healthcare Sector', examines various efforts made by individual or family-based local migrant organizations in the areas of medical education, hospitals, clinics, and medical services, and special programmes. Chapter 3, 'Local Organizations and Education Sector' describes how these individual/family-based organizations contribute to the education sector by presenting cases of the establishment of schools, colleges, and universities, academic research and collaboration, awards and scholarships for meritorious students and needy students, and finally various special programmes for disadvantaged groups across the country. Chapter 4, 'Transnational Organizations and Healthcare Sector' presents an overview of some engagements, especially building of healthcare institutions in India, providing modern medical equipment to hospitals and clinics in India, exchanging of medical professionals from the West to India, and finally launching various special programmes. Chapter 5, 'Transnational Organizations and Education Sector', offers an overview of the engagement of transnational organizations in the education sector by reporting various programmes such as NRI education provision in India, education for vulnerable groups, vocational education and training for skill development, community awareness programmes, provision for modern technology for schools, scholarships and grants for education, and finally various special programmes targeting different underprivileged sections of the society. Finally, the Conclusion summarizes the findings and indicates the directions for future research.

1

Nature, Formation, and Resources

As mentioned earlier, this book deals with both migrant organizations based in India—what we call 'local migrant organizations'—and
Indian migrant organizations formed and run from overseas, referred
to herein as 'transnational migrant organizations'. Our study examined
40 selected local migrant organizations and 50 Indian transnational
migrant organizations. This chapter provides an overview of both
types of migrant organizations, exploring how they differ in terms of
their nature, formation, and resource mobilization. The first section
examines the socio-demographic characteristics of selected migrant
organizations. The second section explores the background to the formation of both types of organizations in India and abroad. Finally, the
third section analyses the ways these organizations mobilize resources
for development initiatives in India.

Profiles of Migrant Organizations

Local Organizations

We identified and interviewed 40 local migrant organizations that have
active programmes primarily targeting the education and healthcare
sectors throughout India. The establishment dates of these organizations span five decades, starting from the 1970s: one organization was

established in 1977; three in the 1980s; eight in the 1990s; sixteen in the 2000s; and the remainder in the 2010s. The pattern of establishment of these local organizations is consistent with the flows of contemporary migration that started mainly in the late 1970s and gradually increased in the 1980s and the 1990s.

In terms of their geographical distribution, seven of the interviewed organizations were in Bihar; Kerala, and Delhi were home to six each; and Karnataka, Punjab, and Tamil Nadu had three each. From Chandigarh, Jharkhand, Maharashtra, and West Bengal, we identified two organizations per state, and one per state in Assam, Gujarat, Madhya Pradesh, and Telangana. It is important to note that the organizations under study also run development activities in other states of India.

Individual migrants, returnees, or family members of migrants (for example, parents or siblings) tend to be behind the establishment of such organizations. From our sample, individual migrants living overseas formed 29 organizations, while returnees and family members founded the remainder. Founders of organizations stemmed from different professional and occupational backgrounds: the founders of 14 local organizations were from a business background and nine from the medical profession. We also found organizations formed by engineers, film directors, technicians, scientists, and other professionals.

Since local migrant organizations require minimal capital investment, single individuals can often afford to form such organizations: from those studied, 26 initially emerged with the help of single individual founders; the remaining 14 came into being as a result of collective efforts. Collective contributions sometimes came from the same family, or else from a community, a locality, or a group of like-minded people. Personal savings were found to be crucial in the initial stages of formation: 17 out of 40 organizations had been established with the help of the personal savings of individual founders. These organizations had no support from any funding agencies or donors. Ten organizations had been established based on personal funding from more than one founder—that is, collaboratively. Eight organizations' establishment relied on contributions received from members. The remaining organizations had been established with the help of funds and contributions from NRI families.

In terms of reach at ground level, the organizations investigated for this study are diverse. Although all of them have a specific focus on working with and helping local communities, each has its own programmes and plans of action. They tend to target underprivileged sections of the society, often focusing on remote areas.

The number and type of beneficiary depends on the level of organizational engagement and the existence of ongoing projects. For example, parents' organizations tend to have 100–50 members and largely concentrate on these members and their children. Most organizations working with fewer financial resources have a relatively small beneficiary base; however, it is important to understand that individuals served by these organizations are mainly from the more deprived sections of the society. One such example is the Parth Foundation, which provides scholarships to economically deprived students in a rural village in Bihar. The foundation's founder is an academic who runs the organization out of his own savings. Another example is the Village Life Improvement Foundation of Chandigarh, Punjab. This organization helps NRIs to develop village infrastructure, running programmes in 10 villages.

Some organizations have a larger-scale focus. The Madina Educational Welfare Trust, based in Bihar, is an individually driven organization which aims to establish a medical, management, and engineering institute in India, and has already initiated basic infrastructural activities. Nevertheless, it operates without access to major funds: the founder manages everything himself and does not receive financial support from any other organization. Another example, the Association for Science and Society, has a significant presence in eight states in India. The founder, a scientist, aspires to promote science education and awareness among underprivileged people in the region.

Overall, the beneficiaries and programmes differ from organization to organization, as discussed in more detail in later sections.

Transnational Organizations

Of the 50 organizations with active engagements in India examined for this study, 36 were established in the USA, nine in the UK, and the remaining five in Canada. Unlike local organizations, which are relatively small and tend to focus on particular social issues, transnational organizations address multiple social issues and often target wider geographic units such as states or even a number of states. In terms of geographic coverage, 16 out of the 50 organizations covered almost all of the Indian states; 22 organizations covered several states; and the remaining 12 organizations focused mainly on one state. We obtained detailed membership information from 10 organizations. Among them, the AAPIO had the most members: over 42,000. The professional and occupational backgrounds of the founders of these organizations varied: from among our sample of 50 organizations, 12 were established by businesspeople, nine by medical professionals, four by academics and other professionals (for example, engineer, scientists, and technicians), and 20 by people of assorted backgrounds.

In terms of levels of engagement, we found that our 50 selected organizations were, at the time of the study, running 2,122 projects in various parts of India—an average (mean) of 42 projects per organization. The activities of these projects involve education, healthcare, childcare, development, community awareness, scholarship, public health, and nutrition and hygiene, among others. Among the organizations covered in the study, the Asian Foundation for Help, a UK-based organization, as of 2018 has 539 projects running in India; the US-based AIF currently runs 449 projects; and Asha for Education has 400 projects running in various parts of the country. Since transnational organizations are based overseas, they identify local partners, especially NGOs, to reach the targeted groups. Other partners include local government bodies and schools. For instance, the Ekal Vidyalaya Foundation is currently running 35 projects with the help of 2,600 government schools, the American India Foundation has a total of 310 partner NGOs in India, while Asha for Education has partnerships with nearly 200 organizations in India. Some of the organizations also run certain programmes directly.

Each of these organizations represents a unique example of organizational engagement. Among these, the AIF presents a useful case study. The organization has a presence in 24 Indian states and is currently running 449 programmes in collaboration with 310 local partners in India. The AIF website claims that the organization has impacted the lives of around 4.6 million people in India: in Delhi alone it runs 42 projects, in the areas of disability, school education, employment training, digitalization, livelihood and others. The focal issues of the AIF are education, livelihood, and public health. It also runs the William J. Clinton Fellowship, which brings young professionals from the US to volunteer in development organizations India, facilitating mutual learning and bringing various benefits to both communities.[1]

The AAPIO also presents an important example of organizational engagement in India. With a total of 65,000 members, including 11,000 patrons/life members, the organization lists various forms of engagements, including the provision of a platform for young physicians, medical students, residents, and fellows—the AAPI Global Clinical Trials Network—which works to educate 60,000 US physicians of Asian Indian origin on late-stage clinical trials and research developments. The AAPIO Charitable Foundation spearheads free clinics and health fairs in India. To date, more than 19 such clinics are active in various states of India.[2]

Another example is the American Foundation of Muslims of Indian Origin (AFMI). Formed in 1989, the AFMI engages with Muslim communities in India, striving to improve the socioeconomic status of underprivileged Indian Muslim minorities through education, with a particular focus on supporting students from poorer backgrounds across all parts of India. Currently the AFMI is working to achieve 100 per cent literacy among Indian Muslims. To achieve this goal, it has built schools in many Indian villages and adopted many others, accommodating students numbering several hundreds of thousands. As a motivation to excel in education, the AFMI has, to date, awarded over 2,000 gold, silver, and bronze medals and certificates to meritorious students in each state of India, as well as provided scholarships to promising students from poorer socioeconomic backgrounds. The organization has also built hospitals, conducted medical camps, and provided relief and rehabilitation during and after epidemics and disasters.[3]

---

[1] See the website of the American India Foundation, https://aif.org, accessed on 18 October 2018.

[2] See the website of the American Association of Physicians of India Origin, https://www.aapiusa.org/, accessed on 12 April 2018.

[3] See the website of American Federation of Muslims of Indian Origin, http://www.afmi.org/about-afmi/, accessed on 29 May 2018.

The American Telugu Association (ATA) was established to assist and promote literary, cultural, educational, social, economic, health, and community activities among people of Telugu origin, as well as to promote exchange programmes between the US, Canada, India, and other countries for Telugu students, scientists, and professionals. With a membership base of 6,000, the ATA provides the opportunity to adopt a village and work on issues such as communications, cottage industries and farming, health, roads, sewage, saving water, and school development. The organization also runs an adopt-a-student programme, alongside many other community services.[4]

Asha for Education is a US-based organization working towards the betterment of community members. The organization has more than 50 chapters all over the world, and currently runs 10 chapters in India. The organization has more than 1,000 volunteers worldwide.

While many organizations are involved in large-scale engagement in India, a few transnational organizations also work on micro-level activities. Hospital for Hope is one of the exceptions. The organization engages in healthcare activities in Jharkhand state, treating 1,200 patients every month; it has thus far helped more than 100,000 people from the state.

Formation of Migrant Organizations

Local Organizations

India is a diverse country with significant developmental variations. Each region has its own difficulties and requires significant intervention. Our study found that organizations established by migrants are having significant impacts in tackling specific issues in local communities. The organizations studied may have been established by individuals or groups from varying backgrounds, but they converge in terms of their orientations and actions. The majority of organizations focused on urgent requirements such as health, education, and public awareness. For example, NRI Forum, established in East Delhi, is concerned with

---

[4] American Telugu Association, https://americanteluguassociation.org/about.php, accessed on 29 May 2018.

the health, hygiene, and education of slum dwellers. Every major residential area has adjoining slums, so many organizations are specifically involved in the welfare of slum dwellers and street children; indeed, the establishment dates of these organizations often correlates to specific needs as they arise. For example, the 2010 Commonwealth Games in Delhi saw a significant increase in the number of workers coming to Delhi from across India. After construction was completed, many such workers decided to stay in Delhi, resulting in an increase in the number of slum dwellers. This increased the demands on non-governmental support systems, which led to establishment of NRI Forum.

All the migrant organizations we investigated were formed with local or regional requirements in mind. One respondent in Assam state had established Parijat Academy, an organization to tackle child labour, setting up a school to provide free education to a significant number of children, helping the region to curb child labour. Meanwhile, the Access Foundation Educational and Charitable Trust, an Indian migrant organization based in Tamil Nadu, was established to disseminate scientific knowledge related to carbon reduction and energy conservation. The founder of the organization, a scientific researcher, is deeply committed to informing the people of his homeland about energy conservation. The organization was formed with a view to conducting scientific research and utilizing the knowledge of Indian returnees. The Association for Science and Society, based in West Bengal, was also established by an Indian scientist, a returnee migrant. The organization was formed to promote scientific awareness in underserved and under-resourced communities. Both these organizations thus aim to raise awareness about environmental issues and green energy, and represent timely interventions by the returnees.

The Athena Educational Social and Charitable Trust from West Bengal is one of many organizations established to promote education in underprivileged communities. Its primary objective is to provide formal education and promote social welfare services for underdeveloped areas of West Bengal and the adjoining states. The organization was established as a result of the individual motivation of an NRI educationist from West Bengal. Bihar Brains is another organization established to provide education to talented but underprivileged students. It was established by a returnee from South Korea, who was inspired by the scientific advancement of that country. It aims to build awareness about education and create a favourable environment for research and development in Bihar.

Certain migrant-driven organizations in India were formed by groups of NRIs from particular communities. The Aleti Charitable Trust is one such example. It was established by a group of young Aleti NRIs who came together to finance and support initiatives targeted at providing education and health services to the disadvantaged Aleti communities in Madhya Pradesh and Andhra Pradesh. A related but slightly different example is provided by the Arkula Charitable Trust, established in the Mangalore region of Karnataka by NRIs from Arkula. The initial motive of the organization was to renovate Arkula Temple. After the restoration was complete, trust members decided to continue with welfare work for the betterment of people in the region. They began with charitable activities to encourage self-employment and empowerment of the local populace. This example shows the diversity of purposes among migrant organizations, from building temples to serving social developmental needs.

The migration of family members creates a vacuum in the traditional family formation; parents' organizations have thus emerged to fill the gap left when family members, who would otherwise fulfil certain traditional roles, are abroad. The members of such organizations consist of parents and other family members of NRIs. This study included three such organizations: the Association of Parents of Indians Resident Overseas (APIRO) in Maharashtra, the Nagarathar NRI Parents' Association in Maharashtra, and the NRI Parents Association (NRIPA) in Karnataka. All three organizations were established to help the parents of NRIs navigate difficulties in everyday life. Initially, parents and other family members gathered informally, over time becoming formal associations. One of their initial objectives was to prevent isolation and loneliness among the parents of NRIs living without family members in India. The APIRO's 'One-by-Two' programme, which provides care, companionship, and support to elderly members, is an example of how such organizations serve traditional roles.

Social remittance is a popular concept in the migration and development literature, denoting the transfer of norms, values, and ideas from the host country to the home country (Levitt 1998). A good example of how social remittance can become a vehicle for change in the migrant's home country is the Agya Wanti Bhalla (AWB) Food Bank, established by a US-based NRI. The idea arose when the founder saw a programme about a food bank in Washington, DC, that procured surplus food from high-end hotels and distributed it to those in need. Inspired by this example, the founder transferred this concept to India by contacting five-star hotels in Delhi. The organization started distributing 50 meals a day and quickly grew to nearly 2,000 meals, mainly for impoverished children.

Some of the organizations emerged to provide advocacy services to migrants. The Global India Association works towards upholding the rights of migrant workers, while the Global Punjabi Society was formed to integrate Punjabis living overseas. The latter is a political organization with established links to Indian political parties. A unique organization found in the course of this study is the Helping Organization for People, Environment (HOPE) & Animal Trust, established in 2000. It was established by a returnee in order to provide animal healthcare facilities in remote places.

We found that the diverse experiences of individual migrants shaped the emergence of the organizations featured in this study; sometimes inspirations are drawn from migrants' early life experiences back in India, sometimes special encounters during family visits or pleas from local community members drive their development, and some are inspired by the experiences of those living overseas.

Transnational Organizations

The formation of transnational organizations typically differs from that of local migrant organizations. As shown in the previous section, inspired by the need to return something to their home country, some founders took the initiative to form an organization collectively, but the majority of local groups were formed by individuals. With transnational groups, the more common model is for migrants engaged in similar occupations or from a shared region of origin, religious, or lingual community to come together to form organizations for transnational engagements. Sometimes, the inspiration for a new group is sparked by events back home. For instance, the AIF was founded in the wake of the Gujarat earthquake of 26 January 2001, to collect and disburse American donations towards the rebuilding and restoration of the region. However, the organization later broadened its scope to include wider developmental activities aimed at bringing about social change across India. The initial spark was given by former US President Bill Clinton, in solidarity with several business stalwarts from the Indian-American community. In February 2001, President Clinton and the then Prime Minister of India, Atal Bihari Vajpayee, held discussions regarding the Gujarat earthquake and potential US aid to mitigate and manage the disaster. The initial engagement in the rebuilding of Gujarat was extremely successful and was built upon with the establishment of 'All India' programmes focusing on employment, public health, HIV/AIDS, and education (particularly women's empowerment and elementary education).

Similar to local organizations, many transnational organizations focus on the urgent needs of local communities, including health and education. Asha for Education was formed by a group of like-minded people in the US, to focus on the improvement of education for Indian children. It began in the summer of 1991 as an Ivy League discussion group set up by three Indian students in their mid-twenties at the University of California, Berkeley. They named the group 'Asha' (Hope), to represent the hope that had brought these individuals together and the hope they wanted to bring to the lives of children in India. Their ideas took shape, and today their organization has a wide reach and a global platform, with significant engagement in various parts of India.

Ekal Vidyalaya Foundation, based in the UK, is another organization working towards improving education in India. The idea for Ekal was born in the early 1980s, when a nuclear physics professor, inspired by the words of Mahatma Gandhi and early Vivekananda workers, travelled to rural areas of Gumla District, in today's Jharkhand state in eastern India. Working with other intellectuals who shared his interest in transforming rural India, the founder concluded that the most effective method to lift people out of poverty was to improve educational access. Due to the lack of accessible public government schools, along with pressing agricultural labour needs, the village children had very limited schooling options. The founder and his team pioneered the idea of the one-teacher school (OTC) in Gumla District.

Another organization which focuses on improving educational access is the Nanubhai Foundation, which was founded in 2004. The initial vision of the organization was to empower the next generation of students in rural India by improving the quality of education. The Foundation's initial focus was the establishment of a school for 2,000 pupils, located in Kadod, Gujarat; however, since then the foundation's mandate has expanded to include other remote villages.

Alongside organizations working towards improving school-age education in India, many organizations focus on higher-level educational development in India. One such organization is the aforementioned American Association of Physicians of Indian Origin. In the 1970s and the early 1980s, foreign medical graduates, including those of Indian origin, were facing increasing difficulties in verifying their professional credentials, procuring residency positions, and obtaining jobs in the US. In 1983, a dozen Indian physicians and their spouses gathered to discuss the issue over a potluck dinner. Initially, the agenda of AAPIO focused primarily on international medical graduates, but now many second-generation Indian-Americans are graduating from American medical schools. The AAPIO continues to expand its programmes, which evolve with the changing times; it is now a well-recognized ethnic organization of physicians in California.

Many transnational organizations with an active role in India have a regional focus. One such group is the North American Telugu Society (NATS), which was established to address issues affecting the everyday lives of Telugu people living in North America by providing social, financial, and educational support services for that community. Another example is the Kashmiri Overseas Association, which originated with the initial meeting of several Kashmiri Pandit families in Maryland and Washington, DC. These families soon came to realize the importance of building a community organization which could grow to include other families, providing mutual support and opportunities. The organization's mission is to promote Kashmiri Pandit ethnic and sociocultural heritage (language, history, art, and so on); to celebrate Kashmiri Pandit religious festivals; to provide financial help to community members in need; to set up educational institutions, places of worship, and shrines—in both the US and India; and to preserve historical monuments and sites of religious and cultural significance in Kashmir.

Child welfare is also often a common focus among transnational organizations. One organization working in this area is Children's Hope, which was started around a kitchen table sometime in early 1992 by a group of professional women in New York who wanted to share their good fortune with disadvantaged children in India. The charitable foundation aims to help impoverished children progress from poverty to prosperity, giving each and every child a chance for a brighter future. It was born out of the recognition that to create lasting change in India there needs to be a balanced combination of education and grassroots efforts to empower women, children, and the community at large.

As observed earlier in the chapter, local and transnational organizations are significantly different in terms of how they are founded. While the majority of local organizations are established by one individual, transnational organizations tend to be established by a group of people. Further, local migrant organizations tend to have a narrower focus and fewer resources, while transnational migrant organizations feature cross-border programmes, have access to more resources, and are typically broader in scope and wider in coverage.

Resource Mobilization by Migrant Organizations

Understanding how organizations mobilize resources to implement their various projects is a vital component in analysing this sector. This section examines the myriad strategies employed by migrant organizations to reach out to compatriots and access resources to support their activities.

Local Organizations

There are two types of resources which can be mobilized for the establishment and operation of local migrant organizations: individual (personal) resources and collective resources. This study further categorizes collective resources into two types: internal and external resources. Internal resource mobilization refers to the utilization of direct financial contributions from one or more founders. External resource mobilization refers to the use of contributions received from those outside the organization, including the broader community and governmental sources.

Mobilization of individual resources usually means the organization was established based on financial contributions from the founder himself/herself; we found 26 local organizations working in various parts of India that were established through individuals' personal savings. One such organization is the Dream and Beauty Charitable Trust (DBCT), a Punjab-based organization established by a returnee. However, the trust later received support from like-minded people in India and abroad and, over time, was able to expand its activities to various sectors, such as healthcare, education, and skill development. Another prominent individual-driven organization is the Sahayata Trust, Hyderabad, Telangana, which also engages extensively in education and healthcare. The trust was established with the personal savings of the founder, but later received support from other international organizations.

In both these cases, individual contributions were the most important source of initial start-up funding. Over time, the organizations began to receive funds from other sources, making them more economically sustainable. Apart from these two, we found a number of smaller-scale organizations working in rural areas of India based on the financial support (personal salary or savings) of a single founder. One such organization is the Parth Foundation, based in Bihar and run day-to-day out of the personal salary of its founder, which is also used to provide scholarships to underprivileged children in the region. Despite its complete reliance on the founder's salary, the foundation has a number of ongoing operations in one of most rural districts of India. Another organization, the Maithili Workers' Charitable Foundation, Darbhanga, Bihar, engages in similar activities, and has also relied on the founders' savings, from its establishment to the present day.

The Jharkhandi Association, a Jharkhand-based organization, was, also, initially completely funded by an NRI who used his own money to develop the basic infrastructure needed for the organization, as well as paying staff salaries. However, over time, with the help of other NRIs, the organization was able to raise INR 50,000 per month. It has also received funds from the Indian government to support its ongoing activities. Similarly, the Kerala-based Shobha Memorial Charitable Trust was founded by a returnee migrant who established it in the memory of his late wife. The organization has three levels of resource mobilization: the personal savings of the founder, which were initially used to take care of all expenditure; nominal fees from people living in a home for old-aged pensioners; and donations received from NRIs and others.

The Chaitanya Gurukul Trust, based in Bihar, also, initially relied upon the personal savings of its founder, who built the organization when he was working overseas. In the beginning, he used his savings on the construction of the trust's building and also for the provision of scholarships to underprivileged students. Later, he returned to India and engaged himself full time with the trust's developmental activities, accepting financial help from NRIs and other like-minded people. Nevertheless, today the school still largely depends on the founder's own savings and resources.

As mentioned earlier, we found that individual motivation is the most visible and significant driver behind the establishment of local organizations. Furthermore, we have seen that it is not always necessary to have external support: in many cases, founders either fund the project entirely by themselves or take on the bulk of the financial responsibility for the organization's long-term sustainability.

Collective resource mobilization broadly refers to the use of resources donated by two or more people, including the primary founders. Of the local migrant organizations in this study, six were established by two or more people. The aforementioned Aleti Charitable Trust was established by a group of younger members of the Aleti community, and were initially supported by financial contributions from family members. The Arkula Charitable Trust, initially established by NRIs from Arkula to renovate the Arkula Temple, was funded, at first, by the founding members and later through the support of other people in the area. Bihar Brains was also formed through the personal savings of a returnee from South Korea, who later received donations and funding from like-minded people to expand activities in Bihar. These days, the organization also works closely with the Bihar government in implementing many projects in the state.

Family relations can also be a mobilizing force in forming and financing these organizations. For instance, three brothers formed the Village Development Forum, based in Bihar. These brothers were doctors, formerly based in the US, who returned to their village to provide healthcare for the local community. They initially used their personal savings to build the necessary basic infrastructure. Later, they charged INR 10 per patient to build funds for other requirements such as staff salaries and clinic maintenance. A good example of collective resource mobilization is the Village Life Improvement Foundation, based in Chandigarh, which was established by NRI doctors based in Canada. The idea for the project arose when, during a visit to his hometown in India, one of these doctors realized there was a serious lack of infrastructure. The doctors initially planned to pay all that was needed for renovation and maintenance themselves, but then they heard about the Punjab government's match-funding scheme for participatory contributions to the development of social services. To access these funds, they established the Village Life Improvement Foundation and contributed 50 per cent of the money needed for the development of a village project, receiving the remainder from the Punjab authorities. After learning about the match funding, many other NRIs expressed a desire to help their own villages, and approached the foundation to contribute funds for this. To date, the organization has completed the renovation of 10 villages, with the development of a further five in progress.

Maharashtra Vikas Mandal presents a slightly different case of collective resource mobilization. In 2008, when a US-based couple visited their home in India, some ordinary people approached them to speak about basic problems they were facing relating to education, healthcare, and many other areas. This couple were not from high-end professional categories; they were ordinary staff members at Walmart. Upon their return to the US, they created a platform to help the villagers. Initially, the organization was established with the help of financial support from the couple, but over time many people came forward to provide economic support. The organization has a number of projects at village level, including education programmes, healthcare programmes, and skill-development programmes.

Transnational Organizations

The resources mobilized by transnational organizations are largely derived from members' contributions and funds from various overseas donor agencies. Transnational migrant organizations also organize fundraising activities such as conventions, conferences, gala dinners, and other events on a regular basis to raise money for their activities in India. These organizations have a wider geographical coverage and more diverse fields of engagement than local migrant organizations, therefore their resource mobilization drives and strategies are commensurately varied and intensive. We found five broad ways of mobilizing resources in transnational groups: membership fees, individual donations (one-off or regular, and including innovative models such as sponsoring a scholar), fundraising events, corporate sponsorship, and social support.

Membership is one of the most important means of securing financial support. Many organizations collect money through a membership fee. The physicians' association AAPIO charges USD 500 for individual life membership and USD 750 per couple. Annual membership of the AAPIO costs USD 100 per person. Another example is the NATS, which offers life membership for USD 50. The Asha Jyoti Community Welfare Society of Canada charges USD 250 for annual membership, or USD 120 for students. The Capital District Malayali Association also has two levels of membership: individual membership costs USD 20 and family membership costs USD 25. The Association of Kannada Kootas of America charges USD 25 for individual membership, USD 50 for family membership, USD 200 for lifetime individual membership, USD 500 for donor membership, USD 1,000 for patron members, and USD 5,000 for grand patrons.[5] Membership fees can raise significant funds for an organization: for example, in 2016 the US-based Kashmiri Overseas Association raised USD 53,251 through membership fees from 665 individuals.

Donations constitute another key component of resource mobilization for transnational organizations. Our analysis revealed two levels of donations: direct donations and alternative models such as sponsoring a child or school. Ekal Vidyalaya is primarily supported by individual donations. The idea of Ekal is to connect families in urban areas with fellow countrymen living in rural and tribal areas to improve education at the grassroots level. Individual donors can be found in all major cities in India and also around the world, across 18 countries. One donor supports one Ekal School and gets direct access to that village, thereby

[5] Association of Kannada Kootas of America, http://www.akkaonline.org/akka_html/join_akka.html, accessed on 28 February 2019.

creating a direct link between the donor family and the village where the school operates. In 2016, the organization raised USD 6,809,883 through contributions.[6] Apart from individual donors, Ekal is also supported by sponsorship from businesses and various charitable foundations.

Apart from sponsoring individuals or institutions, some organizations provide opportunities for members to sponsor broader programmes. In the case of the NATS, global sponsorship is available for USD 24,000 and local chapter sponsorship is available for USD 2,400.

The sponsorship model is also followed by Manjari Sankurathri Memorial Foundation, which asks for INR 9,000 to sponsor a child for a year. Alternatively, one can pay INR 3,000 for one meal for 100 children or INR 4,000 for 100 adults in need. Sponsors can also directly support one cataract operation for INR 3,500.

The US-based Nanubhai Educational Foundation has several ways to collect funds for its activities. Donors can start a chapter, attend events, sponsor a scholar, make a direct donation, and also engage in partnership opportunities. Under the Sponsor a Scholar programme, USD 1,800 pays for the entire college education of a scholar or USD 250 provides a year of job skills training (partial sponsorship is also an option); for those wishing to make a recurring donation, they suggest USD 450 to fund one year's education for one student, or USD 25 to cover the recruitment costs of a scholar.[7]

Many organizations rely heavily on fundraising events to mobilize resources. These can range from glittering galas to cultural events to community picnics. At the high end of this spectrum, the American India Foundation—one of the leading organizations in terms of Indian diaspora engagement, which has raised more than USD 118 million raised USD 1.3 million through its Annual Gala in March 2018.[8]

[6] 'Education Health Skill Development Ekal USA'. (n.d.). https://www.ekal.org/pdf/ekal-usa-annual-report-2017.pdf, accessed on 1 March 2019.

[7] 'Nanubhai Education Foundation | Inspire. Empower. Transform. Mission & Values'. (n.d.). https://nanubhai.org/mission-values/, accessed on 1 March 2019.

[8] 'American India Foundation Annual Gala Raises $1.3 Million to Help Underprivileged in India–AIF'. (n.d.). https://aif.org/american-india-foundation-annual-gala-raises-1-3-million-to-help-underprivileged-in-india/, accessed on 1 March 2019.

Another organization which mobilizes significant resources through events is Children's Hope India: in 2017, they raised over USD 1 million through their Anniversary Gala, which featured an impressive guest list of leading names from the arts, business, and politics, including the Indian Consul General in New York, Sandeep Chakravorty, and noted director Mira Nair.[9] The organization has active projects in seven states across India: in 2016, the organization contributed USD 162,497 to Jeev Sewa Sansthan; USD 98,500 to schools and colleges; USD 70,000 to CH Prayas; and USD 194,000 to other programme and services.[10] It also contributes to US-based projects; under a special programme in 2014, it raised USD 25,000 for homeless people in New York city.[11]

Many organizations run cultural programmes which generate capital through entrance fees. For example, the Association for India's Development runs regular events with entry fees ranging from USD 10 to USD 25. These include Indian classical music concerts, dance dramas, and Bollywood DJ nights, alongside golf fundraisers and an annual conference.[12]

The US-based Association for Indians in America also runs cultural events, the most celebrated of these being their free celebrations for the Hindu festival of Deepawali. Instead of charging attendees, the organization raises money through fees from vendors wishing to set up stalls (USD 700 to USD 3,500 for food stalls; USD 300 to USD 650 for the 'Meena Bazaar').[13] The organization, which relies on sponsorship deals

[9] http://www.indiawest.com/news/global_indian/children-s-hope-th-anniversary-gala-raises-million/article_2d79d522-cc01-11e7-8d36-cf934daf5e8c.html, accessed on 27 July 2018.

[10] https://www.childrenshopeindia.org/about/financials/, accessed on 27 July 2018.

[11] 'Children's Hope India raises $25,000 for New York City's homeless—The American Bazaar'. (n.d.). https://www.americanbazaaronline.com/2014/06/02/childrens-hope-india-raises-25000-new-york-citys-homeless/, accessed on 1 March 2019.

[12] Association for India's Development, https://aidindia.org/events/list/, accessed on 25 September 2018.

[13] Association for India's Development, http://www.theaiany.org/wp-content/uploads/2015/07/AIA-NY-Deepavali-Vendor-Form-2017.pdf, accessed on 25 September 2018.

with major companies like Pepsi and Qatar Air,[14] also organizes events such as investment seminars, fundraisers, charity programmes, and gala dinners.

The Association of Kannada Kootas of America also engages in extensive resource mobilization through events, organizing the high-profile biennial World Kannada Conference. The tenth conference, held in 2018, featured the Chief Minister of Karnataka, eminent religious leaders, and the Maharaja of Mysore as special guests, alongside an impressive array of famous performing artists from the Kannada community including singers, film stars, poets, and musicians, and even a former Federal Bureau of Investigation (FBI) agent, to give talks and concerts. Registration fees are USD 250 (USD 100 for children/students) with special donor packages ranging from USD 1,000 (bronze) to USD 15,000 (Grand Patron). The event is also supported by an extensive array of corporate sponsors whose logos are, in return, featured prominently on the website.[15]

Even small-scale events can have a big impact. Bichitra, a Bengali religious and cultural group, organizes various cultural activities such as picnics, religious celebrations, and cultural activities for its members. The picnic event, which is not merely a fundraiser but also a social event for the community, costs USD 20 for individuals and USD 50 for a family.[16] The organization also sells various cultural products through its online store.[17] Over the past 25 years, Bichitra has helped many non-profit organizations in India, having raised over USD 80,000 to date for social services (mainly education and healthcare).[18]

As well as typical fundraising activities, some organizations also take advantage of the benefits of tax-related laws designed to support charitable giving. For instance, the UK-based Guru Ravidass Educational

---

[14] The Association of Indians in America, http://www.theaiany.org/sponsors/, accessed on 27 September 2018.

[15] 'AKKA WKC 2018—Bringing Kannadigas Together'. (n.d.). https://akkaonline.org/2018/, accessed on 29 September 2018.

[16] See details on https://www.bichitra.org/events, accessed on 29 January 2019.

[17] https://www.bichitra.org/online-store, accessed on 29 January 2019.

[18] https://www.bichitra.org/social-services, accessed on 29 January 2019.

Assistance Trust (GREAT) is registered to claim Gift Aid from the UK tax authorities for funds raised through membership subscriptions, donations from individuals and organizations, and its annual charity function (dinner and dance).[19] The Gift Aid scheme allows charities to reclaim the basic 25 per cent rate of income tax from HMRC (UK Revenue and Customs), for example, turning a GBP 100 donation by a UK taxpayer into a GBP 125 one.[20]

* * *

In summary, local organizations, which are mostly driven by individual initiatives, tend to draw on founders' personal savings to sustain themselves, especially in the initial stages of their establishment. Even in cases of collective resource mobilization, families and immediate community members act as an important support base for their establishment and operation. Transnational organizations, on the other hand, draw upon a number of resource mobilization strategies, which can be categorized under five types: membership fees; direct donations (general or for specific programmes); fundraising events; corporate sponsorship; and grants from governments. These strategies vary widely in terms of both type and scale, but most organizations draw upon a mixture of these strategies to mobilize resources for their development activities in India.

[19] Retrieved 1 March 2019, from http://www.great4education.co.uk/fundraising/.

[20] 'Tax Relief When You Donate to a Charity: Gift Aid—GOV.UK'. (n.d.). https://www.gov.uk/donating-to-charity/gift-aid, accessed on 1 March 2019.

Appendix A1

Table A1.1 Profiles of Selected Local Migrant Organizations in India

S. No.	Name	Year	Location	Coverage	Started as	Immigration status of founder	Professional background of founder	Beneficiary (estimated)	Resource mobilization strategies	Broad activities
1.	Access Foundation Educational and Charitable Trust	2012	Tamil Nadu	Tamil Nadu	Individual initiative	NRI	Not specified	Not specified	Not specified	Education for children, scientific research, and community awareness
2.	Aleti Charitable Trust	2009	Madhya Pradesh	Madhya Pradesh and Andhra Pradesh	Collective initiative	NRIs	Business	Not specified	Family contributions	Healthcare, education, and elderly care
3.	Arkula Charitable Trust	1999	Karnataka	Local	Collective initiative	NRIs	Medical professional, business	Not specified	Contribution of founders	Skill development and community awareness
4.	Association of Parents of Indians Resident Overseas	2010	Maharashtra	Maharashtra	Collective initiative	NRI parent	Retired parents	100 parents total	Members contribution	Alleviate the physical and emotional problems of parents

(*Cont'd*)

Table A1.1 (Cont'd)

S. No.	Name	Year	Location	Coverage	Started as	Immigration status of founder	Professional background of founder	Beneficiary (estimated)	Resource mobilization strategies	Broad activities
5.	Association for Science and Society	2011	West Bengal	West Bengal, Punjab, Bihar, Uttar Pradesh, Karnataka, Haryana, Jharkhand and Odisha	Individual initiative	Returnee	Scientist	Not specified	Personal savings of founder	Education, science education, and community awareness
6.	Athena Educational Social & Charitable Trust	2003	West Bengal	West Bengal	Individual initiative	Returnee	Academician	Not specified	Personal savings of founder	Education and healthcare
7.	AWB Food Bank	1991	Delhi	Delhi, Gujarat, and Haryana	Individual initiative	NRI	Medical professional	2,000 children/day	Personal contribution of founder	Healthcare, child welfare, and medicine bank
8.	Bihar Brains	2004	Bihar	Bihar and Jharkhand	Individual initiative	Returnee	Technologist	10,000 people (appx.)/year	NRI contribution	Education, community development, and advocacy

No.	Name	Year		Location	Nature	Category	Profession	Beneficiaries	Resources	Focus
9.	Dream & Beauty Charitable Trust	1996	Punjab	Punjab and Haryana	Individual initiative	NRI	Business	1,000 people/month	Personal contribution of founder	Healthcare, infant mortality reduction, maternal health, senior citizen homes, and mobile clinics
10.	Chaitanya Gurukul Trust	2011	Bihar	Bihar	Individual initiative	NRIs	IT expert	Not specified	Contribution of founders	Education, child welfare, and rural development
11.	George Educational Medical and Charitable Trust	1977	Kerala	Kerala	Individual initiative	NRIs	Business	10,000 people/year	Contribution of founders	Education, healthcare, and empowering people
12.	Global NRI Welfare Association	2009	Tamil Nadu	Tamil Nadu	Individual initiative	NRI	Engineer	1,000 people/year	Personal savings of founder	Education, skills development, and NRI advocacy

(Cont'd)

Table A1.1 (Cont'd)

S. No.	Name	Year	Location	Coverage	Started as	Immigration status of founder	Professional background of founder	Beneficiary (estimated)	Resource mobilization strategies	Broad activities
13.	Helping Organization for People Environment and Animal Trust	2001	Jharkhand	Uttar Pradesh and Jharkhand	Individual initiative	NRI	Medical professional	20,000 animals and humans/year	Contribution of founders	Healthcare, animal health, and social service
14.	Karnataka Zakat and Charitable Trust	1996	Karnataka	Karnataka, Tamil Nadu, and Andhra Pradesh	Individual initiative	NRI	Medical professional	10,000 scholarships total	Personal Savings of founder	Education, healthcare, and empowering people
15.	Kerala NRI Trust Centre	2010	Kerala	Kerala	Collective initiative	NRI	Business	7,000 people/year	Members contribution	Education, healthcare, and community development
16.	Madina Educational Welfare Trust	2007	Bihar	Bihar	Individual initiative	NRI	Business	1,000 people/year	Contribution of founders	Education, and healthcare

17.	Maharashtra Vikas Mandal	2008	Maharashtra	Maharashtra and Madhya Pradesh	Collective initiative	NRIs	Professionals	1,500 people/year	Contribution of founders	Education, healthcare, and empowering people
18.	Maithili Vikas Sangathan	2007	Bihar	Bihar	Individual initiative	NRI	Medical professional	500 people/month	Personal savings of founder	Education and healthcare
19.	Mehar Baba Charitable Foundation	1998	Chandigarh	Punjab and Haryana	Individual initiative	NRI	Academician	186 villages, 209,339 people total	Personal savings of founder	Education, healthcare, and empowering people
20.	Migration Facilitation Forum	2010	Kerala	Kerala	Individual initiative	Returnee	Business	2,000 prospective workers total	Personal Savings of founder	Education, skill development, and community awareness
21.	Mithila Workers Charitable Trust	2012	Bihar	Bihar	Individual initiative	Returnee	Engineer	200 people/month	Personal Savings of founder	Education, healthcare, and financial literacy
22.	Nagarathar NRI Parents Association	2011	Tamil Nadu	Tamil Nadu	Collective initiative	NRI Parents	Parents	100 Parents total	Members Contribution	Healthcare and elderly care

(Contd)

Table A1.1 (Cont'd)

S. No.	Name	Year	Location	Coverage	Started as	Immigration status of founder	Professional background of founder	Beneficiary (estimated)	Resource mobilization strategies	Broad activities
23.	Non-Resident Jharkhand Association	2008	Jharkhand	Jharkhand	Individual initiative	NRI	Medical professional	7,000 tribal people/month	Personal savings of founder	Education, healthcare, and empowering people
24.	NRI Forum	2003	Delhi	Delhi and Uttar Pradesh	Individual initiative	Returnee	Business	2,000 people/month	Personal savings of founder	Education, healthcare, and empowering people
25.	NRI Parents Association (NRIPA)	1998	Karnataka	Karnataka	Collective initiative	NRI Parents	Parents	175 parents total	Members contribution	Healthcare and elderly care
26.	Palakkad NRI Trust	2008	Kerala	Kerala	Collective initiative	NRIs	Businesses	200 people/month	Members contribution	Education and healthcare
27.	Parijat Academy	2003	Assam	Assam	Individual initiative	NRI	Teacher	522 children/month	NRI contribution	Education
28.	Parth Foundation	2009	Bihar	Bihar	Individual initiative	NRI	Academician	500 children total	Personal savings of founder	Education

29.	Pravasi Bandhu Welfare Trust	2001	Kerala	Kerala	Collective initiative	NRI	Business	Not specified	Members contribution	Education, healthcare, and empowering people
30.	Punjabi NRI Association	2009	Punjab	Punjab	Collective initiative	NRIs	Business	200 families/ month	Contribution of founders	Education, healthcare, and community development
31.	Sahayata Trust	1981	Telangana	Andhra Pradesh and Telangana	Individual initiative	NRI	Scientist	More than 20,000 people/ month	Personal savings of founder	Education, healthcare, and empowering people
32.	Salaam Baalak Trust	1988	Delhi	Delhi	Individual initiative	NRI	Film director	5,000 children/day	Contribution of founders	Education, healthcare, and child care
33.	Shobha Memorial Charitable Trust	2008	Kerala	Kerala	Individual initiative	NRI	Medical professional	1,000 people/ year	Personal savings of founder	Elderly care and healthcare
34.	Village Development Foundation	2012	Bihar	Bihar	Individual initiative	NRI	Medical professional	200 patients/ day	Personal savings of founder	Healthcare

(Cont'd)

Table A1.1 (Cont'd)

S. No.	Name	Year	Location	Coverage	Started as	Immigration status of founder	Professional background of founder	Beneficiary (estimated)	Resource mobilization strategies	Broad activities
35.	Village Life Improvement Foundation	1999	Chandigarh	Punjab and Haryana	Individual initiative	NRI	Medical professional	15 villages total	Members contribution	Healthcare, sanitation, and community development
36.	Global Indian Association	2012	Delhi	Delhi	Individual initiative	Indian	Business	500 people/month	Personal savings of founder	Healthcare, NRI support
37.	Global Punjabi Society	2012	New Delhi	New Delhi and Punjab	Collective initiative	Indian	Journalist	Not specified	Contribution of founders	Community awareness and NRI advocacy
38.	NRI Sabha, Punjab	1996	Punjab	Punjab	Collective initiative	Indian	Business	Not specified	Members contribution	NRI support and advocacy
39.	NRI Welfare Society of India	2006	Delhi	Delhi	Collective initiative	Indian	Politics	Not specified	Contribution of founders	NRI advocacy
40.	Vishwa Gujarati Samaj	1989	Gujarat	Gujarat	Collective initiative	Indian	Business	Not specified	NRI contributions	NRI support

Source: Compiled by the authors from the organizational responses and/or respective websites of the organizations.

Table A1.2 Profiles of Selected Transnational Migrant Organizations Overseas

S. No.	Name	Year	Location	Coverage	Membership	Professional background of founder	Number of projects running in India	Number of partners in India	Number of beneficiaries	Broad activities
1.	American Association of Physicians of Indian Origin	1991	USA	Andhra Pradesh, Gujarat, Haryana, Himachal Pradesh, Jammu and Kashmir, Karnataka, Maharashtra, Rajasthan, Tamil Nadu, and Uttar Pradesh	65,000 Doctors (11,000 patrons/lifelong members)	Medical professionals	15	15	20,000 patients/year	Healthcare, scholarship, community development, and medical education
2.	American Federation of Muslims of Indian Origin (AFMI)	1989	USA	Bihar, Uttar Pradesh, West Bengal, Gujarat, Maharashtra, and Tamil Nadu	Not specified	Medical professionals	33	Not specified	Not specified	Education and healthcare

(*Cont'd*)

Table A1.2 (Cont'd)

S. No.	Name	Year	Location	Coverage	Membership	Professional background of founder	Number of projects running in India	Number of partners in India	Number of beneficiaries	Broad activities
3.	American India Foundation	2001	USA	Himachal Pradesh, Uttarakhand, Haryana, Uttarakhand, Delhi, Rajasthan, Uttar Pradesh, Bihar, Assam, West Bengal, Jharkhand, Madhya Pradesh, Gujarat, Maharashtra, Andhra Pradesh, Odisha, Chhattisgarh, Goa, Karnataka, Tamil Nadu, and Andaman and Nicobar Islands	Not specified	Business	449	310	4.6 million total	Education, livelihood, elementary education, women's empowerment, HIV/AIDS awareness, and Public Health

No.	Name	Year	Country	Location					Focus
4.	American Telugu Association	1990	USA	Andhra Pradesh	6,000 people	Business	6	6	100,000 people	Education, healthcare, and social empowerment
5.	Asha for Education	1991	USA	All States of India	Not specified	Engineers	400	200	291,708 children	Education and child welfare
6.	Asha Jyoti Community Welfare Society of Canada	1995	Canada	Bihar, Karnataka, Haryana, Gujarat, and Punjab	Not specified	Academician	7	Not specified	1,000 people	Scholarship and community service
7.	Asian Foundation for Help	1983	UK	Various parts of India	Not specified	Various sectors	539	105	Not specified	Healthcare, education, and community awareness
8.	Association for India's Development	1991	USA	West Bengal, Tamil Nadu, Andhra Pradesh, Delhi, Jharkhand, and Punjab	Not specified	Scientist	12	Not specified	Not specified	Education, healthcare, and community development

(Cont'd)

Table A1.2 (Cont'd)

S. No.	Name	Year	Location	Coverage	Membership	Professional background of founder	Number of projects running in India	Number of partners in India	Number of beneficiaries	Broad activities
9.	Association of Indians in America	1967	USA	Gujarat	Not specified	Business	5	5	2,000 people	Education, healthcare, and social empowerment
10.	Association of Kannada Kootas of America	1998	USA	Karnataka	4,000 people	Business	14	12	100,000 people	Healthcare, education, and social service
11.	Bichitra	1974	USA	West Bengal	Not specified	Various sectors	4	2	Not specified	Education, child care, hygiene, and vocational training
12.	Bihar Development Foundation UK	2006	UK	Bihar and Jharkhand	Not specified	Various sectors	18	10	70,000 villagers	Healthcare, health awareness, and medical camps

13.	Capital District Malayalee Association	2006	USA	Kerala	150 families	Various sectors	1	Not specified	10,000 people	Healthcare and community initiatives
14.	Child Rights and You (CRY) America	1979	USA	Bihar, Manipur, Odisha, West Bengal, Chhattisgarh, Gujarat, Maharashtra, Rajasthan, Uttar Pradesh, Haryana, Jharkhand, Telangana, Tamil Nadu, Andhra Pradesh, Madhya Pradesh, and Karnataka	Not specified	Various sectors	36	36	660,632 children; 3,350 villages/slums	Education, healthcare, and child care

(Cont'd)

Table A1.2 (Cont'd)

S. No.	Name	Year	Location	Coverage	Membership	Professional background of founder	Number of projects running in India	Number of partners in India	Number of beneficiaries	Broad activities
15.	Children's Hope (India)	1992	USA	Madhya Pradesh, Gujarat, Andhra Pradesh, Jammu and Kashmir, West Bengal, Maharashtra, and Delhi	Not specified	Business	25	24	50,000 children	Education, food, shelter, and health services
16.	Dr Ambedkar Memorial Educational and Welfare Trust	1984	UK	Odisha	Not specified	Various sectors	3	Not specified	400 students	Education
17.	Ekal Vidyalaya Foundation of USA	1989	USA	Various parts of India	Not specified	Scientist	35	52,000 schools	1,848,819 students	Education
18.	Guru Ravidass Educational Assistance Trust (GREAT)	2005	UK	India	Not specified	Various sectors	14	14	175 scholarship	Education

| 19. | Hindu Society of Ottawa-Carleton | 1992 | Canada | Tamil Nadu, Gujarat, Hyderabad, West Bengal, Maharashtra, Odisha, Karnataka, Delhi, Uttarakhand, Uttar Pradesh, Rajasthan, Chhattisgarh, Tamil Nadu, and Madhya Pradesh | Not specified | Not specified | 25 | 25 | 200,000 people (approx.) | Women empowerment, healthcare and education |
| 20. | Hospital for Hope India | 1975 | USA | Jharkhand | Not specified | Various sectors | 1 | 1 | 90,000 people | Healthcare, education, health and hygiene, income generation, watershed development, and agriculture development |

(*Cont'd*)

Table A1.2   (Cont'd)

S. No.	Name	Year	Location	Coverage	Membership	Professional background of founder	Number of projects running in India	Number of partners in India	Number of beneficiaries	Broad activities
21.	India Development and Relief Fund	1988	USA	Various parts of India	Not specified	Medical professionals	47	60	100,000 (approx.)	Education, healthcare, and skill development
22.	India Development Service	1974	USA	Various parts of India	Not specified	Business	253	18	400,000 (approx.)	Education, healthcare, and skill development
23.	Indian Muslim Relief and Charity (IMRC)	1981	USA	Andhra Pradesh, Telangana, Assam, Bihar, Jharkhand, and West Bengal	Not specified	Business	7	1	900,000 people in 2017	Education, healthcare, and community development
24.	Indo-American Charity Foundation	1988	USA	3 States	Not specified	Medical professionals	6	2	10,000 people	Education, health, and children & families of the underprivileged

25.	Indo-American Eye Care Organization	2006	USA	Andhra Pradesh	Not specified	Medical professionals	3	Not specified	1,600 patients	Healthcare and eye care
26.	Indo-Canadian Women's Association	1984	Canada	Various parts of India	Not specified	Various sectors	1	2	45,000 people	Women empowerment and healthcare
27.	Jeevika Trust	1970	UK	Tamil Nadu and Odisha	Not specified	Various sectors	6	6	8,700 people	Education, skill development, employment training, nutrition, and public health
28.	Kashmiri Overseas Association	1983	USA	Jammu and Kashmir	662 people	Various sectors	17	2	5,000 people	Education, healthcare, and community development
29.	Lend-A-Hand India	2003	UK	Maharashtra, Gujarat, Telangana, Andhra Pradesh, Odisha, Delhi, Haryana, and Daman & Diu	Not specified	Various sectors	5	51	10,000 people/year	Education, community development, and skill development

(Cont'd)

Table A1.2 (Cont'd)

S. No.	Name	Year	Location	Coverage	Membership	Professional background of founder	Number of projects running in India	Number of partners in India	Number of beneficiaries	Broad activities
30.	Lohana Community of United Kingdom (LCUK)	1978	UK	Rajasthan and Gujarat	Not specified	Various sectors	2	1	332 children	Education
31.	Maharashtra Foundation	1978	USA	Maharashtra	1,000 people	Business	8	8	50,000 children	Skill development
32.	Manjari Sankurathri Memorial Foundation	1989	Canada	Andhra Pradesh	Not specified	Medical professionals	2	Not specified	250,000 people	Education and healthcare
33.	Mission India Foundation	2010	USA	Haryana	Not specified	Medical professionals	1	1	20,000 children	Healthcare, childcare, and vaccination
34.	Nanubhai Education Foundation	2004	USA	Delhi and Gujarat	Not specified	Academician	1	1	100 scholarships/year	Education

35.	National Federation of Indian American Associations	1980	USA	Maharashtra, Andhra Pradesh, Gujarat, and Kashmir	Not specified	Business	7	1	40,000 people	Healthcare and education
36.	Next Generation Foundation	2001	USA	Various parts of India	Not specified	Technicians	6	6	Not specified	Education, child care, and community awareness
37.	North American Sikh Medical and Dental Association	1992	USA	Punjab	1,000 Sikh medical professionals	Medical professionals	1	1	Not specified	Healthcare
38.	North American Telugu Association	2010	USA	Andhra Pradesh	29 members	Various sectors	6	6	10,000 people	Health, education, and community service
39.	North American Telugu Society	1984	USA	Andhra Pradesh	Not specified	Various sectors	8	Not specified	10,000 people	Education, scholarship, and cultural activities

(Cont'd)

Table A1.2 (Cont'd)

S. No.	Name	Year	Location	Coverage	Membership	Professional background of founder	Number of projects running in India	Number of partners in India	Number of beneficiaries	Broad activities
40.	Rajasthan Association of North America (RANA)	1991	USA	Rajasthan	Not specified	Various sectors	2	2	Not specified	Skill development and community awareness
41.	Rakshak Foundation	2006	USA	Various parts of India	Not specified	Academician	6	6	Not specified	Education
42.	Sakhi South Asian Immigrant Women in NY	1989	USA	Various parts of India	Not specified	Various sectors	1	48	10,000 people/year	Healthcare and women empowerment
43.	SEWA UK	1989	UK	Maharashtra	Not specified	Various sectors	1	1	48 students	Education
44.	Telugu Association of North America	1978	USA	Andhra Pradesh	Not specified	Medical professionals	32	32	Not specified	Healthcare, education, skill development, and community awareness

45.	Eye Foundation of America	1979	USA	Karnataka and Andhra Pradesh	Not specified	Medical professional	1	Not specified	Not specified	Healthcare and eye care
46.	The Loomba Foundation	1997	UK	India	Not specified	Business	1	13	10,000	Education and skill development
47.	Toronto-Calcutta Foundation	1988	Canada	West Bengal	Not specified	Various sectors	11	10	1,000 students/year (approx.)	Health, educational and employability
48.	Upkaar	1997	USA	Various parts of India	Not specified	Academician	Not specified	Not specified	165 students	Education and scholarship
49.	Vibha	1991	USA	Delhi, Uttar Pradesh, Maharashtra, Andhra Pradesh, West Bengal, Rajasthan, Tamil Nadu, Gujarat, Madhya Pradesh, and Karnataka	2,200	Business	37	37	110,000 children	Healthcare and women empowerment
50.	Bihar Foundation of the USA	2018	USA	Bihar	Not specified	Various sectors	1	Not specified	2,000 in 2018	Healthcare and eye care

Source: Compiled by the authors using different online sources and personal connections.

2

Local Organizations and Healthcare Sector

In a country as vast as India, the burden of endemic diseases or public health problems is severe. India has nearly 77 million people with diabetes, and 2.1 million cases of TB, as of 2019 (IDF 2019; WHO 2019). While the number of TB patients has latterly decreased, it is estimated that nearly 1.1 million cases remain either undiagnosed or improperly treated (Tavecchi and Rebecchi 2018: 14). The number of people infected with HIV/AIDS has also seen a significant increase: with 1.5 million cases, India now has the third highest number of people with this condition worldwide. Apart from these, malaria, diarrhoea, and dengue are widespread, while other healthcare issues are still dominant, including high rates of maternal, prenatal, and neonatal morbidity; at the same time, given India's highly uneven process of development, undernutrition and micronutrient deficiencies coexist with obesity and the non-communicable diseases associated with overnutrition (Arora and Gumber 2005: 569).

India thus faces serious issues related to the quality and security of human life. Despite remarkable economic growth in recent decades, in 2016 India ranked 131 on the United Nations Human Development Index (HDI). In 2014 India spent 1.4 per cent of its GDP on healthcare:

given that average public healthcare expenditure worldwide ranges from 6 per cent to 9 per cent of GDP, India is far below the international standard (Jāhāna 2016: 230). According to Capolongo (2018: 11) India is among the five countries with the lowest public health spending. This yawning gap in official provision, in the face of severe need, is the space in which migrant organizations seek to operate.

Medical facilities in India have long been a cause for concern. India has a worryingly low doctor–patient ratio. According to the National Health Profile 2018 (CBHI 2018), there is one allopathic doctor per 11,082 Indians: a ratio nearly 10 times higher than the ratio of 1:1,000 recommended by the World Health Organization (WHO). This figure becomes even more concerning when state-specific details are taken into consideration: in Uttar Pradesh and Bihar, the ratio worsens to 1:30,000. Only if homeopathic and Ayurvedic doctors are included does the ratio seem less critical: inclusion of all categories of doctors brings the overall ratio down to 1:1,596, slightly above the recommended health ratio of WHO.[1] Excluding homeopathic and Ayurvedic medicine—as Western commentators are generally keen to do—India has an urgent need of 500,000 doctors.[2]

Yet these statistics, bleak as they are, arguably mask the true seriousness of the situation. For according to a WHO study (Fan and Anand 2016), 57 per cent of all allopathic doctors practicing in rural India have no appropriate medical qualification; breaking down the overall figure, the report found that 58 per cent of urban doctors had a medical qualification, while for rural doctors the figure was only 18 per cent. Admittedly, this report was rejected by the Indian Government, which pointed out that possession of the MBBS (Bachelor of Medicine and Bachelor of Surgery) degree is a minimum qualification for enrolment as a registered medical practitioner in a state medical register, and

[1] http://164.100.47.190/loksabhaquestions/annex/15/AS48.pdf, Parliament of India, Starred Question No. 48, accessed on 22 July 2018.

[2] 'India Short of 500,000 Doctors, the Doctor-Patient Ratio of 1:1,700 is Worse than Vietnam', NewsGram. 1 September 2016. https://www.newsgram.com/india-short-of-500000-doctors-the-doctor-patient-ratio-of-11700-is-worse-than-vietnam/, accessed on 1 March 2019.

hence all registered doctors do perforce have medical qualifications.[3] Yet, although the response of the Indian Government must be taken seriously, the widespread presence of fake doctors in India cannot be ignored. In one notorious case in Unnao District of Uttar Pradesh, a local fake doctor vaccinated 58 people with an HIV-infected syringe. Similar cases have been observed elsewhere. Thus, while it is a fact that registered doctors will have sufficient medical qualifications, fake doctors continue to operate; and since the WHO report *Health Workforce in India* generally considered fake doctors to be a part of the Indian healthcare workforce, the percentage of doctors without appropriate certification must be considered to be high (Anand and Fan 2016).

This troubling situation persists despite the fact that since 2000, the Government of India has worked towards providing universal healthcare to all citizens (Jāhāna 2016: 11)—two prominent examples being the institution of the Rashtriya Swasthya Bima Yojna (a government-run health insurance for the poor) by the United Progressive Alliance (UPA) government in 2008,[4] and the Ayushman Bharat National Health Protection Mission (AB-NHPM) initiated by the NDA government in 2018.[5]

The lack of quality healthcare cannot, therefore, be ascribed simply to a failure of the government to work towards healthcare development (John 2010: 14); broader factors, extending beyond the facts of population and territory size, must be taken into account. Principal among these factors is the mobility of Indian skilled workers, with migration of healthcare workers to different parts of the world having been a key reality of the post-independence era. From the 1960s, Indian healthcare workers started moving abroad, especially to North America and the UK. As estimated by Supe and Burdick (2006), one-third of medical graduates leave India to seek higher education or practice abroad annually, while between 2 per cent and 5 per cent of new Indian

---

[3] 'http://164.100.47.190/loksabhaquestions/annex/15/AU594.pdf, Lok Sabha', Unstarred Question No. 594, accessed on 22 July 2018.

[4] http://www.rsby.gov.in/, accessed on 5 August 2018.

[5] http://pib.nic.in/newsite/PrintRelease.aspx?relid=177816, accessed on 5 August 2018.

graduates enter the US healthcare system (Aggarwal et al. 2014: 155). India has thus become a major supplier of health professionals, and Indian doctors have made significant contributions in other countries, even while the domestic condition has remained worrisome.

It is in this context that concerns related to healthcare have grown among the Indian immigrant community (Khadria 2012). As observed, healthcare is an important area of engagement for the immigrant organizations we study in this volume, both local and transnational: all the local immigrant organizations working in India are engaged, to some degree, in healthcare development for the needy. Thus the traditional flow of medical expertise out of the country has lately begun to reverse, with successful migrant Indians now turning their attention to the needs of people in the homeland. The government efforts to facilitate the engagement of migrant Indians back home, which we reviewed in the Introduction, should also be seen as part of the State's own efforts to meet the needs of the population: given that it clearly lacks the resources, if not the will, to deploy effective healthcare facilities for the bulk of the Indian population, it is apparently turning to migrant organizations to fill the gap. In this chapter we, therefore, study the engagement of Indian diaspora organizations in supporting healthcare among weaker and needy people in India.

Medical Education

India has one of the largest medical education systems in the world (Aggarwal 2014: 155), with 502 medical colleges spread across the country, of which roughly half are private and half government-run. The state of Karnataka records the highest number of medical colleges (56), followed by Maharashtra (50) and Tamil Nadu (49).[6] The number of colleges has seen a rapid increase: in 2016–17 alone, the Indian Government gave approval for 51 new ones.[7] The total annual

---

[6] http://164.100.47.190/loksabhaquestions/annex/11/AU1735.pdf, Lok Sabha, Unstarred Question No. 1735, accessed on 22 July 2018.

[7] http://164.100.47.190/loksabhaquestions/annex/10/AU4903.pdf, Lok Sabha, Unstarred Question No. 4903, accessed on 22 July 2018.

admissions is about 70,000 undergraduates and 33,000 postgraduates.[8] Competition for these places is high. Admissions to medical institutions is administered by the Central Board of Secondary Education via the National Eligibility Entrance Test (NEET). As per the NEET 2018 results, there were 1.3 million applications for undergraduate places, which is to say for each successful candidate there were 19 applicants (Jain 2018). Efforts have been made to increase the number of students in these institutions by relaxing the student to teacher ratio.[9]

Although the number of medical colleges in India has seen significant growth, their spread remains highly uneven, which in turn has led to imbalances in the regional presence of physicians. According to the High Level Expert Group Report on Universal Health Coverage for India (Planning Commission 2012), there is, for instance, only one medical college for a population of 11.5 million in Bihar and 9.5 million in Uttar Pradesh, compared to Kerala and Karnataka who have one medical college for 1.5 million people.

There are, therefore, two broad problems faced by the Indian medical education system: insufficient output of students, and uneven geographical coverage. As recommended by the WHO and the High Level Committee on Healthcare Services in India, addressing these problems requires the support of other actors, including immigrant organizations. We move, then, to a review of efforts made in this regard.

Among the NRI organizations studied in this research, the establishment of medical colleges has been a principal objective for three organizations in particular: the Sahayata Trust, Palakkad NRI Trust, and Madina Educational Welfare Trust. The Sahayata Trust, established by Mr Manzoor Ghori, an NRI, has multiple levels of healthcare engagement, divided between social ventures (ventures intended to be both sustainable and scalable), social joint ventures (ventures jointly

[8] https://164.100.158.235/question/annex/246/Au760.pdf, Rajya Sabha, Unstarred Question No. 760, accessed on 22 July 2018. https://164.100.158.235/question/annex/246/Au733.pdf, Rajya Sabha, Unstarred Question No. 733, accessed on 22 July 2018.

[9] https://164.100.158.235/question/annex/245/Au4110.pdf, Rajya Sabha, Unstarred Question No.4110, accessed on 22 July 2018.

organized and partly funded), and grants (service support and fund utilization). Besides running a 20-bed hospital in Hyderabad, Andhra Pradesh, the Trust has established the Indo-US Academy of Health and Hospital Administration (IAHHA), offering educational programmes in affiliation with Osmania University, Hyderabad. Its advanced postgraduate diploma programmes in Healthcare are designed for graduates with a view to training them for employment in the healthcare industry. These programmes are of two years' duration divided into four semesters—with theory, practical training, and exams in the first and second semesters and practical training and examinations in the third and fourth.

The hospital and medical institution were initially established with the personal savings of the founder, and over time expanded with the help of donations and other financial resources. Patients are charged a nominal fee, with the level set to suit the financial condition of poor patients. Similarly, students enrolled in the institute are also charged a minimal fee, and the institution helps students by arranging financial support in case of need. Other than direct healthcare engagement, the Sahayata Trust also has joint collaborations such as with the Pushpagiri Eye Institute in Sikandrabad, Uttar Pradesh.

The Palakkad NRI Trust, based in Palakkad, Kerala, has plans to establish a medical institution. The organization came into existence in 2008, originally to bring all Palakkad-based NRIs together under one umbrella to promote the socioeconomic development of the Palakkad District. The trust has since developed programmes of active engagement in four sectors—health, education, infrastructure development, and community service—while also working to motivate other NRIs to engage in community services for the homeland. In addition to its aim of establishing a medical college, the Trust aims to establish hospitals for general medical treatment, for the mentally disabled, and in specific areas of medicine including homeopathy.

The Madina Educational Welfare Trust, established in 2007 in Bihar, is planning to start a medical college in Patna, Bihar. The trust aims to provide quality medical education to meritorious students of Bihar and the neighbouring regions, while also having a hospital to provide medical care to needy people (its wider plan includes institutions for education in engineering and management). At the time of this research, the initial requirements such as land allocation and building planning were already complete and initial infrastructure was underway. The trust is chaired by an NRI based in the Middle East, and, till 2018, now has drawn exclusively on his personal financial resources, although it hopes to enhance the work further with donations from other NRIs and through government support. The organization provides an example of individual-level innovation, driven by the desire of the founder to support meritorious students in the region. As well as aiming to create a medical college, the Trust also seeks to provide scholarships to students so that poorer students can receive an education, with the aim of enhancing self-sufficiency among the needy people of Bihar.

As we have noted in earlier chapters, our survey of migrant organizations is avowedly incomplete; nevertheless, it is striking that we succeeded in identifying only one actually functioning medical college established by a migrant organization; and this is exceptionally striking given that, as we noted above, roughly half of the medical institutions in India are run by the private sector. Whether this indicates the presence of structural barriers to philanthropic interventions in medical education in India, or is simply an artefact of the study design, must await further research.

Hospitals, Clinics, and Medical Services

As discussed earlier, lack of trained healthcare professionals often creates severe problems, especially in rural areas where the coverage is thinnest. Further, although healthcare in urban areas is generally considered to be better, there remain significant questions around quality: even after charging high fees, many private hospitals fail to provide an appropriate service. A study by Panchapakesan, Lokachari, and Chandrasekharan (2014) found that the private hospitals largely fail to provide appropriate service; even though they have expensive equipment, they fail to provide basic necessities such as sanitation, sterilization, wheelchair ramps, etc.

While both state and central governments have taken steps to improve rural healthcare, including monetary and non-monetary incentives, the role of other stakeholders is also significant. Among these stakeholders, migrants with a desire to help their homeland have played an important role, and in many districts and states such people have set up organizations to work with the vulnerable population. Even in urban centres like Delhi, migrant organizations work with vulnerable people such as slum dwellers to provide basic healthcare facilities. Overall, Indian immigrant organizations are working at grassroots level to support the underprivileged and needy sections of the society.

This section presents details about hospital and clinics located in Punjab, Kerala, Andhra Pradesh, and Bihar and are established by Indian diaspora organizations. All these organizations represent unique stories of their own, and all five healthcare initiatives that we review present important examples of Indian diaspora engagement in India, reflecting the specific intentions of NRIs to help the socioeconomically weaker section of the homeland.

Among all the organizations identified as part of this research, five are running hospitals and clinics. These organizations are DBCT; the Sahayata Trust; the Village Development Foundation; the George Educational, Medical and Charitable Society; and the Shobha Memorial Charitable Trust.

The DBCT was established in 1996 to render social service in Ludhiana, Punjab. Founded by a US-based NRI, the trust also receives support from like-minded overseas Indians who are friends and associates of the founder. The organization primarily focusses on the weaker sections of the society, including the interstate migrant population which comes to Punjab from different parts of India.

The trust undertakes two major healthcare initiatives: Karma Medical Care and the Heavenly Palace Senior Citizens Home. Karma Medical Care was established in view of the high infant mortality rate (IMR) and maternal mortality ratio (MMR) in India, seeking to provide a sustained support system for the local community. The hospital was established in 2005 as a mother-and-child care centre. The objective was to provide immediate and timely support to patients who are not able to access premier healthcare services. Over time the organization extended their scope of its work to other healthcare issues, including diabetes, cancer, mental illness, cardiovascular and respiratory diseases, TB, malaria, and HIV/AIDS. With the inclusion of these health issues, the hospital became a multi-speciality hospital, Karma Hospital, which strives to offer comprehensive care with a high standard of excellence.

In addition to the hospital, the trust also started mobile clinics, where a team comprising a doctor, nursing attendant, and a volunteer tour the rural area for general health checks and to provide medicines free of charge. The trust intends to extend the hospital project by setting up primary healthcare centres in the peripheral villages around Ludhiana, aimed at poorer echelons of the community.

The trust is thus a significant example of an individual's dedication towards the homeland. Through the trust, the founder has initiated a social service which is engaged in almost all areas of human empowerment—from skill development to old age homes, health education to school education, and free food to free health services. The objective is to meet the basic needs of the poor and needy people. The organization plans to expand its scope to other states also, while efforts are also being made to expand the hospital.

Sahayata Trust, a Hyderabad-based organization, whose health education work we have already mentioned, also runs clinics for medically needy people. These clinics have been running for the last 10 years. After charging a registration fee of INR 5, it provides free medical consultation and medicines. Under the banner of its 'India Health Initiative', the Sahayata Trust has started medical clinics in areas of economic deprivation, as well as regular medical camps to which it invites 10 doctors every year from the US: these doctors visit the medical camps and provide consultations for thousands of rural patients. In years 2010 and 2011, the trust treated approximately 50,000 patients. The trust's clinics also refer people to the Indo-US Multispecialty Hospital, a full-fledged medical institution which it has established. The trust is also working to open a 100-bed hospital in Hyderabad, with an estimated cost of INR 62.5 million. As of 2018, the construction process was half complete.

Among the organizations interviewed in the course of this study, the Sahayata Trust was only organization found to be engaged with the exchange of medical professionals from the US to India. The doctors invited from overseas also engage in an annual healthcare initiative organized by the Sahayata Trust since 2009, linked to the trust's Indo-US hospital.

Another example of NRI healthcare engagement is the George Educational, Medical, and Charitable Society (GEMS), a non-profit organization registered in Trivandrum, Kerala, and established in 1977.

Notably, the organization claims to be the first NRI initiative of its kind in India. It has helped thousands of underprivileged people both in Tamil Nadu and Kerala.

Although the organization's hospital dates back to 1982, due to lack of financial resources it initially had only two doctors and a rather small staff. Over time, however, it expanded significantly, now having 150-bed capacity and a staff strength of 13 doctors including consultants and specialists, and employing 70 nursing and paramedical staff. As indicated by the respondents to our research, the hospital has served more than a million patients, and recently spent nearly INR 10 million on modernization, expansion of premises, and acquisition of essential medical and surgical equipment.

The long history of GEMS, and its status as one of the first examples of a diaspora initiative in India, is rooted in the region's history. One of the first places to see mass migration due to the oil boom in the Gulf, Kerala today benefits from the significant presence of emigrant households, many of which have worked towards improving the socioeconomic status of needy people. And while its hospital is an important initiative, GEMS has also initiated a number of other programmes which include the establishment of free medical camps, while also actively participating in time of natural calamities. It runs programmes such as schools and hostels, as well as a notable family counselling service. Supported by the Kerala State Social Welfare Board, GEMS's Family Counseling Centre serves the maladjusted, disrupted, and problem-ridden families from the surrounding rural areas, focusing on providing assistance to women and children recovering from atrocities and stressful situations. Extra effort has also been made to extend counseling services through GEMS's medical camps, as well as conducting programmes of social awareness and moral education. Coverage has been increased even further by simultaneously giving free medical as well as psychological assistance to village folk, while official contacts have also been made with police officers, women's welfare officers, school authorities, representatives of Mahila Samajam, etc.

Other than these three examples, another slightly different healthcare initiative is located in Madhubani district, Bihar, where three US returnee doctor brothers have established an organization called the Village Development Foundation. Baleshwar Singh, Sarveshwar Singh, and Singheshwar Singh left their employment in the US in 2012 and returned to help the common people of the region. Finding the medical and other facilities provided by the government unsatisfactory, the three brothers started providing consultation to village people initially with a small clinic, run from their own house. Over time, patients started coming from other parts of the region, increasing the pressure to create a proper hospital building with suitable equipment. After few years they started up a small clinic with necessary medical equipment. Currently, the clinic has a total of five paid employees and 17 volunteers, the latter being local people engaged in managing the day-to-day activities of the hospital. The doctors, we were informed, are particularly popular in that they prescribe very few medicines, and strenuously avoid unnecessary pathological tests. Interestingly, the clinic is situated in a rural area 30 km from the district town, and even so they see more than 200 patients per day. The consultation fee, only INR 10 apiece, is set while keeping in mind the remuneration of support staff and administrative expenses. However, the amount collected from the patients is not sufficient to cover these costs, so every month the brothers draw on money from their savings. Despite this shortfall, the organization intends to expand into other parts of the state, as well as into a wider range of services.

Another Kerala-based organization, the Sobha Memorial Charitable Trust, opened a free Ayurveda and allopathic outpatient clinic in 2011, offering free consultations for the general public on a part-time basis at the moment, with plans to make them full time. The trust was established by P.S. Menon, an NRI, in memory of his wife Sobha, who passed away in August 2007. The intended activities of the trust are to provide all possible physical and financial assistance to the poor and needy people in villages, directed at meeting their medical, educational, and other social needs. The trust has also established an old age home, Tharavadu, which seeks to meet international standards on hygiene, healthcare, and safety, and provide community living for the elderly people who are alone due to circumstances beyond the control of their children. It has also opened a health clinic for the people residing in the old age home, and for the people living in nearby districts. The trust provides charitable assistance to financially weaker families to build and own their own homes, financial aid for the marriage of their children, medical assistance to people who are unable to support their own hospital expenses themselves, etc. The old age home is open to Indian citizens of any caste, creed, or religion, aged 65 years or over in the case of males and 60 years for females. Admission is restricted, however, to persons who do not have children or other next of kin looking after them, and whose children and/or next of kin do not live within a 50-km radius. Tharavadu is housed on a property of about 8,500 square metres of land on long-term lease at Vellanchery, Malappuram District, Kerala.

Provision of medical services by Indian migrant organizations thus seems both widespread and firmly established: as we have seen, such services have in one case been ongoing since 1977. Although the hospitals run by the organizations we have surveyed were, in most instances, rather small, there is no doubt that they provide a significant service, and even more so when clinics and health camps are taken into account. Nevertheless, the scale of the NRI-established organizations' input into India's health needs remains small compared to the governmental or the conventional private sectors. As we have noted in the earlier chapters, the government has made significant efforts to facilitate the engagement of NRIs in India's development needs, so we may expect that the impact of migrant organizations will continue to grow. Yet our survey of initiatives so far has not made reference to the particular comparative advantage that migrant Indians tend to possess: namely, education, training, and work experience in the high-skilled and high-standards environment of the developed countries—environments to which they themselves have made particular contributions, and within which they have well-established networks. Given the shortfall in medical education and skills training in India, and the need for capacity building which we noted at the beginning of this chapter, there is clearly scope for leveraging that comparative advantage. Perhaps surprisingly, though, we found very little evidence of active programmes of exchanges between overseas medical professionals and India.

Direct visits are, undoubtably, an important learning opportunity for medical professionals, and it is surprising that so few of the organizations we contacted are engaged in them; however, many other forms of skill enhancements can also be considered. One among many is online learning for medical students. The concept is new and has not been examined properly, but can be crucial in this area of the global knowledge society. According to O'Doherty et al. (2018: 8), adoption of an e-learning approach can free up a significant amount of time, which can be used by a medical professional to spend more time in other areas of development. Future research would profitably review the use of online tools for promoting skills exchange and development; however, this was not included in the remit of the research reported in this volume.

Special Programmes

Engagement of Indian NRIs in India is mostly voluntary and rarely as extensive or broad as the migrant organizations we have reviewed so far. Alongside the standout initiatives, there are many small-scale organizations addressing many of the critical needs of ordinary people. While hospitals and medical schools deserve serious discussion, it is also essential to attend to the special programmes run by many Indian diaspora organizations. In this section, we list some of these unique activities.

Medicine Banks

Providing free medicine for poor people in low- and middle-income countries has long been a pressing objective for the WHO. On a similar line, India launched its National Health Mission in 2005. Under the National Health Mission, a rural region-specific programme, National Rural Health Mission was launched in 2005. Later, the National Urban Health Mission was launched in 2013 to focus on urban population.[10] These missions provide free health services which include consultations as well as medication for needy people. The project was initiated with budget of USD 5.4 billion and the motto 'free medicine for all' (Bhaumik and Biswas 2012). Under this plan, it is intended that the doctors will prescribe generic drugs where available.[11] However, the project was not very successful, since implementation was left to

[10] National Rural Health Mission (NRHM), http://nhm.gov.in/nhm/nrhm.html, accessed on 5 August 2018.

[11] https://www.livemint.com/Politics/5x1bODGqNASSoFsaBLbqcO/India-to-give-free-medicine-to-hundreds-of-millions.html, accessed on 5 August 2018.

the level of states, many of which had their own healthcare schemes already and so were not keen to implement this project.[12]

This gap in provision has been an opportunity for migrant organizations to make a contribution. One such example is the Agya Wanti Bhalla (AWB) Food Bank, brainchild of NRI Indian American Varinder K. Bhalla, who runs a US-based consulting firm. As informed by one of the Co-founder Brij Mohan Abrol, the idea to establish food bank came in the mind of Bhalla while watching a programme about a food bank in Washington, DC, that procured surplus food from posh hotels and distributed it to needy people. Transferring this concept to India, Bhalla contacted the Hyatt Regency hotel in New Delhi and collected the surplus food.

> Food Bank is a unique concept in India. There may be many such banks in the world, but initiating this kind of institution in Delhi was a difficult job. The work started to distribution of food to fifty children, which has now reached 2000 children.
>
> The food we serve to people needs to be high quality. We cannot serve stale food to any. We collect food from five star hotels and airline canteens primarily. We do not pick used food. Rather we pick left behind packed food.
>
> We have been facing a lot of difficulties from local administration. Most of the time, our vehicles are being stopped by police for regulatory checks. But, even after these difficulties, we are committed to provide food to hungry children as well as grown-ups.[13]

The organization was established in 1991 and currently runs out of the national capital, New Delhi. And while food distribution is a primary objective of the organization, the organization has also initiated a 'medicine bank'. Like the food bank, the medicine bank is also need based, and supports the various orphanages, old age homes, and other needy organizations, with the medicines first being screened by the local

[12] https://www.hindustantimes.com/jaipur/patients-do-not-get-all-medicines-under-cm-free-medicine-scheme/story-GDw0c3VQNuWSqIE5y-RvBQL.html, accessed on 5 August 2018.

[13] Interview, Brij Mohan Abrol, Co-founder, AWB Food Bank, 8 September 2014, New Delhi.

manager, Brij Mohan Abrol. The organization is planning to expand its area of coverage, as well as to start new initiatives which include a toy bank and a clothes bank.

The AWB Food Bank is a unique but much-needed social service currently run by the Indian diaspora in India. Since 1991, the organization has distributed meals to nearly a million people. In 2014, AWB Food Bank donated a motor boat to 125 children in the state of Gujarat, India, who for years had swum across a turbulent 600-metre river using a gohri, a 20-litre brass pot, to keep them afloat, and then walked for an hour to reach school. Along with the motor boat, the organization also hired a retired security professional to train the local youth to use it.

As of 2018, the organization provides support to nearly 15 local organizations, which includes three organizations established to serve people with physical and sensory disabilities. It intends to expend the purview of its current activities, and at the same time is increasingly being contacted by many hotel and airline caterers to offer their surplus food to it.

Financial Support to Local NGOs

Some organizations contacted for this study are not directly engaged with healthcare activities, but rather fund organizations already working in different parts of India. The Karnataka Zakat and Charitable Trust, working from Karnataka and established by a NRI returnee from Oman in 1996, thus has significant healthcare-related activities, being based on the Islamic concept of 'collective zakat',[14] and the belief that such an initiative can bring about a dramatic change in the lives of several of the underprivileged sections of our community, through investment in their education. The trust does not directly engage in healthcare activities, but rather provides support to other organizations working on similar issues. In this way it raises and provides funds for initiatives including reconstructive surgery and rehabilitation for the disabled;

---

[14] As specified by Karnataka Zakat and Charitable Trust, a portion set apart from wealth for the poor and needy is called *zakat*. By giving zakat, a person's wealth along with his/her own '*nafs*' (self) becomes purified. http://www.kzct.org/collective_zakat.html, accessed on 18 September 2019.

youth participation; support for elderly people; women's empowerment schemes; and more. As the founder remarked:

> Indians living abroad have zeal to support their homeland. As an orga-
> nization, we mobilize funds from like-minded people and provide
> support to economically weaker students of our area. Our scholarship
> programmes specifically help students from disadvantage groups.[15]

Medical Camps

Medical camps are often used to address the health problems of populations in remote areas (Thomas et al. 2002: 136), by government,
corporations, and NGOs (Kabra and Narayanan 1990; Singh, Garner,
and Floyd 2000). Sterilization and cataract surgery are two most common themes for such camps, as well as polio and hepatitis treatment,
and blood donation. These medical camps serve significant numbers of
needy people, being mostly free and organized at rural level.

The Kerala NRI Trust Centre organizes medical camps at Gram
Panchayat-level for overseas jobseekers to provide them with advice on
the required level of medical fitness for overseas jobs. These camps are
run with the support of NRIs. The Punjabi NRI Association, established
by three NRIs (Aman Pratap Singh, Sumer Pratap Singh, and D.S. Gill)
from Ludhiana, undertakes healthcare projects for the poorer section
of the society. Currently, 208 NRIs from Punjab are registered with the
association and the association has established an office in the house
of one of the founding members, and two permanent staff and eight
volunteers are working with it.

As noted earlier, the Sahayata Trust has initiated many healthcare-
related activities, and these include health camps and medical clinics in
economically deprived areas. The primary objective of the Trust is to
provide healthcare benefits to those who cannot afford to visit a doctor,
and as we noted these are run in conjunction with the Indo-US hospital,
and with the support of doctors from the US.

The Mehar Baba Charitable Trust organizes health camps for the
needy. The organization runs a number of activities, including education,

---

[15] Interview, Khalil Ahmad, Founder, Karnataka Zakat and Charitable
Trust, 5 October 2014, Hyderabad.

healthcare, and social empowerment. The Trust is working with medical professionals to provide free medical services to the underprivileged people of 187 villages of the region. Fieldworkers of the organization regularly visit these villages, where patients are informed about the service and registered for the medical treatment. It also organizes weekly health clinics and camps for the poor. The camps include facilities for preliminary pathological tests, draw on the support of doctors from the Postgraduate Institute of Medical Education and Research (PGIMER), Chandigarh, and provide free medicines to patients who cannot afford them. The trust also organizes cataract surgery camps as well as general 'health roadshows'. At these roadshows, the trust carries out awareness-raising activities providing health-related information, educating villagers, and communicating ways to combat diseases. Free tests are conducted for high blood sugar, blood pressure, and anaemia in pregnant women.

Maithili Vikas Sangathan, based in Bihar, also regularly organizes health camps to provide healthcare facilities to people with lack of means. The organization generally works towards financial awareness and promoting financial independence. The founder of the organization, an NRI, observed that the remittances sent by the emigrants are usually spent completely, while expenditure on education and healthcare is relatively lower than household and other family-based expenditure. Considering this, the founder initially worked towards promoting awareness of the productive usage of remittances, but the initiative was further extended with the inclusion of health awareness. The initial idea was to make the families more aware about their current health status, since it was observed that many residents avoided visiting hospitals. All the financial responsibilities are being borne by the founder himself; however, he plans to seek official government support, as well as the help of other NRIs.

Tribal Health

Healthcare facilities in tribal areas have long been an area of concern for the Indian medical sector, since these areas are relatively less developed and have lower public awareness of modern healthcare systems. Moreover, participation in modern healthcare systems also depends on one's financial capabilities, and so healthcare financing is one of the major barriers to good health among the tribal communities (John and Kumar 2017). With their reach into the extreme rural level, immigrant organizations comprise a second line of protection for the marginalized tribal people.

The Non-resident Jharkhandi Association was established in 2009 by one returnee NRI from the US, Mohan Oraon, who had worked in the US for 30 years. Till 2019, 102 NRIs from Jharkhand are associated with the organization, and they have established an office in Oraon's house. Three permanent members and 10 volunteers work with it. Some of the focus areas of the organization are education, healthcare, empowering people, infrastructure development of villages, and skill development. The association currently works in Jharkhand, which has a significant tribal population.

The activities of the organization are significant considering that Jharkhand is one of the poorest states of India, and has continuously suffered due to political and administrative turmoil. The condition of tribal people in Jharkhand has never been a focus of official interest, and necessities such as health and education are not available for a significant number of people. In response, the association has established a number of health camps in different parts of Jharkhand, specifically areas where the government has no presence in healthcare. The organization invites doctors from different parts of the world to participate in their camps, although this particular initiative has not seen significant participation by other NRIs.

The ongoing activities of the trust range from health camps to health awareness campaigns. Further, the organization also works towards the establishment of village-level health committees to identify and provide immediate support to needy patients, while also building a pool of volunteers who can work as awareness coordinators. These coordinators are trained in the details of various basic diseases, the idea being to develop paramedical volunteers from the village population. These volunteers are not selected on the basis of their level of education, since the education level is low and it is difficult to get people with adequate education. The motive is to identify people with a working knowledge of the local language who understand the basic medications. The organization plans to remunerate these volunteers should they receive funds in future. Further, these volunteers also include females, so that issues related to reproductive health can also be addressed.

NRI Parents' Organizations

Mental health is an important aspect of human health: according to the WHO (2001), positive mental health is crucial for everyday activities which include social behaviour, decision-making, and interaction with others. The issue of mental health becomes particularly crucial in the case of parents living without children, since low mental health results in lesser interaction with the outside world and hence results in isolation; isolation also has a detrimental effect on mental wellbeing. Therefore, there is an urgent need for an appropriate engagement mechanism for people already suffering with mental stresses or isolation to block this negative feedback cycle. One such mechanism can be the development of self-help groups or collective organizations (Bandyopadhyay 2018: 85).

A number of NRI parents associations have thus formed in India, and this study made contact with three of them: Nagarathar Non-resident Indian (NaNRI) Parents Association, Non-resident Indian Parents Association (NRIPA), and Association of Parents of Indian Resident Overseas (APIRO). These associations were established by the funding provided by the migrants, keeping in mind the difficulties faced by the parents of migrants, including health and psychological issues.

The NaNRI Parents Association was established by the parents of NRIs who are, for the most part, retired professionals. The families left behind by migrants are often in a situation of distress. Considering this, the organization was established to bring together such parents and help them in time of need. The organization meets on a regular basis and connects parents with other parents, and also organizes regular medical camps for them. Currently, the organization has 93 registered members. The organization also provides education, healthcare, and other social benefits to the needy people of the area.

The NRIPA, a voluntary, non-profit, Karnataka-registered association, also works for the betterment of NRI parents. The organization was established in 1998 by T.K. Rao and Ambujan Narayan to address issues concerning parents of NRIs, and currently has about 175 members.

The annual fee is INR 600 for both parents and INR 400 for a single parent. The association has regular meetings to discuss various issues related to parents of NRIs, including stress management, health issues, travel insurances, inheritance laws, and so on. These meetings also serve as opportunities to socialize and discuss issues that are common to NRI parents, who often feel lonely and isolated. The organization has also established an emergency telephone to help parents in distress.

The APIRO was also established by parents of NRIs, and now has 100 active members. Like the other two parents' groups, the APIRO supports parents of NRIs who face physical and emotional problems, and is working to build a self-help group. Emotional support is provided with the help of activities such as group meetings, recreational, intellectual and cultural activities, and the sharing of personal experiences, including problems and possible solutions. The organization also organizes picnics and longer outings, festivals, participation in group events as well as collective visits to theatres, cinemas, and concerts. The organization has also initiated an activity called the one-by-two scheme. Under this scheme, one elderly person gets the companionship of two relatively younger members. The initiative is an attempt to decrease the chances of isolation. The organization also organizes regular health check-up camps for the members and also provides help in case of any other need. Almost all activities of the organization are funded with the help of members' contributions.

Medical Facilities in Slums

The Indian rural population is usually at low risk of developing diabetes and obesity (Gupta, Joshi, and Dave 1978: 148), but after migration to cities rural dwellers face a number of adverse environmental influences resulting in lifestyle alterations: changes from their traditional eating habits; exposure to severe stress; decreased physical activity; and increase in smoking, tobacco chewing, and alcohol intake (Mishra et al. 2001: 1723). Studies from developed countries indicate that the prevalence of established risk factors including obesity and diabetes mellitus are higher among men and women with low level of education as a measure of socioeconomic status. Further, since people living in slums are mostly migrants and have temporary status, local governments do not think about their health. Therefore, the role of NGOs and voluntary organizations becomes crucial.

The NRI Forum is based in Delhi and was founded in 2003 by a businessman working in the UAE. It has been working for the healthcare benefits of people living in slums. The organization interacts with many NRIs from different parts of the world, and is currently run by 17 volunteers. The organization has no space to function independently, and up until now is run out of the house of the founder. Some of the focus areas of the organization are education for the children of the slums, sanitation and healthcare, and providing needs-based vocational training to workers. The eastern part of Delhi has long been a centre of the slum population, since the area is geographically nearer to many industrial localities of Delhi and the National Capital Region (NCR). Many of the workers in these industrial units live in these slums, and most of the labourers engaged in these establishments are illiterate and come from the disadvantaged category. The founder had previously been working for the disadvantaged population of the region, and discussed this issue with other NRIs who expressed their desire to help. The forum was thus founded with the support of many people, and all its activities are undertaken solely on the basis of the contributions received from other members. Indicative of the difficulty in finding support for work in slum areas, the forum originally struggled due to lack of financial means, but latterly has developed a wide base of solid financial support.

Elderly Care

According to the Population Census of 2011, India has an elderly population of nearly 104 million, comprising about 9 per cent of the total population, and recording a growth from approximately 5 per cent in 1961. Many elderly people have lower mobility and need the support of others; yet this support has become less available due to increasing prevalence of the nuclear family (MOSPI 2016: 1). The current era of rapid urbanization and societal modernization has brought in its wake a breakdown in family values and the framework of family support, and hence economic insecurity, social isolation, and elder abuse, leading to a host of psychological illnesses (Jamuna and Reddy 1997). The government has offered facilities for the welfare of senior citizens, but underutilization of the government facilities due to ignorance and other factors remains an area of concern (Joseph et al. 2015).

We have already mentioned the Sobha Memorial Charitable Trust, which set up the old age retreat, Tharavadu. The Dream and Beauty Charitable Trust has also established a senior citizens home. While working towards the upliftment of the employable population, the trust also shared its resources with the retired senior citizens. Seeing the facilities for the aged available in Western societies, the trust felt the need to provide equally good services in India for seniors who are separated from their families due to various personal circumstances.

Child Health

Child heath is an area of deep concern. According to estimates, India contributes 20 per cent to child deaths worldwide, with 1.83 million annually dying before they reach their fifth birthday. Most of these deaths are due to preventable diseases (Billaiya et al. 2017: 13), linked to lack of adequate nutrition for the mother and her education, as well as poor sanitation. Billaiya et al. (2017: 13) have shown that the neonatal mortality rate has shown a significant decrease, dropping from 32 per cent to 21 per cent in only a few years. This change is significant and can be expected to continue. While the Indian government has undoubtedly made a significant contribution to this progress, civil society and non-governmental organizations are also crucial, and immigrant organizations have a vital role to play.

Salaam Baalak Trust, Delhi, is an important initiative undertaken by the Indian diaspora. Similar to NRI Forum, the Salaam Baalak Trust works for the benefit of street children, having been founded and established by Mira Nair, the famous NRI filmmaker, to rehabilitate the child artists of the film *Salaam Bombay!* The organization provides education, basic literacy, and schooling, full-time care facilities for the young (up to 18 years), drop-in shelters for older children, physical and mental healthcare, life-skills education, vocational training, sports, job placement, and counselling in HIV/AIDS and TB awareness. Children on streets live in insanitary conditions and are prone to various infections and diseases; regular medical check-ups are, therefore, provided at the residential centres and contact points run by the trust, which also maintains individual health cards for each child. Children are regularly vaccinated against hepatitis-B and tetanus, and health camps are organized at contact points to strengthen awareness and support the basic health needs. Meals are also served at residential centres and contact points, including protein supplements, additional servings of fruits and milk as prescribed by the doctor.

Aleti Charitable Trust, based in Madhya Pradesh, has also initiated a number of healthcare programmes for weaker sections of the society. The trust was formed by a group of young NRIs who sought to finance and support genuine grassroots initiatives targeted at providing education and health to the underprivileged. They have thus created a platform for individuals to sponsor the cost of education for one underprivileged child. Under its healthcare programme, the trust requests NRIs to bear the cost of living for one elderly parent or to meet the costs of medicine for needy people. Any interested person can become a sponsor with a minimum amount of USD 10 a month.

Health and Sanitation

According to estimates for 2010, 15 per cent of the world population and 19 per cent of people in developing countries defecate in the open without using any toilet or latrine (UNICEF and WHO 2012). Of these 1.1 billion people, nearly 60 per cent live in India (Hammer and Spears 2016: 136). People in India are much more likely to defecate in the open than people in much poorer sub-Saharan African countries; and open-air defecation in India has declined little despite rapid economic growth (Coffey et al. 2014).

Sanitation is thus important for Indian society. While the Government of India has initiated a number of programmes for sanitation and cleanliness, NRI organizations have also worked towards sanitation in villages. One relevant organization is the Village Life Improvement Foundation, established by NRI doctors working in Canada. During a visit to their hometown, the founders became concerned about the infrastructure of their native village. Initially, they contacted the local administration and arranged 50 per cent contribution to a sanitation project, with the remaining amount was paid by the NRI founders. The project having been successful, they decided to help other villages as well, and attracted the support of many other NRIs who were willing to develop infrastructure. The organization has thus far completed the renovation of 10 villages and work on five more is in progress. And while the organization works towards any infrastructural development desired by NRIs, sanitation remains front and centre.

Another West Bengal–based organization, the Athena Educational Social and Charitable Trust also works towards community health, the prime objective being to provide social welfare services for downtrodden and underdeveloped areas of West Bengal. The organization has initiated a number of community health programmes which include community awareness, health and sanitation, and others.

While human health has been the central area of concern in these NRI-driven organizations, some organizations also work for domesticated animals. One such organization is the HOPE and Animal Trust, which has the rare objective of helping animals and the environment, as well as deprived people of the region. The organization works for the protection of the environment and animals, as well as to control the increasing population of street dogs.

Chronic Disease Awareness

Chronic diseases have emerged as one of most notable healthcare deficiencies in India. According to the WHO, approximately 90 per cent of chronic-disease-related deaths occur in low- and middle-income countries (WHO 2014: 11). The issues of chronic disease in a country like India are, therefore, more significant in comparison with other developed countries (Bhattacharjya and Corvino 2014:539). The chronic disease profile for India is extremely serious: the nation is currently home to the largest number of diabetics in the world. Furthermore, as a result of the projected growth in cardiovascular diseases, it is expected that the healthcare burden and related costs will continue to escalate in the future. Hence, like other developing countries, India faces daunting challenges as it looks to allocate limited resources against the galloping demand for access to necessary medical technologies and services. These trends, in turn, will exert even greater pressure on healthcare budgets and the fragmented healthcare delivery infrastructure. In the context of chronic disease care, therefore, immigrant organizations are very important.

The Maharashtra Vikas Mandal, Nagpur, Maharashtra, also works towards healthcare awareness, specifically regarding HIV/AIDS, TB, and other chronic diseases. The organization previously ran a programme in the Mumbai slums to make people aware about infectious diseases, and also runs a health awareness programme in villages in Maharashtra. The organization was established and is still run by an NRI based in the US. The founder established the organization in 2008 to provide basic education, healthcare, and community-specific activities to needy people. The organization attracts contributions from other NRIs and like-minded people and also provides short-term loans for entrepreneur development and vocational training in Nagpur and adjoining areas.

Under its health awareness programme, the Maharashtra Vikas Mandal seeks to raise awareness about chronic diseases in every single village of Maharashtra. While the size of the organization is relatively small and do not have resources to fulfil this objective, the founder is driven by this goal. Further, the founder also wants to proceed at two levels: resource mobilization through other NRIs, and to act as a support system for government initiatives. The founder is of the opinion that the activities should be holistic, and all stakeholders should come together to implement the schemes and programmes. Apart from the health awareness programme, the organization also runs health camps in many villages of the region, providing free health services to the poor and needy patients of the region. As well as this, the organization also runs eye camps in many villages, providing cataract surgery and vision consultation. All these activities are done with the help of financial contributions by the founder.

Health Insurance

Health insurance in India is widely needed yet, equally, widely neglected. More than 80 per cent of Indian healthcare expenditure is paid into the private system, which places a considerable burden on individual households (Breman, Ahuja, and Bhandari 2010: 65; Garg and Karan 2008: 116; Hooda 2017; Mahapatro, Singh, and Singh

2018: 75). On many occasions, expenditure on healthcare exceeds overall monthly income, which results in overborrowing (Breman, Ahuja, and Bhandari 2010: 65). Out-of-pocket expenditure towards healthcare also varies by region, with the rural population seeing relatively higher levels expenditure (Garg and Karan 2009: 116). As indicated at the opening of this chapter, state and central governments have launched a number of health insurance schemes to provide quality healthcare to the poor and needy people, but their impact still awaits evaluation.

There is healthcare insurance (Pravasi Bharatiya Bima Yojana)[16] for immigrants going to countries designated as Emigration Check Required (ECR) category,[17] this insurance being mandatory for ECR passport holders going out for employment. Yet the insurance has no effective implementation mechanism, and coverage is limited to ECR holders only: there is no mandatory insurance scheme for people going for employment under the Emigration Check Not Required (ECNR) category. In the course of the present research we thus found that many local organizations have their own insurance schemes. Among the diaspora organizations working in India, the Global Indian Association works for the rights of NRIs, being one of the leading organizations advocating voting rights for NRIs. The overall objective of the organization is to enhance the living and working condition of disadvantaged Indians, and it provides legal assistance for Indians in foreign jails while also extending help to the families of such hapless people. Under the healthcare programme, the organization provides 'Accidental Insurance Policy' worth INR 100,000 for all its members with the objective of providing support in case of any healthcare-related needs. This represents an important initiative since

[16] https://www.mea.gov.in/pbby.htm, accessed on 5 August 2018.

[17] As per the Emigration Act, 1983, ECR categories of Indian passport holders must obtain emigration clearance from the office of Protector of Emigrants (POE), Ministry of Overseas Indian Affairs for going to the following countries: United Arab Emirates (UAE), The Kingdom of Saudi Arabia (KSA), Qatar, Oman, Kuwait, Bahrain, Malaysia, Libya, Jordan, Yemen, Sudan, Afghanistan, Indonesia, Syria, Lebanon, Thailand, and Iraq (emigration banned).

it focuses on migrant workers and seeks to decrease their healthcare-related vulnerabilities.

* * *

The organizations discussed in this chapter have maintained significant engagement in various parts of India. Even when these organizations significantly differ in terms of geographical coverage and financial strength, each of them is catering the crucial healthcare need to many needy people from remote places to the urban centres across the country. Furthermore, the chapter also highlighted the importance of social remittances in the healthcare system, which include medicine bank, food bank, awareness programmes, and exchange programs for knowledge transfers. The engagement of these organizations has not just stopped with the conventional healthcare services; rather many organizations have also involved in eradicating some root causes of health problems and enhancing the life chances of the underserved people in the country.

Appendix A2

Table A2.1 Local Migrant Organizations in Healthcare Sector

S. No.	Name	Year	Location	Coverage	Started as	Immigration status of founder	Professional background of founder	Beneficiary (estimated)	Resource mobilization	Broad activities
1.	Aleti Charitable Trust	2009	Madhya Pradesh	Madhya Pradesh and Andhra Pradesh	Collective initiative	NRIs	Business	Not specified	Family contributions	Healthcare, education, and elderly care
2.	Association of Parents of Indians Resident Overseas	2010	Maharashtra	Maharashtra	NRI parents initiative	NRI parent	Retired parents	100 parents	Members contribution	Alleviate the physical and emotional problems of the parents
3.	Athena Educational Social & Charitable Trust	2003	West Bengal	West Bengal	Individual initiative	Returnee	Academician	Not specified	Personal savings of founder	Education and healthcare
4.	AWB Food Bank	1991	Delhi	Delhi, Gujarat, and Haryana	Individual initiative	NRI	Medical professional	2,000 Children	Personal contribution of founder	Healthcare, child care, and medicine bank

(Cont'd)

Table A2.1 (Cont'd)

S. No.	Name	Year	Location	Coverage	Started as	Immigration status of founder	Professional background of founder	Beneficiary (estimated)	Resource mobilization	Broad activities
5.	Dream & Beauty Charitable Trust	1996	Punjab	Punjab and Haryana	Individual initiative	NRI	Business	1,000 every month	Personal contribution of founder	Healthcare, infant care, maternal health, senior citizen home, and mobile clinics
6.	George Educational Medical and Charitable Trust	1977	Kerala	Kerala	Individual initiative	NRIs	Business	10,000 people	Contribution of founders	Education, healthcare, and empowering people
7.	Global Indian Association	2012	Delhi	Delhi	Individual initiative	Indian	Business	500 people	Personal savings of founder	Healthcare and NRI support
8.	Helping Organization for People Environment and Animal Trust	2001	Jharkhand	Uttar Pradesh and Jharkhand	Individual initiative	NRI	Medical professional	20,000 animals and humans	Contribution of founders	Healthcare, animal health, and social service

No.	Organization	Year	State	Coverage	Type of initiative	NRI	Founder profession	Beneficiaries	Funding source	Focus areas
9.	Karnataka Zakat and Charitable Trust	1996	Karnataka	Karnataka, Tamil Nadu, and Andhra Pradesh	Individual initiative	NRI	Medical professional	10,000 scholarships	Personal savings of founder	Education, healthcare, and empowering people
10.	Kerala NRI Trust Centre	2010	Kerala	Kerala	Collective initiative	NRI	Business	7,000 People	Members contribution	Education, healthcare, and community development
11.	Madina Educational Welfare Trust	2007	Bihar	Bihar	Individual initiative	NRI	Business	1,000 People	Contribution of founders	Education, healthcare
12.	Maharashtra Vikas Mandal	2008	Maharashtra	Maharashtra and Madhya Pradesh	Collective initiative	NRIs	Professionals	1,500 people	Contribution of founders	Education, healthcare, and empowering people
13.	Maithili Vikas Sangathan	2007	Bihar	Bihar	Individual initiative	NRI	Medical professional	500 People	Personal savings of founder	Education and healthcare
14.	Mehar Baba Charitable Foundation	1998	Chandigarh	Punjab and Haryana	Individual initiative	NRI	Academician	186 villages, 209,339 people	Personal savings of founder	Education, healthcare, and empowering people

(Contd)

Table A2.1 (Cont'd)

S. No.	Name	Year	Location	Coverage	Started as	Immigration status of founder	Professional background of founder	Beneficiary (estimated)	Resource mobilization	Broad activities
15.	Nagarathar NRI Parents Association	2011	Tamil Nadu	Tamil Nadu	NRI parents initiative	NRI parents	Parents	100 parents	Members contribution	Healthcare and elderly care
16.	Non-Resident Jharkhand Association	2008	Jharkhand	Jharkhand	Individual initiative	NRI	Medical professional	7,000 tribals	Personal savings of founder	Education, healthcare, and empowering people
17.	NRI Forum	2003	Delhi	Delhi and Uttar Pradesh	Individual initiative	Returnee	Business	2,000 people	Personal savings of founder	Education, healthcare, and empowering people
18.	NRI Parents Association (NRIPA)	1998	Karnataka	Karnataka	NRI parents initiative	NRI Parents	Parents	175 Parents	Members contribution	Healthcare and elderly care
19.	Palakkad NRI Trust	2008	Kerala	Kerala	Collective initiative	NRIs	Businesses	200 People	Members contribution	Education and healthcare
20.	Punjabi NRI Association	2009	Punjab	Punjab	Collective initiative	NRIs	Business	200 families	Contribution of founders	Education, healthcare, and community development

21.	Sahayata Trust	1981	Telangana	Andhra Pradesh and Telangana	Individual initiative	NRI	Scientist	More than 20,000	Personal savings of founder	Education, healthcare, and empowering people
22.	Salaam Baalak Trust	1988	Delhi	Delhi	Individual initiative	NRI	Film director	5,000 children/day	Contribution of founders	Education, healthcare, and child care
23.	Sobha Memorial Charitable Trust	2008	Kerala	Kerala	Individual initiative	NRI	Medical professional	1000 people	Personal savings of founder	Elderly care and healthcare
24.	Village Development Foundation	2012	Bihar	Bihar	Individual initiative	NRI	Medical professional	200 patients/day	Personal savings of founder	Healthcare
25.	Village Life Improvement Foundation	1999	Chandigarh	Punjab and Haryana	Individual initiative	NRI	Medical professional	15 villages	Member contributions	Healthcare, sanitation, and community development

Source: Compiled by the authors from the organizational responses and/or respective websites of the organizations.

3

Local Organizations
and Education Sector

Post 1947 India has made a significant contribution in the field of technical and professional education. The quality of Indian healthcare education has been considerably high, with the information technology and healthcare professionals have made their presence felt across the world. At the same time, condition of education outside some of these premier institutions is worrisome and needs considerable contribution from government as well as non-government institutions. In terms of public expenditure, India spends 2.6 per cent of its GDP on the education sector (*Economic Survey* 2018: 168), well below the global average of 4.77 per cent (World Bank n.d.). General education in India thus remains an area of serious concern, and is in strong need of support from all stakeholders; once again, therefore, this is an area in which migrant organizations run by NRIs and PIOs have made a considerable contribution, and this chapter presents our findings in this regard.

Indisputably, basic literacy in India has seen a considerable increase. Currently the country has an overall literacy rate of 74 per cent: compared to 1951, the 2011 census reported male literacy as having increased from 27 per cent to 82 per cent and female from 8 per cent to 65 per cent (Census 2011: 102), and such increases have a positive impact on life chances. Yet according to a report by Pratham, a non-governmental organization, 50 per cent of seven-year-olds cannot recognize letters, 20 per cent of ten-year-olds cannot read an entire sentence, and 50 per cent of fourteen-year-olds cannot do division (ASER 2017). As well as poor outcomes from school education, there are also problems regarding employability after graduation, with less than 10 per cent of Indian management graduates considered skilled enough to be employed (Anand 2013).

According to the Annual Status of Education Report (ASER) 2017, published by the ASER Centre, enrolment in elementary education has seen a considerable increase: within a decade, the number doubled, from 11 million to 22 million (Pratham 2018: 3). But these broad statistics concerning enrolment mask serious concerns about the quality of education provided. Less than half of students enrolled in class eight (around 14 years old) can solve mathematics problems formally considered to be of class five level. Further, there are serious worries about the post-elementary enrolment: nearly 7 million students stop studying after class eight.

Education among the tribal populations is also a major concern. Scheduled tribes' enrolment accounted for 5.22 per cent of total enrolment in 2017–18: in absolute terms, 1,913,864 out of a total enrolment of 36,642,378 students.[1] While the Indian government has initiated a number of programmes to enhance tribal education, many immigrant organizations have also focused on this issue, with many of the organizations selected for this study engaged in educational and healthcare activities in tribal areas.

School, Colleges, and Universities

Organizations founded and run by migrant Indians have been frontrunners in the pursuit of social development via education. Many of the local migrant organizations we surveyed had created institutions for education: a few had developed institutes for higher education, while the majority were engaged in school-level initiatives. These schools

---

[1] Higher Education for STs, Lok Sabha Unstarred Question no. 3158, answered on 6 August 2018, http://164.100.47.190/loksabhaquestions/annex/15/AU3158.pdf, accessed on 17 August 2018.

also vary significantly: many provided full-fledged and well-rounded education, while others sought primarily to support the educational infrastructure already existing in the area.

The Chaitanya Gurukul Trust is a non-profit organization established by a returnee NRI, based in Bihar, and working towards the development of education facilities in the remotest parts of that state. The organization's primary objective is to provide education to the rural and marginalized populations, and has established a school with strikingly modern facilities, especially given the remoteness of the region: despite the fact that the region itself has only limited electrification, the school manages to provide Wi-Fi, online teaching from the US and Bengaluru, and an excellent library. With these innovations, the organization aims to nurture talent and create future leaders. The school recruits teachers through a competitive examination and trains them in Bangalore before they start teaching. The trustee members are all NRIs with careers in the fields of software and engineering, and being located all over the world possess significant experience of working in multinational and multi-cultural teams. With school fees kept low to enable underprivileged children to gain access to quality education, Chaitanya Gurukul Trust represents an important innovation in the area of diaspora engagement in the education sector.

George Educational, Medical and Charitable Society (GEMS), as we have seen in previous chapters, can lay claim to being the first NRI initiative of its kind in India. The organization has created two schools: GEMS Residential School, Nedumangad, and GEMS High School, Chadayamangalam, both in Kerala. GEMS Residential School was started in Nedumangad in 2004–5 with a view to providing free education to poor girl children, who were also provided with free food and accommodation. The school was closed in 2010 and all the students of the school were transferred to the GEMS High School complex at Chadayamangalam in Kollam District, which opened in 2006. Classes started in the new school building from the beginning of the academic year 2009–10. Facilities such as computer rooms, library, and a laboratory were provided in the new building. The school has about 600 students, 25 teachers, and three non-teaching staff. The organization also has a hostel and provides health insurance to all students and faculty members.

The Assam-based NRI-funded school, Parijat Academy, was established in 2003 to provide education to the underprivileged, and currently provides free education to 522 children. The primary objectives of the organization include educating underprivileged children, reducing child labour, and providing innovative learning opportunities for students, and it particularly seeks to engage children during the daytime so as to avoid child exploitation and trafficking. The school is a unique initiative given the lack of facilities in the region overall, being located in an area comprising about 10 tribal villages, where access to education is very limited. The school has four rooms, with a tin roof and bamboo walls. The founder has been notably successful in imparting the value of education among children, and sees educating underprivileged children as a first step in helping the community. Establishing the school was difficult, however, since many parents were unwilling to release their children from their labour, and so forego the associated earnings. This was a double barrier, in fact, since sending them to school itself cost money, as well as depriving family of earned income. Thus at first parents showed very low motivation. In order to solve this problem, the founder sought to provide scholarships. The total expenditure of the organization is now 1,800,000 rupees, major source of finances being individual contacts, and donations from NRIs and their organizations in India, and it also runs a sponsor-a-child programme, where one can sponsor a child for INR 425 (USD 7) per month or INR 5,100 (USD 85) per year. The organization also has a weaving programme as well as vocational training activities for women.

Sahayata Trust, whose medical initiatives we have already discussed in earlier chapters, has also established two major schools in Moinabad, Telangana—Challenger International School and Challenger Junior College—as well as a range of other initiatives. Challenger International is a minority school working towards educational betterment of needy students via innovative strategies, while Challenger Junior College is an academic institution established for girls from the 8th to 12th classes (ages 14 to 18) aspiring to become doctors or engineers. Challenger International School, a prestigious education institution, was opened in June 2010 in Moinabad, Telangana. This is an outstanding school, boasting excellent education standards alongside majestic and impressive infrastructure. The massive building includes spacious classrooms, a computer lab, staff room, and other facilities including a basketball court, football ground and play area, a very large auditorium, and green spaces. The Trust has also opened a first-of-its-kind girls residential junior college campus at Moinabad, from 8th to 12th classes aspiring to degrees in medical and engineering streams. Challenger Junior College, meanwhile, combines the state-of-the-art infrastructure and facilities of the Sahayata Trust with its rich management experience and teaching expertise, and includes a fully functional hostel for girls. Established by Sahayata Trust and its members, this is the first minority institution in the area. Currently 129 students are enrolled in the school. The Sahayata Trust has also started a minority English-medium primary school at Bhongir, Odisha, as well as the Jahangirabad Medium Institute in Lucknow, Uttar Pradesh, following on from its engineering college and MBA collage in the same area.

Athena Educational Social and Charitable Trust, an NRI-driven organization in West Bengal, runs two major educational activities: a Bachelor of Education (BEd) college, and nursery and primary schools. The mission of the Trust is to impart formal education and promote social welfare services in the underdeveloped areas of West Bengal and adjoining states, and thus create social awareness, self-reliance and employment, and eradicate illiteracy and poverty. The management team is led by an NRI educationalist who has links with various American and international projects including NASA, General Electric, Boeing, Lockheed, Motorola, and General Dynamics. Besides nursery and primary schools, initiatives have been taken to empower women. The organization also promotes alternative learning, providing support for self-help groups, community health initiatives, and volunteer agencies. The initiatives are, therefore, not purely directed at the education sector but also extend into other sectors such as health and social services, highlighting once again the centrality of education within the overall process of community development.

Along with these examples, two other organizations contacted as part of this research also expressed their intention to start up educational institutions: these are Palakkad NRI Trust and Madina Educational Welfare Trust, which we covered in the previous chapters as well. In particular, the Palakkad NRI Trust proposes to collaborate in creating opportunities for school managements to join together to implement a comprehensive facility development programme of lower primary schools in Palakkad District, Kerala. The objective is to standardize school buildings, furniture, and computer learning facilities within the district, with financial participation by Palakkad-based NRIs, school management, well-wishers, and the local community, including parents.

Academic Research and Collaboration

Aside from the initiatives aimed at providing basic education, which we have reviewed earlier in the chapter, there are other migrant organizations which concern themselves with promoting academic research and collaboration—little surprise, perhaps, given the academic strengths of migrant Indians, on which we have already had cause to comment. The Association for Science and Society was established in 2011 with the goal of promoting and advancing science and technology while creating a universal ethos of tolerance and peace. It seeks to promote awareness especially in the underserved and under-resourced communities, and has established a fully functional lab in Kolkata, West Bengal, while maintaining a presence in 10 Indian states and 16 countries worldwide. One of the activities of the organization is to promote research and training in the fields of Science, Technology, Engineering, and Maths (STEM). The organization also regularly collaborates with other institutions working on scientific issues, and aims to develop a pool of researchers and science and medical practitioners to serve as resources for further knowledge dissemination. The Association has multiple engagements in West Bengal, including significant research and training projects in STEM subjects in Kolkata, as well as hands-on research experiences for inner city and rural youth. Further, it also organizes science streets in fairs and festivals, especially in rural communities and villages in Bengal, as well as a science puja during the Durga Puja Festival, which includes science competitions and panels; and in Sundarbans, the organization has even organized floating laboratories. It has also engaged in science and technology programmes for senior citizens, as well as the creation of energy friendly and plastic-free zones. Under the awareness programme, the organization has initiated the replacement of plastic cups with earthenware cups, and of plastic bags with jute bags.

There are also pilot STEM programmes for Muslim youth conducted in inner city slums and rural Bengal.

In Punjab, the organization has created programmes in STEM research and training including hands-on research for inner city and rural youth similar to Bengal. The coverage includes 50 villages, towns, and cities, 500 schools, and 5,000 young men and women in the Punjab. Similar activities are also being carried out in other states and countries.

Awards and Scholarships for Meritorious Students

Education loans are a significant instrument for supporting poor students' study in India. The interest paid on education loans varies from 8.60 per cent to 11.50 per cent per annum. Given the high rate of interest, and the difficulty which poor students face in accessing education loans, migrant organizations have engaged in a number of activities to support the educational development of students. The Bihar Brains Development Society, commonly known as Bihar Brains, a non-profit organization in Bihar with special focus on education and creating an environment for research and development, has established a scholastic centre to provide support for needy students and develop various projects on issues of urgent social need. As the founder told us,

> I came from South Korea to enhance the educational capabilities of children and young students from the weaker community. Since 2004 we have been working hard to provide focused educational support to the needy in Bihar and Jharkhand. We could not receive appropriate support from the local government; however, non-resident Indians, especially non-resident Biharis, provided overwhelming support. This organization acted effectively with the support of Indians living abroad.[2]

The society came into existence in 2004 and has established its office in Patna, run by Bihari and other NRIs and the educated people of Bihar. Initially, the scholastic centre was established with online library facilities including magazines and international journals subscribed to by Bihar Brains, and not easily available for public. This facility was

---

[2] Interview, Bibhuti Bikramaditya, 26 August 2014, Patna.

made available at a cost of INR 50 per month. The scholastic centre also provides training for the Graduate Record Examinations (GRE)/ Graduate Management Admission Test (GMAT)/Test of English as a Foreign Language (TOEFL) examination, for which regular students pay INR 21 per month to access all the requisite facilities at the centre. The centre also provides a forum for debate, group discussion, and regular seminars or daily lectures on the preparation for these exams. Members of the organization are encouraged to choose any village school/college and scholarships to deserving schools or students. The scholarship is disbursed by the Bihar Brains subsequent to members depositing the relevant amount in the society.

Bihar Brains aims to develop Bihar as a technical hub for research and development, as well as a centre of learning for formal and non-formal education. Under its programme of education work, initiatives are undertaken for school and college infrastructure development and building an environment for an all-round development. The objectives include providing career guidance to youngsters, jobseekers, and those engaged in higher studies and research, as well as organizing seminars and symposiums, orientation programmes, short- or long-term training programmes on cutting-edge technology, life sciences, and human sciences. The programmes are organized with an objective to uplift impoverished but meritorious students. It also plans to establish training and design houses, and give assistance to government and university or college departments to develop labs and start research and development (R&D) activity.

The Parth Foundation, another Bihar-based organization, also provides scholarships and awards to meritorious students, as well as running a school. The founder, an educationist, works in the Middle-East and runs the organization with the help of his own earnings. The scholarship programme, named the Aryawart Intellect Scholarship, was initiated in 2010. The beneficiaries of the scholarship are chosen through a competitive examination, with selected students receiving a monthly scholarship of INR 100, and a few other students also receiving a one-off scholarship of INR 600. The organization has so far disbursed this benefit to more than 500 people. In order to motivate children to apply, the organization organizes prizes for the best students, and helps nearby schools maintain the quality of their midday meals. The organization also runs an annual programme of organizing cultural events including cultural and sports activities for children, and periodic vocational training camps for the benefit of people living nearby. All these programmes are aimed to enhance the employability of people living in the region. Its overall annual expenditure is INR 50,000.

Awards and Scholarships for Needy Students

The Karnataka Zakat and Charitable Trust (KZCT) is a community social enterprise based on the concept of collective *zakat* (Islamic charitable giving), which among its other activities also provides educational scholarships to the poor and needy students. The organization collects zakat from NRIs, especially through online donations, and runs the KZCT Scholarship Program to provide financial aid to students who exhibit academic potential but do not have the means to pursue their education. Applicants are selected on the basis of their academic performance and socioeconomic background. Currently 12 districts are included under the programme.

The founder of the Trust observes that the social and economic challenges of recent years have focused public attention on the availability of skills and learning opportunities for the young. Formal secondary schooling is still the most effective way to develop the skills needed for work and life, yet despite a global increase in enrolment numbers, the gross enrolment ratio at secondary school level in India was just 52 per cent, leaving millions of young people to face life without the foundational skills they need to earn a decent living. Furthermore, there is a major gender disparity in literacy rates, with girls facing larger obstacles and being more likely to be pulled out of school. The organization focuses on education, considering the fact that economic growth per se does not necessarily imply a reduction in economic inequality. Combating poverty necessitates having equal opportunities to engage in economic activities and a more equitable distribution of incomes; and while education on its own cannot solve the problem of economic inequality, it is one important tool in promoting equal opportunities for all, including for children from marginalized backgrounds as well as women. The educational initiative of the organization is implemented to motivate students who have excelled during the academic year under the Trust's support. These students are awarded medals and prizes to encourage them to continue into higher education. Further, the Trust also aims to help the Government in its efforts to reach the underprivileged communities by running awareness campaigns.

The Parth Foundation, mentioned earlier for its merit-based scholarships, also works for the education of underprivileged and needy people. The objectives of the organization include provision of financial help to children in need, as well as quality midday meals in government schools. In 2015, the foundation distributed scholarships of INR 100 per month to six students and of INR 50 per month to one student.

Sahayata Trust also runs a number of educational programmes for the betterment of needy students, including scholarships of INR 600 per year to deserving students, as well as education loans of INR 8,000 to INR 15,000. The Parijat Academy, Assam, also provides monthly scholarships of INR 300 to needy students. These are provided in particular to help reduce child labour.

Special Programmes for Disadvantaged Groups

Many of the Indian diaspora organizations in different parts of India are undertaking special programmes designed to enhance the lives of disadvantaged people. In this section we review some of these activities.

Vocational Training

Vocational education greatly enhances employment chances, and the Government of India has launched schemes such as the Skill India Mission aimed to provide training for needy students. Specific ministries also have their own skill development programmes, with more than 40 schemes in 20 different ministries now providing a variety of skill development training programmes throughout the country.[3] Nearly 5 per cent of Indian youth are currently receiving some form of

---

[3] Employment Oriented Education to Students, Lok Sabha Unstarred Question No. 3079, answered on 6 August 2018, http://164.100.47.190/loksabhaquestions/annex/15/AU3079.pdf, accessed on 16 August 2018.

vocational training or related job-oriented courses. This number also includes students currently in school and colleges. The majority of students pursue vocation courses of under 6 months' duration (Pratham 2018: 56). While these initiatives are important for the employability of the youth, considering the vast population there is always a scope for more engagement, and many immigrant organizations have thus initiated programmes along the same lines.

Access Foundation Educational and Charitable Trust, in Tamil Nadu, is one such organization. This is a not-for-profit organization involved in carbon services and energy conservation with a zero-waste investment plan for government and private sectors, while also providing training and employment opportunities to educated unemployed youth in the field of energy conservation, carbon services and renewable energy, solar power generation, waste to energy, smart grid, and smart metering services. The organization trains engineering and management students in the field of renewable energy, carbon credits, and energy management technology.

Dream and Beauty Charitable Trust also works towards enhancing the 'soft' skills of the younger age group so that they become more employable. In 2003, DBCT initiated the Market Aligned Skills Training programme in Ludhiana, in collaboration with the American India Foundation. Today, the trust runs this programme independently under the banner Marg Darshan. The programme targets slum dwellers and school dropouts. It sends social workers, employed by the trust, into the slums to spread the information about the programme and to encourage parents and their children to join the three-month course. The curriculum includes basic computer skills, spoken English, coupled with a specialization in sales, marketing, and hospitality. Special attention is also given to equip young minds with effective communication skills, and attitudinal and behavioural training for work readiness. Under another programme, adult women are taught skills that would make them economically self-reliant. A dedicated placement team has also been created to place the institute's graduates in the industrial and service sector, providing support to the graduating students and the prospective employers both before and after the placement. To date the programme has trained over 3,000 students, most of whom today are gainfully employed and their families are financially better off.

Maithili Vikas Sangathan also works towards providing education to the poor and needy people. Located in the eastern part of Bihar, the organization has 70 members, two paid employees, and 18 voluntary workers. The founder of the organization returned to India from the US to help uplift the common people, seeing this as a unique initiative to bring together people from the Mithilanchal region,[4] who had migrated overseas, and motivate them to contribute towards homeland development. The objectives of the organization include sponsoring meritorious children, skill development, and vocational training. The organization initially worked towards financial awareness and promoting financial independence, in particular as regards the use of remittances, but this initiative was further extended with the inclusion of a skill development programme focused towards enhancing employability skills among the poor and the needy people of the region. The organization has purchased computers to provide technical literacy among local youth, and also trains local people in the use of the banking system through basic computer-based financial literacy. These activities are currently organized without any outside financial support, all financial responsibilities being borne by the founder himself. However, he plans to seek government funds as well as soliciting contributions from other NRIs.

The Punjabi NRI Association, established by three NRIs from Ludhiana, also works towards skill development for the underprivileged population, its activities including vocational training and skill development. People from other parts of Punjab, such as Jalandhar, Amritsar, and Chandigarh, had been working for the betterment of their homeland, and the organization was formed with the view that there was an urgent need for Ludhiana-based NRIs to help in these efforts. The Punjabi NRI Association, with its development-oriented objective, thus seeks to be a platform to facilitate development activities by NRIs.

The Non-Resident Jharkhandi Association, established by a returned NRI, also works on the educational development of common people. Having worked in the US for 30 years, the founder established the organization in 2009. Currently 70 NRIs from Jharkhand are associated

---

[4] The Mithilanchal region roughly include Madhubani, Darbhanga, Sitamarhi, part of Samastipur, and a part of Muzaffarpur districts of Bihar.

with it. The organization primarily focuses on empowerment of disadvantaged people of the region, in particular by providing education facilities and vocational training to tribal people, keeping in mind the aspect of employability. The organization has established a number of skill-development programmes in different parts of Jharkhand, specifically areas where the Government has little, if any presence. The Village Life Improvement Foundation, Chandigarh, also works towards providing skill development training aimed to enhance employability, as does Maharashtra Vikas Mandal, Nagpur, which provides a number of vocational training programme, free of cost, to people in need.

Sponsor-a-Child Programmes

Many NRI organizations also provide opportunities for other NRIs to sponsor the costs of education for children. The diaspora organization Aleti Charitable Trust works to develop opportunities for underprivileged children through education. It promotes and catalyses universal education among underprivileged children, seeking a sustainable means to include these children into the mainstream. 'Our organization has been an important support for local community people. Through this organization, we aim to help needy people especially people hailing from the Aleti community. This way, we are connecting ourselves to our homeland and sending message to the next generation.'[5]

The objective of their education programme is to sponsor the education of children who are at risk of discontinuing their schooling due to impoverished circumstances or due to changes in the family situations. The organization broadly covers Aleti community members living in Madhya Pradesh and Andhra Pradesh.

Community Awareness Programmes

Migration Facilitation Forum works towards providing pre-departure training to prospective migrant workers. The founder of the organization is a returnee NRI, who established the organization in 2010

---

[5] Telephone interview with staff member (Anonymous), 19 October 2014, Madhya Pradesh.

because he was unhappy with the level of training and information people received prior to migration. The pre-departure orientation has been an important issue of concern for many of the sending countries. Many workers face life-threatening problems on arrival due to lack of information about rules and regulations. The forum's aim, therefore, is to inform people about the possible difficulties they may face in other countries, providing workers with information about regulations in the destination country as well as other information needed for safe migration.

Financial Literacy

Financial literacy in Indian society is generally considered to be poor. A significant part of the Indian population has no or negligible information about how financial systems work. The Mithila Workers Charitable Trust, in Bihar, thus works towards the financial education of the rural population. The organization was established in 2012 by a returned NRI from the US. Later, more NRIs in the region joined the founder, most of whom had been working as scientists and doctors in North America. Vacationing in their hometowns, they felt there was an urgent need to tell migrant workers about the best usage of remittances and their potential impacts on their life. The founder established the organization with a view of informing migrant workers about the best ways to use the money they would go on to earn. Currently the organization has seven registered and 23 unregistered members, and up to the present it is run from the house of the founder.

Migration from Bihar, especially international migration, has seen huge increases, and this trend has equally increased the vulnerability of workers in the host country. The Trust was established with a view to create a welfare-oriented forum for potential or existing migrant workers in the region. In particular, there are acute issues concerning the economic costs of migration, since most migrants must borrow money from moneylenders as usurious interest rates. Over time, people have grown to understand the advice offered by founders, and increasingly grasp the importance of financial institutions.

The Mithila Workers Charitable Trust organizes events with the help of village sarpanches to motivate people to establish community

banks, provides informal training before migration, and informs workers about difficulties they may face. Most of the events planned by the
organization are focused on the poor people of the region, and up until
now 200 people have benefited from its initiatives. The establishment
of community banks in many villages is one of the organization's major
achievements, and it is planning to establish a fully functional office in
the near future.

Women's Empowerment

Many of the diaspora organizations run educational programmes
directed at the empowerment of women. Mehar Baba Charitable Trust
aims to bridge the urban/rural gap in education, medical care, and
employment opportunities in Punjab, and to support children of parents below the poverty line. The trust specifically works towards development of women through skills and computer training, healthcare,
and enhancing social awareness.

The Trust is working towards empowering women in rural areas
by making them into independent and knowledgeable entrepreneurs.
The objective is that women should become economically empowered
and independent. The training provided to women includes vocational
training, computer studies, and spoken English programmes. Women
are trained in marketable skills such as garment making, phulkari craft,
machine embroidery, aari zardozi embroidery, and rug making. Already
more than 500 women are in gainful employment, thanks to the
programme, working from their homes and in local boutiques, and
few enterprising women have started their own garment boutiques.
Some have formed self-help groups to produce phulkari garments and
imparting training to other women.

The Trust has developed significant infrastructure to provide training to women, including a large community centre, farmhouses, and a
high-tech high school which is in development. The community development centre in Punjab contains a computer centre, language lab,
vocational centre, and a women's empowerment enterprise and convention centre. Known as 'Phulkari Makers of Bassi Pathana', here women
are encouraged to work towards gaining commercial knowledge of
their product including packing, finishing, and marketing. Along with

employability training, the trust also works towards development of sports skills among underprivileged children between the ages of 6–10. Initially, former national and international players provided children with hockey training.

The Trust has opened a learning centre and a spoken English lab in Punjab to train girls in basic computer skills, networking, spoken English, and manual and computerized accounting. It also plans to establish training centres in other villages which can become production hubs, creating employment opportunities for poor rural women. The trust currently serves a population base of 200,000 underprivileged women, living in 186 villages in district Fatehgarh Sahib, Punjab, India.

Education for Slum Dwellers and Street Children

The NRI Forum was established by two brothers who had returned from UAE, where they had been working as businessmen. In 2003, they established the forum with a view to helping people living in the slums. The focus area of the organization is the slum population itself, which is located near to many labour-intensive areas. Most of the labourers engaged in these establishments are illiterate and come from disadvantaged communities. The annual expenditure of organization depends on contribution by members. Initially the organization faced financial problems because of a lack of support from NRIs; many did want to donate, but there was no clarity about regulations. Now on a firm footing, the organization has expended their work to other parts of Delhi also and plans to increase the scope to other parts of Delhi and India.

The Salaam Baalak Trust is an important initiative which we introduced in the previous chapters. Besides its medical work, it also carries out educational work for the benefit of street children. Street children can be classed as among the most marginalized sections of the society. The Trust works with street children to transform them into capable and thinking individuals, principally through enabling access to education, and empowering children with skills. Children come to the Trust from different parts of the country and even abroad, bringing with themselves a myriad of experiences—social, cultural, economic, and emotional. Most are first-generation learners who have either no experience of education at all or, worse, a bad experience including bullying and exclusion. Therefore, the Trust engages in three forms of education—formal school, non-formal education, and open school—and makes them available to the children as per their need and their capability as assessed at the time of first contact. To deal with this efficiently, different curricula with relevant teaching staff have been implemented. The teachers play the role of parents, attending parent-teacher meetings, and ensuring that the child is not discriminated against in school. The Trust imparts vocational training for employable skill development and capacity building for growing children. Children above 16 years of age or those who pass their Class 10 board exam qualify for vocational training. The choice of vocational training course for a child is made by career counsellor and staff members, keeping in mind the child's interests as well as a realistic assessment of his/her abilities. A careful attempt is made to match the child's skill and ability with the training course opted for. The Trust's team makes efforts to enrol children in quality training courses in reputed institutes: popular choices of courses have been Desktop Publishing, web and graphic designing, multimedia animation, film editing, C++ software, caregiving, house-keeping, puppetry, karate, theatre, macramé, and photography.

* * *

This chapter described the engagement of 24 local migrant organiza-tions in the education sector in India. Migrant organizations not only offer formal education but also provide various skill development programmes to cater to the need of the disadvantaged sections of the society. They run a wide range of programmes such as financial support schemes for meritorious children, modern technology education, vocational training, and skill development programmes even in the remote countryside.

Appendix A3

Table A3.1 Local Migrant Organizations in Education Sector

S. No.	Name	Year	Location	Coverage	Started as	Immigration status of founder	Professional background of founder	Beneficiary (estimated)	Resource mobilization	Broad activities
1.	Access Foundation Educational and Charitable rust	2012	Tamil Nadu	Tamil Nadu	Individual Initiative	NRI	Not Specified	Not Specified	Not Specified	Education for children, scientific research, and community awareness
2.	Aleti Charitable Trust	2009	Madhya Pradesh	Madhya Pradesh and Andhra Pradesh	Collective Initiative	NRIs	Business	Not Specified	Family Contributions	Healthcare, education, and elderly care
3.	Association for Science and Society	2011	West Bengal	West Bengal, Punjab, Bihar, Uttar Pradesh, Karnataka, Haryana, Jharkhand and Odisha	Individual Initiative	Returnee	Scientist	Not Specified	Personal Savings of founder	Education and science Education and community awareness

(Cont'd)

Table A3.1   (Cont'd)

S. No.	Name	Year	Location	Coverage	Started as	Immigration status of founder	Professional background of founder	Beneficiary (estimated)	Resource mobilization	Broad activities
4.	Athena Educational Social & Charitable Trust	2003	West Bengal	West Bengal	Individual Initiative	Returnee	Academician	Not Specified	Personal Savings of founder	Education and healthcare
5.	Bihar Brains	2004	Bihar	Bihar, Jharkhand	Individual Initiative	Returnee	Technologist	1,0000 (Appx.)	NRI Contribution	Education, community development, and advocacy
6.	Dream & Beauty Charitable Trust	1996	Punjab	Punjab and Haryana	Individual Initiative	NRI	Business	1,000 every month	Personal contribution of founder	Healthcare, infant care, maternal health, senior citizen home, and mobile clinics
7.	Chaitanya Gurukul Trust	2011	Bihar	Bihar	Individual Initiative	NRIs	IT Expert	Not Specified	Contribution of founders	Education, child care, and rural development

No.	Name	Year	State	Area	Initiative	NRI	Profession	Beneficiaries	Funding	Focus
8.	George Educational Medical and Charitable Trust	1977	Kerala	Kerala	Individual Initiative	NRIs	Business	10,000 people	Contribution of founders	Education, healthcare, and empowering people
9.	Karnataka Zakat and Charitable Trust	1996	Karnataka	Karnataka, Tamil Nadu, and Andhra Pradesh	Individual Initiative	NRI	Medical Professional	10,000 Scholarships	Personal Savings of founder	Education, healthcare, and empowering people
10.	Kerala NRI Trust Centre	2010	Kerala	Kerala	Collective Initiative	NRI	Business	7,000 People	Members Contribution	Education, healthcare, and community development
11.	Madina Educational Welfare Trust	2007	Bihar	Bihar	Individual Initiative	NRI	Business	1,000 People	Contribution of founders	Education and healthcare
12.	Maithili Vikas Sangathan	2007	Bihar	Bihar	Individual Initiative	NRI	Medical Professional	500 People	Personal Savings of founder	Education and healthcare
13.	Mehar Baba Charitable Foundation	1998	Chandigarh	Punjab and Haryana	Individual Initiative	NRI	Academician	186 Villages, 2,09,339 People	Personal Savings of founder	Education, healthcare, and empowering people

(*Cont'd*)

Table A3.1 (Cont'd)

S. No.	Name	Year	Location	Coverage	Started as	Immigration status of founder	Professional background of founder	Beneficiary (estimated)	Resource mobilization	Broad activities
14.	Migration Facilitation Forum	2010	Kerala	Kerala	Individual Initiative	Returnee	Business	2,000 intending workers	Personal Savings of founder	Education, skill development, and community awareness
15.	Mithila Workers Charitable Trust	2012	Bihar	Bihar	Individual Initiative	Returnee	Engineer	200 People	Personal Savings of founder	Education, healthcare, and financial literacy
16.	Non Resident Jharkhand Association	2008	Jharkhand	Jharkhand	Individual Initiative	NRI	Medical Professional	7,000 Tribal	Personal Savings of founder	Education, healthcare, and empowering people
17.	NRI Forum	2003	Delhi	Delhi and Uttar Pradesh	Individual Initiative	Returnee	Business	2,000 People	Personal Savings of founder	Education, healthcare, and empowering people

No.	Name	Year	State	Area	Type	NRI	Founder	Beneficiaries	Funding	Focus
18.	Palakkad NRI Trust	2008	Kerala	Kerala	Collective Initiative	NRIs	Businesses	200 People	Members Contribution	Education and healthcare
19.	Parijat Academy	2003	Assam	Assam	Individual Initiative	NRI	Teacher	522 Children	NRI Contribution	Education
20.	Parth Foundation	2009	Bihar	Bihar	Individual Initiative	NRI	Academician	500 Children	Personal Savings of founder	Education
21.	Punjabi NRI Association	2009	Punjab	Punjab	Collective Initiative	NRIs	Business	200 Families	Contribution of founders	Education, healthcare, and community development
22.	Sahayata Trust	1981	Telangana	Andhra Pradesh and Telangana	Individual Initiative	NRI	Scientist	More than 20,000	Personal Savings of founder	Education, healthcare, and empowering people
23.	Salaam Baalak Trust	1988	Delhi	Delhi	Individual Initiative	NRI	Film Director	5,000 Children / Day	Contribution of founders	Education, healthcare, and child care
24.	Village Life Improvement Foundation	1999	Chandigarh	Punjab and Haryana	Individual Initiative	NRI	Medical Professional	15 Villages	Members Contribution	Healthcare, sanitation, and community development

Source: Compiled by the authors drawing on the interviews of organizations and/or official websites and other online presence of the organizations.

4

Transnational Organizations and Healthcare Sector

Healthcare is one of the largest economic sectors in India, both in terms of revenue and employment. The industry is expected to grow in size from USD 160 billion in 2017 to USD 372 billion by 2022; the hospital industry, meanwhile, stood at USD 61.79 billion (INR 4 trillion) in 2017 and is expected to increase at a rate of 16 per cent to 17 per cent annually in order to reach USD 132.84 billion (INR 8.6 trillion) by 2023 (IBEF July 2018).[1] The private sector has emerged as a driving force in India's healthcare industry, lending it both national and international repute, and now accounting for 74 per cent of the country's total healthcare expenditure—notably because for the last two or three decades, India has relied more on private healthcare initiatives than on the public sector. While private sector institutions have received ever-increasing concessions and subsidies, government healthcare has been largely ignored, and deprived of funding or political attention (Chakravarthi et al. 2017: 50). It is within this context that many small, medium, and large healthcare enterprises have been established, with a particular emphasis on larger organizations (Santilli and Vogenberg 2015).

[1] India Brand Equity Foundation, https://www.ibef.org/industry/health-care-india/showcase, accessed on 15 February 2019.

According to Mukhopadhyay et al. (2015), there are 13,413 private hospitals, amounting to almost 95 per cent of the total population of healthcare institutions. Healthcare infrastructure in India was estimated to be worth USD 100 billion in 2015, and expected to grow to USD 280 billion by 2020, an annual growth rate of 22.9 per cent; healthcare delivery, which includes hospitals, nursing homes, diagnostics centres, and pharmaceuticals, is expected to see a corresponding rise (Chakravarthi et al. 2017: 50).

Transnational migrant organizations engage with the Indian healthcare sector in broadly two ways: setting up healthcare institutions through foreign direct investment (FDI), and supporting and funding local organizations. These developmental initiatives by overseas citizens have steadily become more significant: during 2000–17, India received USD 4.99 billion in FDI for hospitals and diagnostic centres (IBEF June 2018).[2] Indians living overseas have extended their interaction with the homeland via remittances, knowledge exchange through professional networks, and permanent return to help local communities with their skills and expertise (Tejada et al. 2014: 39).

As we have noted in previous chapters, the migration of healthcare workers from India to North America has been a reality for quite a long time (Walton-Roberts et al. 2017: 2). Indians constitute one of the largest segments of the US healthcare professional workforce: cumulatively, Indians make up approximately 20 per cent of the 'International Medical Graduates' (or foreign-trained doctors) who are operating in the US. Considering the fact that Asian Indians constitute less than 0.6 per cent of the US population, they clearly represent a disproportionately high presence in the country's medical professions (Pandey et al. 2004: 8).

This chapter discusses healthcare initiatives in India undertaken by Indian diaspora organizations established in different parts of the world. The chapter attempts to include details about major organizations engaged in the health sector in India, with information about the organizations gathered from a wide range of sources, including organizational websites, social networks, newspapers, personal contact, and more.

[2] India Brand Equity Foundation, https://www.ibef.org/industry/healthcare-india.aspx, accessed on 15 February 2019.

Building Healthcare Institutions in India

All the migrant organizations we have surveyed have their own modes of engagement in India. Those dealing with healthcare seek to establish hospitals, clinics, and medical colleges, while others have developed particular programmes to serve the poor and needy. While some aim to reach rural people through medical camps, many others provide financial support to existing organizations.

The AAPIO was established in the US by Indian migrant doctors in 1982, and had established 15 clinics across India (The Times of India 2003). The clinics vary in size and type, treating an average of 20,000 patients every year. Thus far, more than a million patients have received medical care in India with the help of on-site and outreach programmes conducted via these medical clinics.

The clinics established by AAPIO's work towards improvements in rural healthcare, and are centred on the needs of the rural population. The AAPIO has a number of clinics currently running either as independent initiatives or in collaboration with local organizations. One such activity is the AAPI Preventive Health Clinic of Jagtial, Telangana, established in December 2005 with the mission to improve the health and wellbeing of villagers in the area, focusing on what is known as the ABCD (AIDS, blindness, child-mother health, deafness, diabetes screening and education, safe drinking water, and sanitation). The AAPI Tamil Association of North America (TANA) Hospital Trust, Kadapa, Andhra Pradesh, another joint venture, is engaged in eye care, performing vision support and eye surgery for many local patients. The Thakar Datta Charitable Trust, Gurugram, Haryana, also works for poor and needy patients in the area, providing free medical care to the disadvantaged and the underprivileged. Statistics for this initiative allows us to gauge the impact of the AAPIO's outreach: in 2009, a total of 17,915 patients were examined by this clinic alone.

AAPI Charitable Clinic, Mandi, Himachal Pradesh, another medical clinic run by the AAPIO, provides primary and preventive health services. The clinic provides consultations to local communities concerning prevalent diseases and disorders, and also organizes specialty health camps and health fairs, and distributes free medicines to the needy.[3] Shirya Bhatt Mission Hospital and Research Centre, also AAPIO-funded, organized medical camps for flood victims in 2009 after an on-the-spot assessment of the situation of flood victims. Jigani Clinic Hospital, another AAPIO hospital, provides services for needy patients in Karnataka, offering both outpatient and inpatient facilities, and is equipped with an ambulance to transfer patients to referral centres in Bangalore.

Similar to the AAPIO, Children's Hope India also funds organizations to initiate various healthcare activities. Started by a group of professional women in New York in 1992, Hope India began its activities with an initial fund of USD 1,000 to support one preschool project for 25 children. Over time, the organization has increased its initiative to over 25 projects reaching 50 thousand children, and has raised millions to support a multitude of projects across several major cities in India, providing education, food, shelter, and health services. In New York, Children's Hope has given 50 per cent tuition scholarships to students from India, Pakistan, and Bangladesh to assist them in pursuing their academic and career goals through college education. In 2012, Children's Hope India collaborated with the K K Eye Institute and the Sadhu Vaswani Mission, Maharashtra, to expand the screenings and corrective procedures via the Sight for the Sightless project. Areas covered under the programme include Maval Taluka, Maharashtra, and the villages of Kamset, Khandala, and Kanhe Phata (all in Maharashtra). In Kolkata, the organization has partnered with the Society for Indian Children's Welfare to arrange heart surgery for around 50 children every year. In Mumbai, Children's Hope India has partnered with Ek Asha, to provide a programme which concentrates on education for children, support of parents, and community development. The programme provides education (preschool to Grade 10), nutrition, medical camps, and skill development. In Mount Abu, Rajasthan, the organization has collaborated with Global Hospital to distribute aid to students in remote

---

[3] 2014. 'Nearly Two Dozen AAPI Physicians Render Free Service', *American Bazaar Online*, 23 February, https://www.americanbazaaronline. com/2014/02/23/nearly-two-dozen-aapi-physicians-render-free-service-treat-thousands-patients-rural-gujarat/, accessed on 17 August 2018.

village schools and support each school through hiring an extra teacher. A health component also provides for regular check-ups for students and the distribution of medicine, as well as nutritional supplements to needy students. The entire village population also benefits, through the distribution of medicines (via mobile clinics) and a water connection in one of the supported schools. The programme aims to improve the nutritional status of students by distributing supplements during schooling hours, which also encourages school attendance and reduces dropout rates. School aids enhance the children's interest in the learning process and ensure that children have access to essential aid irrespective of their economic background. Health check-ups nip diseases in the bud and teach children about basic hygiene. The nutritional project for school children sponsored by Children's Hope India was short-listed in the top five of the Americas' Foundation Spirit of Humanity Awards 2011.

In New Delhi, Children's Hope India has established a preschool and health clinic providing primary healthcare for children and parents in the community. Classrooms have been created for students, along with kitchens and bathrooms, and early years' education is given for children aged three to six years. The facilities provided by the school include midday meals, medical care, community medical services and afternoon tuition, promoting education, discipline, honesty, courtesy, and sharing. Overall, Children's Hope India provides support to 19 organizations working in different parts of India.

Child Rights and You (CRY) India works to help children across 20 states in India, addressing the root causes of deprivation that constrain the rights of children. By mobilizing these communities, and working alongside with over 300 NGO partners, CRY India has enabled over 2 million children across India to gain new opportunities. It has received support from over 150,000 individual donors and 10,000 institutional donors from within India and overseas. In just nine years of its existence CRY America has transformed the lives of over 411,300 children living across 2,254 rural, tribal, and urban communities through the support of 56 projects.[4]

[4] CRY India, India NGO Awards 2007, p. 16. Available at http://bookings. resource-alliance.org/documents/casebook_2007.pdf, accessed on 17 August 2018.

Child Rights and You supports several organizations in the implementation of various programmes related to childcare. One such initiative is Peoples Action for People in Need (PAPN), which ensures that children in the programme area have access to quality education. The organization enhances reproductive and child healthcare and nutrition in the Transgiri region. The organization provides community awareness on the importance of immunization, birth registration, and issuance of birth certificates. It also liaises with the district administration to raise issues related to healthcare services. Further, it provides community awareness on the functioning of Anganwadi centres with the objective of tracking all children aged 0–6 years for health and nutrition assessments.

Janarth, also supported by CRY, promotes non-discriminative attitudes about differently abled children in society. It engages in advocacy at state level for the provision of medical treatment and therapy to all disabled children identified in the intervention blocks and villages. The organization also ensures that differently abled children enrol and are retained in regular schools. Further, it ensures they receive a disability certificate, and it also works towards providing Aaganwadi services linked with 20 villages to provide nutritious food supplements. Mahila Abhivrudhi Mattu Samrakshana Samasthe (MAMSS), of Belgaum district, Karnataka, is also being supported by CRY to provide healthcare benefits to children. Currently, CRY India runs 20 projects in support of different local organizations.

The India Development Service (IDS), another Indian diaspora–driven organization, works in the areas of education, environment, healthcare, empowerment, and income generation. The projects supported by the organization run in Andhra Pradesh, Assam, Bihar, Haryana, Kashmir, Madhya Pradesh, Maharashtra, Odisha, Rajasthan, Tamil Nadu, Uttar Pradesh, and Uttarakhand. The organization runs an International Village Clinic (IVC) to provide healthcare in the Uttar Pradesh region, and employs skilled medical personnel in an area where illiteracy and disease are widespread. As a result, the clinic has made impressive progress in reaching out to villages and providing both curative and preventive healthcare. The IVC's proactive efforts to treat medical conditions, cure illness, and prevent disease include: mobile clinics; ambulance services for emergency transportation to nearby city hospitals; treatment for common diseases; inpatient wards for seriously ill patients; screening for heart, eye, and kidney diseases; and 24-hour emergency services seven days a week. The clinic also offers diagnostic services such as X-rays, ultrasound, EKG technology, and basic laboratory services. The IDS preventive programme supports the ongoing wellness of its participants through vaccinations, nutrition, education, childbirth services, and family planning. The IVC, as of 2017, was serving 36 villages and planned to expand to 100 in two years. It also had an effective vaccination programme for polio, tetanus, diphtheria, hepatitis, cholera, and other such diseases in place. Additionally, IVC offers balanced nutrition programmes for children and pregnant women who have vitamins, proteins, and other nutritional deficiencies. The clinic offers basic health education seminars, preventive and educational maternity services, and childbirth and family planning services. The organization also runs a mobile medical and health kiosk in rural Rajasthan. The organization initiated the kiosk, locally referred to as Arogya Ghar, to treat common ailments and prevent diseases in rural Rajasthan. After extensive training, high-school students who venture to become social entrepreneurs can function as health workers as well as owners and operators of the kiosks. In the fall of 2012, Sustainable Innovation received additional grant funding and cooperative support from the National Rural Health Mission (NRHM), Rajasthan. With the support of NRHM, great strides were made in furthering the Sustainable Innovation healthcare initiative to work with primary healthcare centres. The NRHM instructed primary health centres and district administrations to extend full cooperation to Sustainable Innovation; the organization also recommended the pilot programme be extended to 50 additional villages, which would total 100 villages as part of the programme.

As well as this programme, the organization runs the Nutritional Supplementation Program in partnership with Sodhana Charitable Trust in Andhra Pradesh. With IDS funding, Sodhana seeks to provide 600 children with nutritional supplements in the form of two eggs per week, for the duration of the school year at a cost of USD 6 per child. The IDS funds are used to address the two-fold health and nutritional needs of infants and toddlers from birth to five years of age, as well as to help prepare them for school. Mothers are not only the primary but also the first and most significant teachers for this age group. As such, the focus of the grant is to address the needs of mothers in order to improve their overall health and well-being, as well as their efficacy as caregivers. To improve the health and nutritional status of the children, the organization will implement a participatory growth-monitoring programme and create awareness among women regarding the importance of a balanced diet. The programme engenders school readiness in children by building upon the capacities of the mother as primary caregiver and by improving the teaching skills of the Anganwadi worker.

Hospital for Hope aims to fund the construction of a hospital in an extremely underserved area of the rural Indian state of Jharkhand, where the population is approximately 100,000. For a total cost of USD 100,000, Hospital for Hope plans to construct and establish a self-sustaining hospital. Run primarily on patient fees, the hospital will be community planned and community operated, working their partner Jagriti Vihara, a well-respected local NGO.

Association for India's Development (AID) supports grassroots organizations in India and initiates efforts in various interconnected spheres such as education, livelihoods, natural resources including land, water and energy, agriculture, health, women's empowerment, and social justice. Throughout India people are struggling to defend their rights to healthy living conditions as well as to access healthcare. Joining hands with some of these efforts, AID supports village health workers in remote and rural areas, trains government health workers to work more effectively and sensitively, and engages in direct interventions in areas such as children's nutrition, eye care, malaria, or mental illness. The AID has supported a number of organizations in India to build healthcare institutions. One of these is Jan Swasthya Sahyog (JSS), founded by a group of doctors committed to developing a compassionate, high-quality, and low-cost health programme for rural India. The JSS has a three-tier system with 104 trained village-level health workers working in 55 remote villages, three sub-centres with health workers, and a 60-bed rural hospital in Ganiyari, Chhattisgarh, complete with an operation theatre, radiology, and lab services. The JSS is involved in development of diagnostic technology appropriate to rural areas. It has developed kits for diagnosis of anaemia, urinary infections, pneumonia, sickle cell disease, and diarrhoea, among others. The JSS conducts action-based research in childhood illnesses, TB, malaria, and leprosy. It runs training programmes for other organizations as well as for the government's own health workforce, acts as a Technical Resource Group for the Government of Chhattisgarh and the Planning Commission of India, and engages in advocacy for primary healthcare and a rational pharmaceutical policy, as well as highlighting the centrality of chronic hunger as India's most important and persistent public health problem.

Also supported by the AID, the JSS Village Clinic Support seeks to create a system of primary healthcare which builds a continuing and mutually enriching dialogue with the people and derives its strength and long-term sustenance by providing appropriate, low-cost healthcare services, identifying medical problems which demand scientific scrutiny, and working on them on a long-term basis and sharing the findings, including appropriate solutions to common health problems.

The AID also works in the areas of leprosy, a notorious chronic and debilitating disease. The idea that it has been eradicated, or at least exists in very low numbers, is largely a myth promoted by successive governments to underplay its seriousness.[5] The disease is highly contagious and affects the social and economic well-being of patients and their families. The government programme for leprosy patients is ineffective and private treatment is very expensive. The objective of the AID programme is to provide services for leprosy-affected patients of the Bilaspur district and the surrounding areas, documenting the treatment to show the government that leprosy continues to be a significant public health problem in Chhattisgarh state.

Unmesh Child Protection Centre,[6] another healthcare initiative supported by AID, works in the area of child trafficking and violence against children. It aims to prevent child trafficking and violence against children. The Voluntary Health Association of Tripura (VHAT) works

---

[5] The website of the Center for Disease Control, run by the US Government, provides a summary of the modern burden of the disease (known today as Hansen's disease), while also noting that the disease is not as serious as the myths would make out. See https://www.cdc.gov/features/world-leprosy-day/index.html, accessed on 7 August 2018.

[6] 'Unmesh' means 'sprouting of new life'.

on the same issue in Agartala, Tripura. Both organizations rescue, reha-bilitate, reintegrate, and provide medical help for victims. More than 50 children in the age group 7–18 years are directly being benefited through this programme. Unmesh Child Protection Centre provides shelter and care to child labourers, street children, ragpickers, children rejected by the parents especially the father, orphan children, victims of sexual and physical violence, insurgency, and differently abled children. Under the programme, basic healthcare services are provided including regular health check-ups, immunization, and medical facilities. Further, formal or non-formal education from class 1 to 10 is also provided.

In order to provide adequate healthcare, AID also runs the Alternative Health Care for Marginalized Women. This project is designed to enable people to address various interconnected issues of individual and community health. Ayurveda doctors and herbal medicine experts will instruct, validate existing practices, demonstrate, and help in iden-tification, collection, and preparation of herbal medicines by women volunteers. Preparation of medicines is accompanied by discussion of factors affecting health and nutrition. Under the programme, voluntary clinics are run by trained women and there is periodic dissemination of health information to women from these villages through the women volunteers and leaders. The programmes are organized to make women in villages into a collective force of change, so that they can be made aware and take ownership of health issues, equal wages, land rights, etc.

The AID also trains local health workers in Maharashtra, where geographic and climatic factors hamper access to medical facilities in several villages of the Chiplun taluka (Ratnagiri district, Maharashtra). To address this problem, the project (Amhi Amchya Arogyasaathi) aims to select a total of 20 women from 10 of these villages to serve as arogyasakhis (health workers) in their own villages. The primary function of arogyasakhis is to provide basic medical assistance for common ailments such as colds, fever, diarrhoea, and Renal Tubular Acidosis (RTA). They also provide referral services, spread awareness of preventive health, and address key issues such as the right to health. The project is monitored by the Nav Maharashtra Community Foundation (NAVAM) and run by an organization called Sanwad, based in Chiplun, Maharashtra, which has been working in this region since 1995. Support for Advocacy and Training to Health Initiatives (SATHI), an organization engaged in training and advocacy initiatives in the health sector, trains the selected health workers.

The Bihar Development Foundation, a UK-based Indian diaspora organization which we have also discussed in the earlier chapters, has significant healthcare engagements in Bihar, India. The Foundation coalesced in 2007 following efforts by professionals in the UK, most of whom had their cultural origins in India and in Bihar in particular. These professionals had for some years been supporting individual projects and causes for educational, social, and medical developments in Bihar. The Foundation had started many projects, one of which, the Healthy Heart Project, educated communities about heart diseases, hypertension, diabetes, hypercholesteremia by holding health check-up camps and educating, screening, and advising villagers. The Foundation has conducted several such camps, and given people, suffering from the above conditions, the appropriate dietary and medical advice. This project has received help from the British Heart Foundation and Diabetes UK.

The Dr Mahendra Narain Diabetic Retinopathy Project, Patna, Bihar, aims to create awareness in the general population concerning diabetes and diabetic retinopathy. The focus of the Project is to screen at least 5,000 people every year for diabetes, and thus to estimate the prevalence of diabetes and diabetic retinopathy in the urban and rural population of Patna. The Project provides free or subsidized treatment to patients with diabetic retinopathy who are underprivileged. The Project emphasizes the importance of maintaining a diabetic register by all concerned in the management of diabetes (government hospitals, diabetologists, physicians, paediatricians, ophthalmologists, and pathologists). The focus of the Project is to prepare a computerized databank of the entire diabetic population, collecting data from the various diabetic registers. Some other activities of the project are to train general physicians and general ophthalmologists to detect early diabetic retinopathy changes.

The British Indian Orthopaedic Society (BIOS) UK aims to provide educational support to orthopaedic surgeons of Indian and British origin who are currently in training or practicing in the UK, as well as those who, at any time, have been trained in the UK but are settled in India or other countries. The BIOS organizes various meetings, courses, and social events at local and national level, as well as acting as a forum for informal discussion amongst members on issues of mutual interest. The BIOS plays a key role in liaising between the Indian Orthopaedic Association and the British Orthopaedic Association. The Indo-British Travelling Fellowships sponsored by the BIOS are now well established and are receiving wider recognition. Indian Summer and British Autumn scientific meetings initiated and arranged by the BIOS provide an excellent platform for scientific exchanges between British and Indian orthopaedic professionals. The BIOS is currently developing short- and long-term fellowships for British trainees in BIOS-recognized centres of excellence in India.

The Manjari Sankurathri Memorial Foundation (MSMF), Canada, a registered charity, has taken on the mandate to promote rural community development through education, healthcare, and disaster relief programmes. The organization established the Srikiran Institute of Ophthalmology in 1993 in Andhra Pradesh to provide quality eye care.

The North American Sikh Medical and Dental Association was established in 1992 by the Indian diaspora in Canada, and strives to provide a platform for the Sikh medical and dental professionals to network and interact with each other while promoting the ideals and the mission of Guru Nanak. The organization has established the Guru Nanak Mission Hospital in Punjab, a 250-bed hospital run by the Guru Nanak Mission Medical and Education Trust. The North American Sikh Medical and Dental Association sends specialists in the field of orthopaedics to the hospital, who have spent significant time there and have helped in improving the delivery of orthopaedics.

The Toronto–Calcutta Foundation (TCF) began in 1988 when a group of Torontonians in business, teaching, and academia came together to consider ways to help alleviate poverty and need in Calcutta (now Kolkata). The Foundation has initiated a number of projects in India, one of which is the Dr R.N. Bhaduri Memorial Health Centre in West Bengal. The centre has a waiting room, consulting room, laboratory, and a small office, and its regular medical staff includes two physicians (one of whom donates his services), a nurse, and a field clinic assistant. The doctors provide diagnosis in basic health, gynaecology, dermatology, and cardiology. The foundation has also established medical field clinics, for which patients pay a small fee to attend. Medicines are free, to the extent that TCF can afford it, together with pathology tests. Patients are made aware of common diseases and preventative actions.

These initiatives and organizations are representative, since all the organizations working in India have some kind of engagement in India. We found three broad categories within the organization-building activities of these migrant groups: (a) building clinics, where it is evident that the clinics established by these organizations are located in areas of urgent need and serve specific population groups; (b) development of collaborative clinics and hospitals, notably in this category the work of AAPIO; and (c) provision of funds and grants to these organizations in the previous categories, where many transnational organizations provide grants to the local organizations in particular to establish hospitals.

Providing Modern Medical Equipment to India

The provision of modern healthcare is heavily dependent on technological innovations including access to suitable healthcare equipment (WHO 2011: 8). Middle- and low-income countries often have shortages of such medical equipment, which creates needless delay in providing adequate healthcare. In many developing countries, access to modern technology largely relies on donations and individual contributions. In many countries, these donations can count for up to 80 per cent of the available equipment (Gatrad, Gatrad, and Gatrad 2007: 90). Following similar trends, many transnational organizations also donate equipment to Indian hospitals. While many studies (Gatrad, Gatrad, and Gatrad 2007; Perry and Malkin 2011; WHO 2011) have highlighted the usability of these equipment, on many occasions the equipment become outdated and useless. These are the challenges addressed by diaspora organizations in the area of healthcare, many of which provide modern medical equipment to organizations already working in India.

The AAPIO, for instance, has made significant contributions of modern equipment to India. During the Gujarat earthquake tragedy of 2001, the AAPIO donated a minivan for the relief operation, and also raised nearly USD 23,000, which paid for an ambulance that was donated to the Bochasanwasi Akshar Purushottam Swaminarayan Sanstha (BAPS) relief centre in Bhuj, Gujarat.

The India Development Service bought a Philips HD6 Ultrasound System for the Halo Medical Foundation, enabling them to provide a daily ultrasound service for patients from rural India. Thanks to the donation, the annual detection and diagnosis rate of critical cases has increased by 25 per cent from 2007 to 2011. The Halo Medical Foundation conducts a monthly medical camp on the second Sunday of every month. A diagnosis and report are provided to each camp participant for INR 100 (roughly USD 1.5 as per the 2019 conversion rates), half what they would pay during the rest of the month, and the service is free to women and girls from underprivileged communities. Patients have thereby saved INR 625,000 (USD 12,500) in direct costs, minimized loss of wages, and reduced transportation expenses and other miscellaneous costs indirectly.

The North American Telugu Society (NATS) collaborates with the Pushpagiri Vitreo Retina Institute (PVRI), Telangana, a healthcare initiative of the Sahayata Trust. The objective is to organize Eye Camps, which it currently does in 20 villages at a cost of USD 2,500 per village and in 25 schools at a cost of USD 600 per school. An additional objective is to set up a library within the PVRI with an investment of USD 10,000.

The Telugu Association of North America (TANA) has also donated equipment, specifically EKG equipment to the Kuchipudi clinic in Andhra Pradesh, as well as video libraries to the eight medical colleges in Andhra Pradesh: Singapore Airlines shipped these to India free of cost. All these activities in India were conducted with zero cost to the TANA treasury: all volunteers met their own travel expenses and all the equipment was as individual gifts. Indeed, for the fifth TANA conference, all travel expenses and telephone bills were borne by volunteer committee members including the convener.

Asian Foundation for Help, meanwhile, donated 25 ambulances and medical vans to a number of organizations to assist patients, while the AID, which established the JSS, also funds priority medical equipment for JSS. The three outpatient clinics (serving remote parts of the Bilaspur district in Chhattisgarh) are to get their own microscopes, which hitherto had to be carried from the Ganiyari campus (20 km from Bilaspur) each time they were needed to diagnose blood smears for infectious diseases such as malaria. Apart from the microscopes,

JSS will use funds from AID to replace their haematology analyser, an instrument that performs automated counts of various blood cell types. They also plan to purchase a laminar flow hood for their microbiology tests, a wall unit that will enable the laboratory personnel to work in a safe and sterilized environment.

The Maharashtra Foundation has partnered with Vijay Shikshan Sanstha, Mumbai, Maharashtra, on a hearing aid project, providing behind-the-ear (BTE) digital programmable hearing aids for children to reduce background noise and understand speech better at a cost of approximately USD 600 per student. The Maharashtra Foundation will support 10 students at a cost of USD 6,000.

These examples aside, the contribution of modern medical technology and equipment by transnational organizations is not very common, and relatively few organizations have received such equipment. Further, the Government of India also discourages the transportation of expensive equipment from outside the country, and the relevant parts of the taxation system are not very clear and generally act as a barrier. In the main, donations are used to enhance and modernize existing medical technology and equipment rather than to provide completely new services from scratch.

Exchanges of Medical Professionals from the West to India

Exchanges of professionals from one country to another have often been treated as processes of skill accumulation, conferring a net benefit for the homeland. Some of the major activities of transnational diaspora organizations under this heading include exchange programmes, fellowships, and scholarships. The activities differ on the basis of enrichment and size: a few organizations offer scholarships to needy students and young professionals who wish to start their careers in a third country. Other organizations support students in their education and simultaneously provide skill development programmes to students in the homeland. These activities are performed by both local as well as transnational organizations.

The AAPIO has initiated an Indo–US physician exchange programme: the American Professional Exchange Association (APXA) provides a free service that matches US physicians with physicians in

India for a voluntary and mutually agreed reciprocal visit. Under this programme, hosts provide free lodging, boarding, and professional interactions to their visiting guests. These exchanges prove beneficial both professionally and culturally.[7] The APXA considers that US physicians can play an important role in improving medical education and healthcare in India, and in turn will learn about local traditional medical practices. The visiting Indian physicians also become acquainted with the US healthcare system, and such exchanges also result in joint projects benefiting both India and the US. The APXA matches physicians based on specialty and interest: of the 950,000 practicing physicians in the US, approximately 45,000 are of Indian origin, and some of these physicians would like to visit India and provide their services and expertise. Similarly, some of the physicians in India (especially from among the 70,000 specialists) desire to visit the US to avail themselves of the state-of-the-art knowledge and practice in their specialty. The APXA thus provides an organized framework for physicians' exchanges.

The AIF has links with the William J. Clinton fellowship scheme to support service in India, which is a significant scheme for supporting development exchanges between the US and India. As per the website:

> The Fellowship pairs a select number of highly skilled young professionals with leading NGOs and social enterprises in India in order to accelerate impact and create effective projects that are replicable, scalable, and sustainable. Through ten months of service and fieldwork, Fellows gain knowledge of development on the ground in the fields of education, livelihoods, public health, and social enterprise, honing and harnessing their growing skills as change agents capable of effecting lasting change.[8]

---

[7] This programme is supported by the US State Department (Office of Professional and Cultural Exchanges); the American Medical Association (AMA) [International Medical Graduates (IMG) Section]; the World Health Organization (WHO—Global Health Workforce Alliance—GHWA); the Government of India; and the AAPIO. See the list of partner members, https://www.who.int/workforcealliance/members_partners/member_list/apxa/en/, accessed on 17 August 2018.

[8] University of Pennsylvania website, https://www.curf.upenn.edu/content/aif-clinton, accessed on 22 August 2018.

The AIF has also started the India Medicorps Fellowship, launched on World AIDS Day of 2005, to connect US-based healthcare professionals with recipient institutions in India so as to expand the overall medical responsiveness to the HIV/AIDS crisis.

The BIOS, UK, is running a number of Indo-British fellowship or scholarship programmes. Some of these programmes are the Indo-British IOSUK Fellowships, Arthroplasty Fellowships (Junior), Arthroplasty Fellowships (Senior), Junior Arthroplasty fellowship, Junior Arthroplasty fellowship, and Arthroplasty fellowship. These fellowship opportunities are aimed to help medical professionals from India and facilitate skill upgrade through exchange programmes.

Special Programmes

Maternal and Child Health

The AIF engages in the healthcare sector in India in several ways. Its maternal and child health clinics provide essential medical services to those who would otherwise not have access due to the remoteness of their location. Camps are organized on a fortnightly basis targeting a cluster of six to seven villages at a time, consisting of a team of a doctor, nurse, and medical technician. The project is being implemented with the assistance from Tata Steel's Rural Development Society, its philanthropic programme focused on development in rural areas, which provides a majority of the staff and funds 50 per cent of the programme. The programme has seen a 19 per cent decrease in mortality rates, and AIF expects to begin implementing it in other areas of India once a decline in rates can be demonstrated over four years.

Mission India Foundation (MIF) is a US-registered not-for-profit organization working in the field of education and healthcare, particularly maternal and child health (MCH) in India. Mission India Foundation focuses on newer vaccines that the local health authorities do not provide under their schedule. The WHO calls such vaccines newer and under-utilized vaccines, and the organization provides such vaccines that are recommended by the Indian Academy of Pediatrics and WHO for the Indian population. Mission India Foundation operates from a local organization called 'Vaccine Centre', which has provision to supply vaccines like Measles, Mumps, and Rubella (MMR), Hepatitis B, and Typhoid to children and teenagers. It hopes to reach 16,000 doses of vaccines. The Vaccine Centre has been sponsored by a number of organizations, including Biological E. Limited, which has donated 1,947 vials of hepatitis B vaccine (paediatric dose), while Bharat Biotech International Limited, a biotechnology company, has donated 2,500 doses of Typhbar (typhoid) vaccine, and Singapore-based EPICS has donated INR 27,500 to Mission India Foundation to support 500 vaccines. EPICS is primarily a fund-raising entity that collaborates with individuals, universities, and corporations for the benefit of social enterprises and community groups catering to children's education and healthcare. Shantha Biotech, an India-based biotechnology firm credited with manufacturing the first India-made hepatitis B vaccine, has also donated 2,500 adult doses of hepatitis B vaccine to Mission India Foundation.

Sewa UK, based in Birmingham, is a charity of Indian origin that came to prominence in the 1990s when huge natural disasters struck the subcontinent. Working in partnership with business leaders, politicians, civic society, and local communities, Sewa UK has raised substantial funds for various calamities internationally. It is committed to working in areas which suffer from humanitarian disasters and tragedies, providing immediate relief and rehabilitation by mobilizing technical assistance to relief operations, and investing in building infrastructure and services in the aftermath of such tragedies. In partnership with Northern Cleft Foundation (NCF), London, Sewa UK provides cleft lip and palate surgery for children and adults in India who would otherwise be unable to access specialized treatment. Each year a team of medical and nursing volunteers travels to India with the NCF to provide high-quality cleft surgery. Sewa UK and Dr Hedgewar Hospital of Aurangabad, Maharashtra, are joining hands with the NCF to cater to those with cleft and pallet deformities.

HIV Awareness Programmes

Another healthcare programme being implemented by the AIF is related to HIV/AIDS awareness, operating under the moniker Positive Care. The programme aims to ensure equal opportunities for children living with HIV by developing a high standard of care and a common platform for orphaned and vulnerable children. Through a comprehensive assessment of the standards and practices of childcare institutions in high HIV prevalence states, Positive Care works to build the capacities of childcare institutions and families and strengthen the linkages between institutions and existing services, to ensure children get the care, support, and treatment they need while enjoying a stigma-free childhood. While frequently motivated by compassion, childcare institutions focused on orphaned and vulnerable children often lack the technical skills to focus on the overall development of a child. A comprehensive training manual for the capacity building of care home staff, based on assessment results from the experiences of different care home and childcare organizations, will be launched in the three states with high prevalence of HIV—Maharashtra, Karnataka, and Andhra Pradesh. The manual's holistic approach provides institutional caregivers with a range of skills, practices, and applications to better care for and support children throughout their development. The training manual serves as the basis for the project's comprehensive training programme in institutional and community-based care settings.

The Association of Indians in America (AIA) is a non-profit organization established in 1967 with a vision to improve and strengthen understanding between peoples through cultural and social activities. The AIA established its Project India charter to support causes in India, with a focus on health and specifically on AIDS Awareness and Prevention. In 2005, the association collaborated with Gujarat AIDS Awareness and Prevention (GAP), an NGO in Ahmedabad, Gujarat, which is highly active in the field of HIV/AIDS. The association has also collaborated with the Brooklyn Hospital Center, known for its Programs for AIDS Treatment and Health Center.

As of 2019, with the help of its partners, the organization works in 20 villages within 100 km from Ahmedabad, Gujarat, where there is no medical assistance. The AIA's Project India has contributed over USD 100,000 to GAP, to fully fund the rural outreach programme, focused on prevention of HIV/AIDS through education and awareness. The programme has touched the lives of over 600 patients who probably would not have survived without AIA's financial contribution, and the work of the GAP volunteers, assisted by the medical experts from the Brooklyn Hospital.

The TANA also works on various issues related to HIV/AIDS and other chronic diseases. As it relates on its website:

> TANA Foundation witnessed from very close quarters the devastating impact it has on families and communities. Met women, children and other well educated individuals whose lives were changed overnight, thrown out of their homes without food or shelter. There are children being born who will not know what life is without HIV/AIDS. Women in addition to not receiving basic medical care during the childbirth did not even get baby napkin to wrap the new born. These are innocent victims facing heart wrenching discrimination and isolation. After these encounters, one cannot sit back and think life goes on and it is the disease of others.[9]

The Lepra Society, Telangana, the TANA's partner in its AIDS Project, is an internationally known organization dedicated to the eradication of leprosy, malaria, TB, and HIV/AIDS. Their joint project seeks to establish a comprehensive model designed to empower people living with HIV/AIDS, provide them with essential medical and nutritional support, and build their self-esteem. The beneficiaries, in turn, will be the 'foot soldiers' in taking the fight to the community. The TANA Foundation also engaged in work it calls 'Healthier Highways', erecting informational billboards by the side of the road to explain preventive practices to at-risk groups like truck drivers.

The Jeevika Trust, UK, also works in the area of HIV/AIDS, through a specialized healthcare project called Mithra. Project Mithra works across nine villages, working with 165 families with HIV/AIDS to build their capacity to generate income from candle-making, making embroidered greetings cards, and goat rearing, which it supports with a crèche facility for their children while the parents work. It also provides ongoing income-generation training and market outlets for the candles and cards.

The TCF sends a doctor to Boral village in Kolkata, West Bengal, every week, where there are several sex workers. While attending to basic health problems, the doctor stresses the importance of condom

---

[9] Website of the Telugu Association of North America, http://www.tana. org/foundation/aids-awareness, accessed on 22 June 2018.

use and generally educates the women about the prevention of sexually transmitted diseases. Periodically, a woman 'peer educator' meets with the sex workers, encouraging them to express their concerns and allowing the foundation to better understand their needs.

Sanitation and Hygiene

The America Telugu Association is another organization established to promote cultural, educational, religious, social, economic, health, and community activities among people of Telugu origin, as well as to promote exchange programmes for students, scientists, and professionals of Telugu origin between the US, Canada, India, and other countries. Currently the America Telugu Association is running an awareness programme on fluorosis, a disorder which is prevalent in Nalgonda and surrounding districts in Andhra Pradesh. In Nalgonda District, nearly one million people are living on the verge of death due to an overdose of naturally occurring fluoride delivered through the ground water. Five hundred villages in the district are gripped by fluorosis, among which 165 are severely affected. This disease is more prevalent in areas where the underground water resources are tapped and pumped out through pipes. Such water contains fluorine which gets dissolved, making it a hazard for people who consume it. This disease is also known as 'reservoir-based disease'.

The Ekal Vidyalaya Foundation, based in Texas, US, also works towards sanitation and cleanliness. The foundation aims to eradicate illiteracy from rural and tribal India, and has created a movement comprising tens of thousands of teachers, as well as voluntary workers, and field organizations across 22 Indian states. With this tremendous human force, Ekal Vidyalaya strives to create a network of literacy centres that aim to educate and empower children in rural and tribal India. The Foundation is a charitable trust that initiates, supports, and runs one-teacher schools (popularly known as Ekal Vidyalayas) all over the country. With the participation of numerous non-profit trusts and organizations, this programme has now become the greatest education movement in the country.

The Foundation's activities also seek to provide healthcare education to villagers. The Ekal teachers collect data concerning the villagers, healthcare facilities, disease incidences, and common health issues. These are then reviewed by upper-level management teams of the Ekal Vidyalaya Foundation, and a plan is designed to provide healthcare education, services, and access to facilities in the village. The teacher is then trained to provide education and awareness on areas such as personal hygiene, sanitation, nutrition, awareness, and identification of diseases such as malaria and diarrhoea. The healthcare education and awareness activities are done through training camps and health centres (*Chikitsa Kendras*) in the villages or at district level. The trained teacher provides several levels of education or awareness to the children, villagers, and housewives to empower them take care of their own and their families' health. In many cases the teacher takes an active role in leading the change towards cleaning up the village, constructing toilets, or creating other sanitation facilities. Depending on requirements, the teacher is also trained as a primary health worker to serve the villagers in time of need.

Preventive Healthcare

The NATS has significant engagement in India in sectors including healthcare, education, and community welfare. Along with the Rotary Club and the Gates Foundation, NATS has initiated a programme to eradicate polio, aiming to raise USD 5 million through networks of friends and corporations. Further, NATS and the Ghazal Charitable Trust have jointly adopted villages of Uddanam area in the Srikakulam district of Andhra Pradesh where there are high rates of kidney failure and death due to poor quality of drinking water.

The Maharashtra Foundation works in particular on the issue of breast cancer, organizing a ten-month patient assistance course. The Foundation seeks to enhance the quality of lives of the under-privileged by supporting programmes in the fields of healthcare, education, welfare, and development of women and children. For issues related to breast cancer, it is collaborating with the Maina Foundation, Mumbai, Maharashtra, to provide funds to more cancer patients admitted to the Tata Memorial Hospital, seeking to increase the number of in-patients from 10 to 40, at a cost of about USD 500 per patient.

Health Camps

Many Indian diaspora organizations have initiated needs-based health camps in rural areas, one such organization being the Indo-American Eye Care Organization. The organization was formed in 2006 to provide eye care in India in collaboration with other like-minded non-profit organizations and local eye care providers. The organization has conducted a 'mega' eye camp at Shamshabad, Telangana, sponsored by other US-based NRIs. The objective of the camp was to serve over 1,250 people from the Greater Hyderabad region around Shamshabad.

The TANA Foundation, whose donations of medical equipment we noted above, also works in the areas of eye care, as well as spending millions of dollars each year in the Indian state of Andhra Pradesh on literacy, education, sanitation, disease prevention, health promotion, and rehabilitation. The many projects sponsored by TANA include libraries, schools, temples, roads, and protected water supply systems, and it has also founded a rehabilitation home for street children in Vijayawada. In 2005 and 2009, TANA helped build colonies of homes for people's whose lives and livelihoods had been devastated by tsunamis and floods.

The TANA's Project Envision is well known for the help it has provided in restoring eyesight to thousands of rural people. The Foundation is working with eye hospitals in Andhra Pradesh to handle the problems of cataract-related blindness amongst the elderly and correcting the vision of school-age children. The eyesight project is making steady progress in Andhra Pradesh, with cataract surgery camps being conducted on a regular basis. By the end of 2006, according to their records, the organization had completed 247 cataract surgery camps and 17,366 people had recovered their eyesight since the inception of the project in 2002. The staff of these hospitals is trained to screen large numbers of patients at eye-screening camps. Buses or trains then transport the patients who need surgery to the hospital's modern facilities, where surgeries are conducted on a mass scale by qualified ophthalmologists. Similar efficient techniques are being employed to screen the vision of large numbers of schoolchildren, where those children who need vision correction are provided with eyeglasses.

An eye-screening camp is a systematic way of reaching rural patients who would, otherwise, not travel to the nearby city for eye care. The camps are conducted as a partnership between TANA Foundation, the Eye

Hospital, and relatives and friends of the donor who live in or near the village where the camp is conducted. The relatives of the donors living in the village take on the responsibility for arrangements of the venue, spreading the word in the surrounding villages, and organizing the camp. A team of ophthalmologists, ophthalmic assistants, and camp coordinators from the hospital visits the village where the camp is held. The patients are provided with free food and accommodation during their three-day stay at the hospital, and then provided with post-operative medication, and two follow-up visits.

The organization also screens high-school children. The screening is done in two phases: following the initial screening, an eye-screening camp is held at the school. The hospital staff visits the school and conducts a more detailed examination of those who are found to be in need of vision correction by the school staff. Modern optometric equipment is used to check the vision and arrive at an eyeglass prescription. The cost of conducting the screening and vision testing works out to USD 1 per student.

The Asian Foundation for Help (AFH) was established in 1983 to work as a link between those who can help and those who need help in Asia and the Third World countries, and now has significant engagement in the healthcare sector in India. As well as collecting more than GBP 1 million over the last 17 years, it has also sent tons of used clothing to India, Ethiopia, Ghana, Tanzania, and Uganda. The AFH has major dealings with other prominent organizations in India, and has also sent help for the needy through the Royal Commonwealth Society, Sight Savers, Oxfam, the Save the Children Fund, Action Aid, and the St John's Ambulance Service. The Foundation is involved in a wide range of services, which include eye camps, provision of clothes, financial support for people in emergencies and distress, etc.

The Kashmiri Overseas Association has established the Shriya Bhat Mission Hospital and Research Centre, Durganagar, Jammu, where a workforce of consultants in internal medicine, neurology, general surgery, urology, orthopaedics, and dermatology is in regular attendance. Patients are registered for examination and treatment throughout the week. The mission hospital has so far rendered its services to more than 35 thousand patients. All the patients receive a free 3–4 week supply of medicines. A mini-laboratory helps with some basic investigations, again conducted free of charge for the patients. Like the other organizations we have looked at so far, the association also runs medical camps, and these take place from time to time both within the premises as well as in refugee camps. They cover the most prevalent diseases like diabetes, hypertension, asthma, heart disease, osteoarthritis, urological and endocrine disorders, dermatological conditions, and nutritional syndromes. So far more than 45 camps have been held, drawing patients from refugee camps and non-camp habitations. Further, the association also provides vaccinations for needy people. The organization has undertaken and completed vaccination drives in two refugee camps, covering 1,800 camp inmates. It hopes to cover the whole displaced Kashmiri population over the coming months and years under this programme.

The Hindu Society of Ottawa-Carlton is a registered charity incorporated in Ottawa, Canada, and is recognized as a non-governmental organization by the Government of Canada. The society contributes to the improvement of tribal and children's welfare through health, elderly care, and health programmes. With Bharat Sewashram Sangha, Kolkata, West Bengal, the society provides operational support for tribal welfare through programmes at hostels, orphanages, and health centres. Another associated organization, the Bombay Leprosy Project in Mumbai, works on comprehensive Leprosy Care Management covering social support, medicines, and mentoring. Another project, 'Mobile Hospital Covering' has provision for operation of mobile infrastructure, health/hygiene related education programmes, and medical services including medicine. 'RK Math Mangalore, Karnataka' provides operational support of for orphanages operated by the partner at Mangalore with focus on shelter, education, and health covering provision of food and clothing, and medical services including medicines.

Other Activities

The Capital District Malayali Association, New York, USA, currently runs the Jeevan Fund, a charitable fundraising wing of the association, established in 2006, whose mission is to assist Keralites who are unable to afford medical expenses, especially those who are suffering from terminal illnesses.

The AAPIO Foundation is planning to establish charity clinics in India under the umbrella of the AAPI charitable foundation, although funding will be responsibility of local/state chapters.

In 2009 the AIF initiated a programme called MANSI (Maternal and Newborn Survival Initiative), a pilot programme to improve maternal and newborn survival rates. MANSI is currently targeting 174 villages in the Seraikela district of the Indian state of Jharkhand, a remote rural area with a tribal population of 78,000 that has little or no access to basic healthcare. MANSI's approach has two components, one which trains community workers to educate and assist women before and immediately after childbirth, and another which organizes mobile health clinics to provide essential medical services.

The home-based neonatal care component is based on an approach innovated by the Society for Education, Action and Research in Community Health (SEARCH) Gadchiroli, an NGO based in Maharashtra which serves as a technical partner to the project. SEARCH was able to achieve a 62 per cent decrease in mortality rates over a seven-year period by training community workers known as Sahiyyas to educate pregnant and lactating women on health issues pertaining to childbirth and neonatal care, and assist them personally during childbirth and the first month thereafter. They are paid government workers, usually from the villages they serve, and are trained to perform all the basic health procedures for pregnant women and newborns. MANSI has trained over 200 Sahiyyas to cover 167 villages in the Seraikela district.

* * *

This chapter has thus looked at the healthcare engagements of transnational organizations in India. As we have seen, through their extensive engagement in almost all healthcare-related issues, these organizations emerge as the hidden backbone of the Indian healthcare system. Further, a number of activities aimed at the provision of preventive healthcare go beyond current private provision, and are able to provide significant help to people in need. One of the most prominent features we observed during our study is the geographical location for their activities, with a clear focus on the neediest areas, such as tribal areas of Jharkhand or slums in Delhi. Our survey of migrant organizations, although avowedly incomplete, is sufficient to indicate the importance of these organizations in the development of India.

Appendix A4

Table A4.1 Transnational Migrant Organizations: Healthcare Sector

S. No.	Name	Year	Location	Coverage	Membership	Professional background of founder(s)	Number of projects running in India	Number of partners in India	Beneficiaries (estimated)	Broad activities
1.	American Association of Physicians of Indian Origin	1991	USA	Andhra Pradesh, Gujarat, Haryana, Himachal Pradesh, Jammu and Kashmir, Karnataka, Maharashtra, Rajasthan, Tamil Nadu, and Uttar Pradesh	42,000 doctors	Medical professionals	15	15	20,000 patients/ year	Healthcare, scholarship, community development, and medical education

2.	American India Foundation	2001	USA	Himachal Pradesh, Uttarakhand, Haryana, Delhi, Rajasthan, Uttar Pradesh, Bihar, Assam, West Bengal, Jharkhand, Madhya Pradesh, Gujarat, Maharashtra, Andhra Pradesh, Odisha, Chhattisgarh, Goa, Karnataka, Tamil Nadu, and Andaman and Nicobar Islands	Not specified	Business	449	227	Not specified	Education, livelihood, elementary education, women empowerment, HIV/AIDS awareness, and public health
3.	American Telugu Association	1990	USA	Andhra Pradesh	6,000	Business	6	6	100,000 people	Education, healthcare, and social empowerment

(*Cont'd*)

Table A4.1 (Cont'd)

S. No.	Name	Year	Location	Coverage	Membership	Professional background of founder(s)	Number of projects running in India	Number of partners in India	Beneficiaries (estimated)	Broad activities
4.	Asian Foundation for Help	1983	UK	Different parts of India	Not specified	Different sectors	539	105	Not specified	Healthcare, education, and community awareness
5.	Association for India's Development	1991	USA	West Bengal, Tamil Nadu, Andhra Pradesh, Delhi, Jharkhand, and Punjab	Not specified	Scientist	12	Not Specified	Not specified	Education, healthcare, and community development
6.	Association of Indians in America	1967	USA	Gujarat	Not specified	Business	5	5	2,000 people	Education, healthcare, and social empowerment
7.	Bihar Development Foundation UK	2006	UK	Bihar and Jharkhand	Not specified	Different sectors	18	10	70,000 villagers	Healthcare, health awareness, and medical camps

8.	Child Rights and You (CRY) America	1979	USA	Bihar, Manipur, Odisha, West Bengal, Chhattisgarh, Gujarat, Maharashtra, Rajasthan, Uttar Pradesh, Haryana, Jharkhand, Telangana, Tamil Nadu, Andhra Pradesh, Madhya Pradesh, and Karnataka	Not specified	Different sectors	36	36	660,632 children/ 3350 village/ slums	Education, healthcare, and child care
9.	Children's Hope (India)	1992	USA	Madhya Pradesh, Gujarat, Andhra Pradesh, Jammu and Kashmir, West Bengal, Maharashtra, and Delhi	Not specified	Business	25	24	50,000 children	Education, food, shelter, and health services

(Cont'd)

Table A4.1 (Cont'd)

S. No.	Name	Year	Location	Coverage	Membership	Professional background of founder(s)	Number of projects running in India	Number of partners in India	Beneficiaries (estimated)	Broad activities
10.	Ekal Vidyalaya Foundation of USA	1989	USA	Different parts of India	Not specified	Scientist	35	52,000 schools	1,848,819 students	Education
11.	Hindu Society of Ottawa-Carleton	1992	Canada	Tamil Nadu, Gujarat, Hyderabad, West Bengal, Maharashtra, Odisha, Karnataka, Delhi, Uttarakhand, Uttar Pradesh, Rajasthan, Chhattisgarh, and Madhya Pradesh	Not specified	Not specified	25	25	2,00,000 people (approx.)	Women empowerment, healthcare, and education

12.	Hospital for Hope India	1975	USA	Jharkhand	Not specified	Different sectors	1	1	90,000 people	Healthcare, education, health and hygiene, income generation, watershed development, and agriculture development
13.	India Development Service	1974	USA	Different parts of India	Not specified	Business	253	18	4,00,000 (approx.)	Education, healthcare, and skill development
14.	Indo-American Eye Care Organization	2006	USA	Andhra Pradesh	Not specified	Medical professionals	3	Not specified	1,600 patients	Healthcare and eye care
15.	Jeevika Trust	1970	UK	Tamil Nadu and Odisha	Not specified	Different sectors	6	6	8,700 people	Education, skill development, employment training, nutrition, and public health

(Cont'd)

Table A4.1 (Cont'd)

S. No.	Name	Year	Location	Coverage	Membership	Professional background of founder(s)	Number of projects running in India	Number of partners in India	Beneficiaries (estimated)	Broad activities
16.	Kashmiri Overseas Association	1983	USA	Jammu and Kashmir	662	Different sectors	17	2	5,000 people	Education, healthcare, and community development
17.	Maharashtra Foundation	1978	USA	Maharashtra	1,000	Business	8	8	50,000 children	Skill development
18.	Manjari Sankurathri Memorial Foundation	1989	Canada	Andhra Pradesh	Not specified	Medical professionals	2	Not specified	2,50,000 people	Education and healthcare
19.	Mission India Foundation	2010	USA	Haryana	Not specified	Medical professionals	1	1	20,000 children	Healthcare, childcare, and vaccination
20.	North American Sikh Medical and Dental Association	1992	USA	Punjab	1,000 Sikhs medical professionals	Medical professionals	1	1	Not specified	Healthcare

No.	Name	Year	Country	State						Focus
21.	North American Telugu Society	1984	USA	Andhra Pradesh	Not specified	Different sectors	8	Not specified	10,000 people	Education, scholarship, and cultural activities
22.	SEWA UK	1989	UK	Maharashtra	Not specified	Different sectors	1	1	48 students	Education
23.	Telugu Association of North America	1978	USA	Andhra Pradesh	Not specified	Medical professionals	32	32	Not specified	Healthcare, education, skill development, and community awareness
24.	Vibha	1991	USA	Delhi, Uttar Pradesh, Maharashtra, Andhra Pradesh, West Bengal, Rajasthan, Tamil Nadu, Gujarat, Madhya Pradesh, and Karnataka	2,200	Business	37	37	110, 000 children	Healthcare, and women empowerment
25.	Eye Foundation of America	1979	USA	Karnataka and Andhra Pradesh	Not specified	Medical professional	1	Not specified	Not specified	Healthcare and eye care

Source: Compiled by the authors from the organizational responses and/or respective websites of the organizations.

5

Transnational Organizations and Education Sector

Immigrants' engagement with their homelands has become an internationally recognized subject, and—as we have already had occasion to note in the course of this research—has now firmly broken free of the rubric of remittance payments, under which heading it was once exclusively considered. Multilateral forums like the International Organization for Migration (IOM) or the Global Forum on Migration and Development have become international spaces to connect immigrants to their homelands (Omelaniuk 2016:19), and new initiatives are constantly emerging at country level to marshal overseas citizens to support developmental activities at home. India's active overseas citizen's integration policy puts it firmly with the frame of these initiatives. As we have seen, the attempts were largely made after the turn of the millennium, when a high-level committee was formed to look into possible engagements with the Indian diaspora. Later, with recommendation from the committee, a specialized government ministry was established to review issues pertaining to overseas Indians, and an agency was also established, the OIFC, to act as a focal point for diaspora engagement in major sectors such as health, education, infrastructure, science and technology, and others.[1]

After the millennium, the financial engagement of NRIs in India was considerably enhanced, eventually dividing into three major streams: full-fledged establishment, share-holding, and philanthropy. The philanthropic engagement of NRIs in India can be further divided into two parts; individual and organizational.

As is evident from the reviews of different sectoral engagements which we have provided in previous chapters, the development contributions of overseas Indian organizations are multilayered. There are microprogrammes which include building colleges, schools, or technical institutions, and others such as providing scholarships or supporting exchange programmes. All the migrant organizations working in India provide significant skill-oriented and community awareness programmes as well. Many of them run skill-development programmes to enhance employability, while their community awareness programmes are intended to empower rural populations. It is in this context that the present chapter outlines the educational engagements of transnational migrant organizations in India. Sections are divided according to specific activities undertaken, and the discussion is based on information provided by the organizations themselves.

NRI Education Provision in India

India has a vast population spread over a vast area, and thus faces severe challenges in meeting the universal right to education. The Indian Government has initiated a number of programmes to provide formal education to every children of the country, but these are clearly insufficient as they stand. Programmes like the Right to Education and Sarva Siksha Abhiyan[2] have been implemented to provide free education to poor and needy children, and the Government has taken steps to ensure

---

[1] Website of the Overseas Indian Facilitation Centre, http://pib.nic.in/newsite/PrintRelease.aspx?relid=90491, accessed on 22 June 2018.

[2] An initiative to provide free universal primary education. See the website at https://mhrd.gov.in/ssa, accessed on 12 February 2020.

there is at least one school at every gram panchayat level and a secondary school and government college at block level. Yet despite these efforts, the paucity of education provision remains palpable. Many of these schools face a scarcity of teachers and a lack of trained educational professionals. Non-governmental actors, therefore, become crucial, yet while the numbers of private schools have increased significantly, the fees are generally high and they remain inaccessible to India's very large poor and rural populations. In view of this, immigrant-driven institutions have become crucial, with overseas Indians providing inexpensive (often free) education to vulnerable populations in the homeland.

In view of the fact that they have a relatively low presence in India, and generally no scope to engage in frequent visits, overseas Indian transnational organizations tend to rely on partnerships in running their activities. We found very few initiatives that are run entirely by the organizations by themselves; more often, they act as supportive or enabling institutions. One such example is the MSMF, which promotes rural community development in India through education and vocational training, healthcare, and disaster relief. Since its inception, MSMF has been working with the Sankurathri Foundation, an Indian NGO. In partnership they have established a primary school, since Sarada Vidyalayam aims to provide free education to local children. In addition to the standard curriculum it offers, the school focuses on promoting self-discipline and the overall development of the child. Children receive free school supplies, uniforms, nutritious midday meals, regular health checks, and medication when required.

Where transnational organizations do engage in independent activities in India, they usually start up a small venture which can be managed in their absence. Compared with local organizations, the organizations do not venture into bigger institution building; local organizations, in contrast, are able to engage in major institution-building initiatives, since they have time and contacts which transnational organizations are unable to muster.

The chapter is divided into six broad headers which discuss the various activities of the transnational organizations: (a) education for vulnerable groups, (b) vocational education and training for skill development, (c) community awareness programmes, (d) provision of modern technology for schools, (e) scholarships and grants for education, and (f) special programmes: institution building (under which we consider: community-based education, innovative learning initiatives, alternative education, tribal education, hostels for needy students, educational awareness programmes for youth, education for slum dwellers, education for minority communities, community-specific initiatives, strengthening school education, and education for the physically disabled).

Education for Vulnerable Groups

We noted earlier that transnational organizations tend to rely on local partners for the implementation of their proposed activities: in some cases, the extent of such partnerships is striking. The AIF and Asha for Education, both based in the US, maintain partnerships with more than 200 organizations working on different issues, generally pertaining to communities living in areas of multiple deprivation.

Asha for Education supports the running costs of several children's homes. Typically, the support provided covers daily living expenses and schooling for the children. In certain cases, the homes receive referrals and partial support from the state government as well. Among the 57 local partnerships designed to provide support in the area of education, one key collaboration is with Aadarana, an NGO based in Hyderabad, Telangana, which helps orphans by providing them with accommodation, education, knowledge, and much-needed affection.

The AID has collaborated with the Society for Education of the Crippled (SEC), Mumbai, Maharashtra, to provide a residential school for differently abled children from rural communities. The school provides educational facilities to the children of daily wage earners, and teachers, physiotherapists, and social workers work with the children and their families for physical rehabilitation, academic education, encouraging creativity, and helping them lead independent lives.

The IDS has been working since 1974 to be a catalyst for change, and has thus far assisted more than 150 projects in 22 states with the support of over USD 2 million in financial contributions. The IDS has initiated a project entitled 'Primary Education for Rag Pickers' in partnership with the Indian Pollution Control Association (IPCA), New Delhi, a non-profit organization that has worked for more than a decade to help people who are involved in waste management enterprises. The IPCA has developed strong relationships with ragpickers and their families, and during the last few years has been dedicated to improving their health, education, and social well-being. The funds from the IDS grant are used to develop moral and social responsibility among ragpickers' children by using learning activities as a vehicle for primary education. The primary goals of the project are to educate the ragpicker community about general healthcare and sanitation, to improve their social status and quality of life, and to ensure that only children who really aspire to it will become ragpickers.

The IDS has also launched the School Readiness Programme in partnership with the Watershed Organization Trust, Pune, Maharashtra. The IDS funds are used to address the twofold health and nutritional needs of infants and toddlers from birth to five years of age, as well as help prepare them for school. Mothers are not only the primary but also the first and most significant teachers for this age group. As such, the focus of the grant is to address the needs of mothers, in order to improve their overall health and well-being as well as their efficacy as caregivers. To improve the health and nutritional status of the children, the organization seeks to implement a participatory growth-monitoring programme and create awareness among women regarding the importance of a balanced diet.

Lend-a-Hand India, a UK-based organization, has implemented Project Swadheen (meaning 'self-motivated'), which provides vocational training and career guidance to young boys and girls from urban and rural communities in pre-identified trades as part of the secondary school curriculum. Introductory training is provided in twenty different skills, such as poultry farming, garage mechanic, fabrication, carpentry, electric maintenance, tailoring, construction, and pathological analysis. Girls and boys in the age group of 14 to 16 years, who are studying in secondary schools, participate in these training programmes, with full or partial scholarships provided to deserving participants. Project Disha, another initiative of the organization, provides career guidance to young boys and girls from rural communities, since career guidance and counselling facilities are usually available only in urban centres and rural students are deprived of them. Career counselling includes aptitude testing, individual/group counselling, and year-long capacity-building workshops. Ongoing contact through events organized every month, feedback from career counsellors, and mentoring from professionals from diverse backgrounds all help the participants to make appropriate choices about their future career. A quarterly publication is also planned to reach out to larger numbers of students.

The educational engagement of the AIF can be understood as dividing into two layers. The first is its focus area, the second its active engagement in the different Indian states. The Foundation maintains educational engagements with children as well as community stakeholders. One such programme is the Learning and Migration Approach Programme (LAMP), launched in 2003, which educates and nurtures children in areas of high seasonal migration. Having identified seasonal migration as a critical issue for the provision of consistent and reliable education, the programme now functions in some of the most remote regions of the country, present in highly neglected communities that lack access to education. For these children, most of whom are the first in their families to receive an education, LAMP provides access to continuous, quality, and age-appropriate education, as well as resources to attend local schools, stable home and educational environments, as well as safe and structured care in seasonal residential hostels during the migration season.

The Lohana Community of United Kingdom (LCUK) was founded in 1978 to form a UK national body whose main objectives are to promote the cultural, religious, social, linguistic, and economic welfare of Lohanas in the UK. Since then it has grown steadily, and today all 21 regional Lohana Mahajans are members of the LCUK. The LCUK has sponsored the costs of building two primary schools (Shakta Sanala and Mota Bhela) with the aid of the Lions Club International in the Morbi district of Rajkot. These schools were rebuilt after the major Gujarat Earthquake and reopened in March 2004. They have a total of 332 boys and girls, most of whom are from local underprivileged families, and are getting a good education from the 12 teaching staff employed by the school. The Gujarat Government has recently provided seven computers to the Shakta Sanala Boys Primary School to hold special IT classes. The LCUK is looking at a further project to sponsor some refurbishment and refurnishing work at the schools and provide funds for IT teachers as well as more computer equipment.

Vocational Education and Training for Skill Development

Employment is a critical issue in Indian society. India has one of the largest working populations in the world, yet the majority do not possess the skills to achieve economic success. Many transnational organizations also have significant skill development programmes for poor and needy people. Among these, Asha for Education is working with partners through different types of educational programmes, aimed at a range of initiatives that have a positive overall impact on the community. Asha has supported the costs of providing drinking water facilities, seed funding for women's self-help groups, small-scale fisheries, and other types of community-based activity. Among the several programmes and initiatives which it runs, the Asha Darshan Trust, Assam, was established to promote education in a poverty-striken rural area by funding related infrastructure and midday meals. The emphasis is on providing vocation skills that will raise the standard of living and spread awareness about peoples' rights and responsibilities. Asha Darshan is an 'Asha Stars' project[3] run by the Asha Silicon Valley chapter, and operates in an insurgency-ridden area to provide education and organize self-help groups. The project runs 13 centres (pre-primary, primary, and lower secondary) in the Tamulpur and Kumarikata areas and has over 300 self-help groups under its wing. The centres provide a crucial source of schooling to about 1,300 children in this area, since there are no schools close by. Other than this, 105 other projects are currently being run by Asha for Education in different parts of India.

The AID discovered that even though Tamil Nadu had an excellent school system, thus eliminating the issue of access to schools, the quality of education provided in those schools remained a concern. Ineffective teaching methodologies, no focus on basic skills, lack of resources, and low community involvement were major causes of the lack of quality. Bringing together all the ideas from various initiatives, AID Chennai

[3] The Asha Stars programme of the organization includes group of likeminded individuals to take responsibility for a specific project.

is now spearheading a state-wide effort through its Eureka Quality Improvement Programme, which aims to improve the quality of the education offered.

The AID has also initiated a project in partnership with Medha in Lucknow, Uttar Pradesh. Medha, as its website explains, 'better prepares youth for life after school. We provide 21st-century skills training, career counselling and workplace exposure, and ongoing job placement and alumni support to students at their existing educational institution.'[4] In this project, Medha first collaborates with educational institutions to deliver its services within the existing system. Next, it works with leading employers to ensure that graduates meet their needs. Lastly, it delivers employability services to students. Recently, Medha secured partnerships with three local colleges—Jai Narain PG, Avadh Girls' Degree College, and Babasaheb Bhimrao Ambedkar University. The colleges introduced Medha to their students and granted it access to their classrooms and computer labs for two hours each afternoon. Medha also developed a curriculum which entails over 300 hours of experiential learning activities and 150 hours of on-the-job training. Currently, Medha is focus-testing the curriculum on more than 30 students from a local training institute and government job exchange. Medha has built up a core team of professionals to support its activities during the pilot year, and in addition a full-time volunteer from the US assists with a comprehensive monitoring and evaluation plan.

The IDS has set up the Skills4Girls project in partnership with Going to School, which also operates in Bihar. Going to School is a non-profit organization that empowers impoverished children to transform their lives through education and entrepreneurship. Skills4Girls utilizes narratives to teach entrepreneurial skills to around 600 school-age girls in 10 government secondary schools in Bihar.[5] The project follows the skill-learning journey of each girl for two years, during which time students regularly read stories with their teachers, play skills games in the classroom, and create and develop their own skills projects. Through

---

[4] See website at http://medha.org.in/about/, accessed on 2 August 2018.

[5] Extract from 2014 IDS Annual Report, http://idsusa.org/projects/current-projects/education/skills4girls/, accessed on 2 August 2018.

the implementation of skills-driven projects, Skills4Girls hopes to prevent girls from dropping out of school. In Bihar, 86 per cent of adolescent girls drop out of school by tenth grade. There is an evident lack of female role models who have completed their education and work outside of their domestic situations. This project, therefore, intervenes in a cycle of poverty that prevents women from becoming employable and independent due to societal constraints.

Vibha works to ensure every underprivileged child attains his or her right to education, health, and opportunity. Vibha's mission is to educate, empower, and enable all individuals who wish to make a positive difference in the life of the underprivileged child. Since its inception in 1991, Vibha has impacted over 150,000 underprivileged children in India and the US, by enabling, empowering, and encouraging more than 190 social entrepreneurs and projects in India and the US through over USD 8 million in direct funding. Vibha funds 28 projects across India, notably a project called Alamb, providing education and vocational training for slum-based girls in New Delhi. Alamb was established in 1992 by a group of experienced professionals who had been working in the development field for a long time. The main aim of the organization is to help people (the specific target group being women and children of socio-economically weaker sections of society) become aware of their rights to education, good health, and self-respect.

Sakhi for South Asian Women, based in New York, has initiated a Youth Empowerment programme for girls aged seven to 12 years, and in 2011 it expanded its reach and impact by providing services to young women aged 13 to 18 years. The youth empowerment programme was designed to expose youth to leadership, self-exploration, and advocacy skills through social, emotional, and academic support. Hosted as an after-school programme, the group takes the form of group sessions during which topics are discussed such as peer pressure, health and wellness, body image/self-esteem, and relationships. Another key component of the Youth Empowerment programme is to provide an environment where girls and young women feel comfortable talking about issues they would otherwise not speak of.

The TCF is registered in India to receive foreign funds and runs a wide range of projects, one of which is a basic literacy and needlework skills programme via Uttaran, a tailoring school for women that supports trainees to become self-sustaining through skills provision, and by implementing a microcredit system.

The Asha Jyoti Community Welfare Society is a nonprofit, secular, and charitable organization originally with the sole purpose of providing educational scholarships to the children of economically strained communities in India. Later its scope was expanded to include self-help community development projects for the benefit of the underprivileged in India. Asha Jyoti is managed by a Board of Directors who is elected by the general membership each year. They all work as volunteers and receive no remuneration or benefits in any form. The Society runs programmes in different parts of India: in Bihar, some tribal women were given formal training to produce and market handloom products—this project and the associated scholarship plan made Asha Jyoti a household name in this part of Bihar. Another Asha Jyoti initiative for women was initiated in Karnataka, where a vocational training centre including 24 sewing machines was established to teach tailoring to a group of widows and poor women. The scholarship fund provides them with necessities such as books, tuition fees, stationary, school uniforms, shoes, transportation, winter clothes, and basic medical care.

Jeevika, another UK-based Indian diaspora organization, works on educational development, and is currently undertaking more than 10 projects in Tamil Nadu and Odisha, benefiting over 15,000 villagers in more than 25 villages, as well as extending the organization's support in the northern state of Uttarakhand and in south-west Uttar Pradesh. One of these initiatives is Project Madhu, an ongoing beekeeping initiative for 100 tribal women who live in the Chandaka Tribal Forest Area. By providing self-help group development, livelihood training, and equipment for honey production as well as for vermicomposting, medicinal herbs, and kitchen garden production, women beekeepers are providing honey for their families, selling the surplus at the village market, and contributing to household income. These bee colonies also make a vital contribution to the pollination of fruits and crops and help sustain the local ecology.

Community Awareness Programmes

Many organizations work on issues related to community awareness. Asha for Education, for instance, is currently running community awareness programmes with the support of many allied organizations. These programmes provide education aimed at raising awareness on various sociopolitical issues and creating an informed society capable of generating social change. These programmes are located both in rural (tribal) communities as well as cities. They cover a broad range of issues including agriculture, general health, women's education, and community rights.

In the last eight years, Asha for Education's Aasra Sewa Santhan project has focused on a number of things including children's education, public rights, and employment guarantee. This is done primarily through NGOs using and enforcing the Right to Information Act of 2005 and the National Rural Employment Guarantee Act (NREGA). The organization works primarily with the Mushahar tribe, and underserved and unheard group. Along with this, 10 other projects are being initiated by Asha in different parts of India.

In collaboration with the Muthamizh Education and Rural Development Society (MERDS) in Tamil Nadu, the AID runs a programme entitled 'Awareness Education through Cultural Performances in Villages'. The MERDS is a registered non-profit organization that is engaged in creating a positive impact through building a collective movement within the rural population. This project is aimed at spreading awareness about HIV/AIDS in villages, through street theatre, music, and folk arts. In the process, it also seeks to identify high-risk individuals via health surveys and subsequently tests them for HIV/AIDS.

Vibha runs a project entitled Society for Education and Action (SEA), which educates and empowers children in fishermen's community in Tamil Nadu. Here it supports motivation centres, bridge courses, and parent-teachers associations. Motivation centres help students in their studies and general development, and encourage them to continue education. The extracurricular activities conducted by SEA in these motivation centres allow these children to discover their talents and learn new things. Bridge courses enable dropouts to get into mainstream Government schools.

Sakhi for South Asian Women, which we discussed earlier, runs the Economic Empowerment Programme, seeking to provide financial stability and economic security to survivors of domestic violence from the South Asian Diaspora. Sakhi recognizes the close links between domestic violence, economic control, and self-sufficiency, and sees the importance of the ability to make choices that create safety for women and their families. Realizing the need for services aimed at improving survivors' economic opportunities, Sakhi has provided skills-enhancement activities since the mid-1990s under the banner of the Economic Justice Project. In 2001, the organization's efforts were formalized under the Economic Empowerment Programme. The organization currently provides case management, workshops and training, and scholarships to women so that they can access public benefits, jobs, credit, banking, and other forms of support, and thus reach their goals of self-sufficiency and safety.

Bharat Sevashram Sangha (BSS), a Canada-based Indian diaspora organization which operates more than 100 institutions providing quality education to disadvantaged children, has organized health awareness camps in its schools and educational institutions. A total of 6,116 students have been examined till 2018 and treatment has been given to them when necessary. Special clinics have been held for the care of tribal groups, benefitting over 3,000 people. As well as a charitable dispensary, BSS operates a free multispecialty hospital at its ashram in Barajuri, this being the only medical facility within an area of 12,000 square km. The hospital has recently introduced an ambulance service, extending its geographical reach. Four mobile medical units operating at 64 locations provide healthcare facilities to 200,000 people under the Government of India's Grant-in-Aid programme. Awareness campaigns are organized to make tribals more conscious of health risks. Interactive aids such as audio-visual presentations are used to educate tribals on issues of health and hygiene. The organization also has social-service-based education programmes which combine with vocational training programmes to empower the youth to be self-sufficient and economically independent. The Sangha runs institutes for formal and non-formal education which include primary schools, night schools, junior basic schools, junior high schools, high schools, and colleges.

Provision of Modern Technology for Schools

Education in India can be broadly divided into two categories: government and private. Although there are also other categories of school, including religious schools and schools run by trusts, these are very much in the minority compared to government and private ones. One of the most visible differences between private and government schools is presence of modern educational equipment. Most of the private schools today are furnished with modern educational equipment such as computers, while the government is generally yet to provide such measures for the children in its schools. Considering this, the role of non-governmental organizations such as transnational immigrant organizations emerges as very important, since these organizations engage in various activities to provide appropriate technological education to needy children. In this section, we document the role of transnational organizations in enabling children to access modern means of education.

The AIF holds 'Digital Equalizer' programmes, equipping each participating school with a computer centre, an educational laboratory to enhance student learning that reaches approximately 400 students per site. Targeting secondary students in grades 6–10, the programme trains educators in basic computer literacy, internet research, and pedagogical methodologies that bring creativity, diversity, and real-life examples into the school curriculum through the use of technology. The Digital Equalizer curriculum ensures that teachers and students are equipped with practical digital literacy skills that enhance both their classroom and out-of-school learning. Digital Equalizer schools demonstrate improved learning outcomes in subject learning alongside a marked increase in the utilization of technology for teachers and students alike. The impact of Digital Equalizer extends well beyond the classroom: by inspiring students to take charge of their education, parents and communities increasingly support keeping their children in school. The AIF is also partnering with state governments to scale up its work and sustain it long term.

Asha for Education supports educational resource centres which aim to improve the quality of schooling provided by both government and non-government schools. These resource centres serve the important role of documenting and disseminating information on teaching and learning techniques and learning aids. They also serve as centres for exploring ideas related to pedagogy, and for disseminating information and training affecting the quality of the schooling experience. The organization also provides mobile laboratories that provide children with the ability to perform practical experiments in science and other subjects. The mobile laboratory is placed in a bus or van and driven from school to school, and also carry books, videos, and other educational materials.

Asha is working with organizations such as the Tamil Nadu Science Forum to produce and disseminate educational and science communication videos that can be used in schools, by NGOs, and by science movement activists in villages. The organization is also involved in a collaborative effort to develop supplementary curriculum material, supporting the production costs of material for further distribution. Asha works with organizations such as World Computer Exchange and Friends of Young Minds to collect working computers from corporations and individuals in the US, and ship them to India where they are put to educational use, mostly in government schools which do not have such facilities.

Since 1997, Eureka Child, a key initiative of the AID, has focused on innovative and enduring interventions in the area of education. Over these years, the AID has developed many techniques for teaching basic science, mathematics, and reading. The techniques have been in the form of subject-based learning modules, built up through extensive work with school children and field experimentation. In 2006, the Government of Tamil Nadu requested the AID to train its teachers to improve the quality of education. Within a period of six months, the AID reached out to 7,300 schools in five districts in Tamil Nadu and trained the teachers on a novel approach to learning. The AID was able to achieve an improvement in reading skills by 30 per cent in that period.

The IDS has implemented a project in collaboration with the Himalayan Education Foundation (HEF) in Kumaon region of Uttarakhand. The IDS awarded USD 5,000 to HEF for work in the Kumaon region. In partnership with Avani, a local NGO that develops and disseminates technologies utilizing solar resources, HEF installed a 20W/20Ah solar LED system with 17 light fixtures. The installation provides uninterrupted lighting in classrooms, the library, dormitories, dining hall, offices, and teachers' quarters. The lighting system solved an ongoing and long-standing problem of the erratic power supply, which directly contributes to the livelihood of the community and its utilization of solar resources. Two hundred school students and staff benefit from this initiative, while it also has the symbolic benefit of a reduction in deforestation and carbon emissions.

The IDS is implementing another project named 'Supplemental Remedial Education' in partnership with the Sharda Mahila Vikas Society in Bharuch District, Gujarat. The IDS funds supported tutorial classes to improve the education of impoverished children whose parents are unable to afford private tuition. Teaching materials are provided and storytelling, action songs, puppets, games, and CDs and DVDs are utilized to simultaneously improve language skills and make learning enjoyable and interesting. The society focuses on students' health as well as their education. Every student receives a yearly health check-up, and treatment and medicine are dispensed as needed. In addition, students are taught personal hygiene and life-building skills. Skills include basic grooming (such as washing hands and trimming fingernails) and basic mending (such as sewing patches and buttons on clothing and putting protective coverings on books), to illustrate the importance of cleanliness and hygiene in their daily lives. Children are also taught to recycle and make useful items out of discarded materials such as vegetables, broken bangles, waste paper, and woollen clothes by turning them into Diwali cards, rakhis, paper caps, and other craftwork.

The NATS has worked with the Andhra Pradesh State Government and the local panchayat to set up digital libraries. Under the project, panchayatas are donating land for the buildings, while the state Government is engaged in the maintenance of facilities.

Under the school development programmes, and in collaboration with JBVS, AID has initiated a project called 'Computer Education for Rural Children and Youth'. The JBVS is a non-profit organization committed towards providing quality computer education to young people living in villages. The organization aims to provide basic computer literacy, furnish a computer as a tool for learning in schools and home, and offer training in hardware support. Currently JBVS runs six computer centres in different locations providing basic computer literacy, with around 115 students participating. The JBVS and a collaborating organization are also running computer education programmes in schools in rural areas, currently operating in three schools. Many students get job opportunities after going through the JBVS programme, notably in reputed firms, schools, and computer centres.

Scholarships and Grants for Education

While discussing the engagement of local immigrant organizations in the education sector, we provided examples of organizations located in the interior regions of India which provide scholarships to needy children. While local immigrant organizations play a very important role in supporting education among economically weaker people, their ability to engage in outreach is relatively low. However, some transnational organizations engage in extensive scholarship distribution activities in India, and this section lists some of the major activities.

Asha for Education runs a fellowship programme that supports individuals 'of the highest quality and unquestionable dedication'. The area of support includes (but is not limited to) education, income generation, women's empowerment, and integrated rural or slum development, addressing dominant social concerns like child labour, bonded labour and other areas (Bhatt, Ghopal, and Barghava 2006: 100).

The Indian American Forum for Political Education (IAFPE) has initiated the IAFPE Summer Political Fellowship Programme, which seeks to increase the engagement of Indian American students in the Massachusetts state political system by placing applicants in two- or three- month political fellowships, with the requirement that they engage in a structured community project thereafter.

The IDS runs a project in partnership with PUKAR Monsoon in Mumbai, the latter being a platform in which participants in PUKAR's Youth Fellowship Programme have an opportunity to present action research projects conducted with Mumbai's disenfranchised population. PUKAR is an independent research collective that trains youth to use participatory, community-based research as a tool for alternative pedagogy, advocacy, transformation, and intervention. The presentations teach presenters and attendees how to analyse problems and synthesize information to find solutions. The PUKAR Youth Fellowship Programme trains 300 'Barefoot Researchers' every year with financial support from IDS. Barefoot Researchers are youth who have become empowered with the knowledge and skills required to conduct research in their communities, thereby democratizing the research and knowledge-building process. In 2013, PUKAR Monsoon helped 30 Barefoot Researchers present research topics to 5,000 youth in various educational institutions and communities in Mumbai.

The Upakar Foundation, created in 1997 in the US by a group of Indian-American leaders from the Washington DC area, also helps disadvantaged Indian-American students to achieve their educational goals, gives four-year renewable scholarships, acknowledging academic excellence and consider financial need.

The NATS has a scholarship project called the Society for Rural Scholars (SFRS) to sponsor disadvantaged students across the country who demonstrate academic excellence and strong leadership skills. These scholarships assist students in meeting the cost of attendance at the school of their choice. Scholars who choose to pursue studies in the areas of mathematics, finance, science, languages, engineering, and medicine are eligible to receive funding. While the state continues the difficult work of creating high-quality institutions from which all students graduate and learn to face global challenges, the organization aims to remove the financial barriers that prevent low-income students from pursuing higher educational goals. Private assistance, so NATS claims, is a critical measure in bringing true equality to the Indian educational system.

The TANA, meanwhile, provides its TANA Foundation Graduate Scholarships, open to Telugu students who are currently residing in Andhra Pradesh and wish to pursue higher education in the US. The TANA has also set up an endowment to award scholarships to financially disadvantaged but meritorious students who aim to pursue higher education and so overcome their poverty. This endowment covers about eight scholarships based on current returns. However, the Foundation is trying to find more sponsors. Each scholarship recipient will be directly connected with his/her sponsor so that sponsor can monitor the student's progress and mentor him or her. Meritorious students are selected from low-income families, and do not belong to any reservation category and as such do not receive any financial support from the Government. According to the current policy in Andhra Pradesh, the Government reimburses tuition fees for professional studies for such students; however, many are left without any support. Though the

Government reimburses their tuition fees, their economic background poses barriers in finding resources for books and other living expenses. The TANA Foundation gives such aspiring students a scholarship which enables them to complete their professional degrees.

Sakhi for South Asian Women provides the Swarna Chalasani Scholarship Fund, established in 2002 in memory of a volunteer who died in the atrocity of 9/11. The scholarship advances the ability of survivors of violence to complete higher educational goals and supports them in obtaining the necessary licensing and vocational certificates in order to obtain and retain jobs. The fund has supported women through nursing school, college, postgraduation programmes, and in other programmes that have enabled them to provide for themselves and their family.

The National Congress of American Indians (NCAI) also offers many scholarship programmes. Under the NCAI Internships, students enrolled in institutions of higher learning are invited to apply for semester or summer-long internships (for which most institutions will offer college credit), with one to two applicants selected for each term. The NCAI interns work with various staff on issues that concern them. The NCAI Wilma Mankiller Fellowship Programme for Tribal Policy and Governance Fellowship provides an opportunity for young professionals in India to work with national leaders engaged in shaping in tribal policy. By developing a cohort of native health professionals who are ready to lead in formulating and promoting health policies and practices that meet the unique needs of both American Indians and Alaska Natives, the NCAI Native Graduate Health Fellowship aims to address the stark disparities in the health of tribal populations. The Fellowship provides for a financial award of USD 5,000, and professional development in tribal health policy. The NCAI also offers internships and fellowships to young leaders from India, so that they may serve on the forefront of legislative action and policy development. All interns and fellows are selected through an application and interview process.

The Asha Jyoti Community Welfare Society provides the Asha Jyoti educational scholarship, which allows children to continue their education and realize their ambitions for a better future. The scholarship fund provides for books, tuition fees, stationery, uniform, shoes, transportation, winter clothes, and basic medical care. Preference is given to high-school students who are orphans, fatherless, or from large families with only one earning member. No consideration is given to gender, caste, creed, religion, or the place of origin of the applicant. Asha Jyoti is entirely privately funded, with sponsors donating a fixed annual amount determined by the Board of Directors. Asha Jyoti also receives donations from the public, and organizes fundraising events. In addition to educational scholarships for the needy, as mentioned on its homepage, Asha Jyoti supports small community projects for under-privileged communities.

As noted in Chapter 4, Children's Hope India has given out 50 per cent tuition scholarships to several South Asian students from India, Pakistan, and Bangladesh to assist them in pursuing their academic and career goals through college education.

The Guru Ravidass Educational Assistance Trust, an Indian diaspora organization based in the UK, provides financial help for poor and needy students whether engaged in primary school or in higher professional courses.

Special Programmes: Institution-Building

We observed at the outset of this chapter that the majority of migrant organizations are engaged in providing support for existing initiatives, often working in partnership with local agencies. This strategic approach reflects the positional strengths and weaknesses of migrant organizations, being located in countries which confer considerable social and financial capital, but lacking the local contacts and networks which would allow them to be really effective solo actors within India itself. Nevertheless, some migrant organizations have engaged in the challenging process of building up entirely new education institutions within India itself. This section reviews some of these projects.

Community-Based Education

Basing education facilities within the communities that need them has long been a major area of concern for the Indian government as well as for non-governmental organizations. There are attempts to provide education 'on the door-step' or at least near to populations living with multiple deprivation. One such activity is being run by AIF: as we saw earlier, this organization provides education for children of migrant labourers. Working directly with communities, AIF also forms village councils and trains community members to improve school management and planning, thus fostering trust between community leaders, parents, and families, and establishing community-wide ownership of the education facilities provided for their children.

The TCF runs two full-time pre-elementary schools in Kolkata, West Bengal (for children aged 3–7 years) and a basic education programme for mothers. The two pre-elementary schools operate in Ghutiari Sharif (60 students), and Chakjaggaddal (30 students), each run by two teachers. The programme also includes monthly health check-ups, and one daily snack plus school uniforms. The mothers' basic education programme is focused on reproductive and child health, food and nutrition, intestinal diseases, and sanitation problems. The mothers are involved in selecting food for the pre-elementary schools through a parent–teacher committee, guided by staff with experience in teaching general hygiene, and school administration. Seminars are held twice a year on health and hygiene. Once the year ends, new mothers are educated in collaboration with women's group specializing in public health, women empowerment, microcredit, self-help groups, and disease prevention.

Innovative Learning Initiatives

Educational innovation enhances the learning capabilities of students. Innovation can be at any level, including innovative learning methods adopted by teachers within or outside of the classroom. The AIF is adopting one such innovative learning approach, fostering cross-cultural understanding and social good by connecting students, educators, and artists in India, Pakistan, and the US through multimedia, music, dance, and theatre. As the Foundation explains, this global engagement platform inspires young people to embark on a path of learning and discovery about themselves, their culture, and the issues that impact their families, their neighbourhoods, and the world itself. Collaborative project-based learning, resulting in original artistic and multimedia works, empowers young people to critically understand their own identities, the issues that affect their lives—and take action in their communities to foster cultures of service and responsibility. In building connections between local cultural groups in different parts of the world, the project fosters cross-cultural understanding through collaborative dialogue. The Foundation has a significant presence in rural parts of India.

The AID also runs a number of innovative education projects in India, notably through Eureka Child, its key initiative. Over the years, AID India has developed innovative techniques for teaching basic science, mathematics, and reading, and engaged in extensive upskilling within the education sector in Tamil Nadu, as mentioned earlier in this chapter. The AID has also established a number of schools, while also aiming to improve the quality of education provided by the middle schools in the regions where it operates. One of the schools it runs in Uttar Pradesh provides free education to the children of migrant labourers in Kanpur. There are currently more than 600 students across the 25 Apna Skool centres.

Alternative Education

Asha for Education works with a variety of project partners and community groups on many education- and development-related matters. The organization looks at issues concerning access to education, but also aims to ensure that every child has access to an education that is meaningful. The alternative education schools that Asha supports not only seek to address the pitfalls in the conventional education system, but also to ensure that children from poor socioeconomic backgrounds are not deprived of the opportunity of high-quality education. The schools also assist children in taking the mainstream government exams.

Asha for Education has also set up the Jambuni Child Growth Centre, which is a centre for extended education, entertainment, moral development, physical development, and value-building among young children. The centre adopts innovative methods of teaching, such as barefoot education that involves utilizing local resources and materials to teach children, and ensuring that they learn more from nature and their surroundings than simply from books. Moral, physical, and cultural development is given equal importance. The children are also given routine health check-ups, alongside inputs to develop their cultural orientation. The teachers undergo rigorous training on teaching methods by well-known resource persons in the field of education and child growth. The project also provides basic education materials to the centres. The website of Asha for Education gives sense of the scale of their operation, as well as their ambition.

> Asha for education also provides support to Parijat Academy, one of the diaspora-driven schools in Assam. Parijat Academy is a school located near Guwahati for underprivileged children of an area called Pamohi. The area where the school is located comprises a number of tribal villages and most of the people living in the villages are poor farmers and daily wage workers working in nearby stone quarries. Before this school was opened, the children of these stone quarry workers were seen spending most of their time during the day in and around the quarries. Since its inception in 2003, Parijat Academy has grown to about 300 students. Currently the school has students from Nursery through Class VII. Also the students of Kindergarten, Class VI and Class VII are currently housed in temporary rooms. The goal of this project is to provide for the funds to construct classrooms for Class VIII, KG, Class VI and Class VII. The class rooms will have concrete floors, wooden doors and windows, tin roofs and bamboo walls. Along with the project mentioned above, the organization has currently 24 projects spread all over India. Further, the organization has also established 102 formal or informal schools in all over India.[6]

Tribal Education

Child Rights and You India acts as the link between grassroots-level initiatives in India that are doing excellent work with children but are short on resources, and people and organizations in America that have the resources to help. One such activity supported by the organization is Mahan Sewa Sansthan, formed in 1989, which works with the tribal families of 20 villages spread over four Panchayats. Initially the focus of intervention was to address discrimination and deprivation through a strengthening of education system. Later with broadening of

[6] Website Asha for Education, https://atlanta.ashanet.org/past-projects/, accessed on 12 February 2020.

perspective, experience, and experimentation, the organization focused more on community mobilization and working towards the rights of children, advocating for the rights of displaced communities and creating a just society. The organization now reaches approximately 6,000 families and covers approximately 42,000 people. The project area contains villages predominantly inhabited by tribal communities (almost two-thirds).

The India Development and Relief Fund (IDRF) also provides affordable, holistic education to students across India with a special emphasis on girls and tribal children. The IRDF supports programmes that cultivate students' minds and their sense of social responsibility. For 25 years, students have excelled in IDRF-supported classrooms and become advocates for progress in their own communities. The organization runs a number of projects for educational development, one such project being Shiksha Bharti in Uttar Pradesh, an innovative residential school for tribal girls from the Northeast. Sahaj Seva Samsthan, Andhra Pradesh, meanwhile, runs schools for children from slums and children with special needs. The organization also has the Udavi School in Tamil Nadu which provides holistic, value-based education for rural children, and in Madhya Pradesh, it runs Sewa Bharati Bhopal, providing dormitories and educational support for tribal children. In Uttar Pradesh, in collaboration with Nagauri School, the organization serves 1,000 children from 25 scattered villages, while in Jammu Kashmir, the Disha and Ved Mandir Hostels have been established to provide homes and education support for boys and girls who have lost their families in war or insurgency. The Swami Keshwanand Trust, Rajasthan, is also being supported to establish dorms, scholarships, and vocational training for girls. There are other collaborations are also being carried out to enhance the quality and availability of education.

Hostels for Needy Students

The IDS also supports economic and social development in India, and has established a boarding school for children in partnership with the George Foundation in Krishnagiri District, Tamil Nadu. The school, Shanti Bhavan, provides boarding facilities for children from deprived backgrounds. Given proper care, support, and educational opportunities, these children have a good chance of achieving success. The founder of Shanti Bhavan believes that through such institutions many poor people can overcome the cycle of poverty and social deprivation. Through the multiplicative effect of education, the experiences at Shanti Bhavan will impact the lives of families for generations to come. Currently, Shanti Bhavan cares for 248 children in its boarding school and another 45 in its college. For the last three years, the Council for Indian School Certificate Examinations (CISCE) has recorded the entire tenth grade class of Shanti Bhavan has having secured First Division in the nationally accredited ICSE examination, while the twelfth grade graduated first class, and over 60 per cent achieved a distinction. Sixteen years after Shanti Bhavan started, its first group of students graduated from higher education, and other students have been receiving job offers from top organizations such as Goldman Sachs, Ernst & Young, etc. These children come from homes with no running water or bathrooms, and they face severe hardships; their astounding outcomes have confirmed the validity of the Shanti Bhavan model.

The Next Generation Foundation (NGF), a US-based organization, was founded to develop a network of people around the world who would work for the empowerment of children by the virtue of honest help. One of the major projects NGF has undertaken in India is the National Integrity and Responsibility Complex (NIRC) Project, which seeks to provide the best possible residential education for orphan and underprivileged children.

Educational Awareness Programmes for the Youth

In partnership with Pravah in Delhi and in other parts of India, the IDS is implementing a project entitled Community Youth Collective (CYC) Learning and Leadership Journey, which takes as its principle that to build a more peaceful, equal, inclusive, and just society, youth need to be at the helm of change. Opportunities for youth must be created in order for them to engage in the social context of change, and investment in neighbourhoods and communities, as well as stakeholder involvement, are an active part of this process. The CYC encourages every young person to realize his or her full potential, as well as to benefit society, through active citizenship. Annually, the initiative supports 15–25 youth activists and is seeking to strengthen their capacities to develop and implement context-specific community projects.

The Gandhi Foundation (based in the UK) exists to spread knowledge and understanding of the life and work of Mohandas K. Gandhi (1869–1948). The organization's most important aim is to demonstrate the continuing relevance of Gandhi's insights and actions today. Gandhi, one of the most significant figures of modern times, began as an individual with no particular talents and gradually emerged as a remarkable human being. He considered that everyone has the potential for ethical and spiritual growth, and that community is the most effective basis for organizational development. Gandhi's ideas have relevance beyond his own time. His approach was holistic and evolved through experience. In order to assist educators, the Gandhi Foundation has produced a presentation 'Gandhi—A Life in Pictures', designed to be used at high school level, while the Gandhi Speakers Network provides a list of speakers available to address schools and community groups around the country. The British Library appointed the Gandhi Foundation as a UK touring partner for its Gandhi Travelling Exhibition, comprising six roll-up panels, printed with photographs depicting events in the life of Gandhi.

Education for Slum Dwellers

Vibha supports the Alamb education project, which we have already covered earlier in this chapter. In another of its projects, Gramin Shiksha Kendra (GSK)-Uday Pathshala, it is planning to set up three high-quality learning centres and schools in the Sawai Madhopur and Khandar blocks of Sawai Madhopur district, Rajasthan, to help communities see what quality in education actually means. In addition, through a community outreach programme, it encourages communities to demand a better quality of education from the existing governmental school system and the private sector. The organization will also design, develop, and implement a curriculum and develop a pedagogy which makes education more relevant to people's lives in rural areas and gives them the information necessary to take informed decisions about their livelihoods and their future.

As well as its work in marshalling funding, CRY India also runs programmes in a slum of Pandav Nagar in West Delhi, where the socioeconomic status of the residents is far below the poverty line. The population comprises migrants from Rajasthan, Bihar, Uttar Pradesh, and Andhra Pradesh who earn their living through arts like acrobatics, folkdance, puppetry, etc. The project provides immunizations and has provided a pulse polio drop to large numbers of children.

The AID is implementing the Disha Project in Gurgaon, India, which it began in January 2009. Project Disha followed Project Unnati, which built a school in the slum areas of Jharsa village; the second project thus appealed to the community because they were familiar with the presence of AID in the area. The AID's beneficiaries in the slums were mainly construction workers, daily wage workers, or domestic workers. The new school was assembled on the site of an old community centre, with the dedicated help of many community members, especially the youth who took a leading role in the construction. However, the school had a low supply of desks, books, stationary, electrical fittings, and teaching aids. The functioning and the expansion of the project were thus threatened by a lack of funds.

Education for Minority Communities

The AFMI focuses on improving the educational status of Indian Muslims. The organization started with bottom-up strategy, supporting schools and students at primary level. Since 2000, it has helped hundreds of primary schools across India from where thousands of students have graduated. The help has included construction and renovation of school buildings, providing staff salaries, and scholarships and other financial aid for students. The work has paid off, and the organization now claims an overall improvement in the enrolment of Muslim students at primary level. To continue strengthening the primary school base of Indian Muslims while also expanding the organization's support for students at the higher grades of school, efforts are being made in Kolkata, for instance, to construct a high school. In order to implement its plans, AFMI reaches out to the American Muslim community, and Indo-American Muslims in particular, persuading them that they have a special responsibility in this regard. If help is not forthcoming, then there is a chance that the progress of past two decades will stall, yet the organization expresses its confidence that, even despite the financial crisis of 2008, it will succeed in driving down levels of illiteracy among Indian Muslims.

Following a suggestion made at the Kashmiri Overseas Association (KOA) National Camp in 1994, that the best way to extend help to the community back in India was to help needy students in their pursuit of higher education, the KOA now runs several educational programmes. Their education work is done in partnership with Kashmiri Pandit Sabha, Jammu, which assists in the receipt of applications from needy students, as well as with the distribution of funds. The programme is advertised in a widely read regional newspaper, the Daily Excelsior.[7] Another project by the KOA, the Rishi Memorial School was started in the mid-1990s with contributions from a group of US-based Indian-Americans concerned for the future of indigent children. What is today a remarkable experiment in social self-service began with only about a dozen students and one teacher.

Community-Specific Initiatives

The American Telugu Association runs a programme in Andhra Pradesh to provide financial assistance for eligible students during their high school and junior college studies. Students who receive benefits under this programme sign a pledge that they will help two other students after they finish their education and establish themselves in their career. To adopt one child for educating under this programme costs USD 1,500. The students who receive benefits are required to stay in personal contact with their benefactors.

Strengthening School Education

The Ekal Vidyalaya Foundation, which has been cited more than once already in this research, aims to eradicate illiteracy from rural and tribal India. Although its stated completion date of 2015 has arguably

---

[7] Drawn from the KOA website, http://koausa.org, accessed on 2 August 2018.

been missed, Ekal Vidyalaya remains a movement of prodigious size, counting over 51,000 teachers, 6,000 voluntary workers, 35 field organizations (across in 22 Indian states), and eight support agencies as of August 2013. With this tremendous human force, the Ekal Vidyalaya movement strives to create a network of literacy centres that will educate and empower children in rural and tribal India, and alongside its network of schools it engages in substantive community development efforts.

The Maharashtra Foundation, a US-based diaspora organization, acts according to a motto of 'enhanced quality of life for the poor and vulnerable, and a sustainable and long-term solution'. The Foundation seeks to enhance the quality of life of the underprivileged by supporting programmes in healthcare, education, welfare, and the development of women and children. The Foundation also has a focus on the use of technology, vocational training, and entrepreneurship, and empowers women and minorities with a view to their economic improvement. Rare among the organizations we have canvassed for this research, the Foundation also engages in environmental protection by helping communities combat deforestation and promote environmental consciousness.

The Nanubhai Education Foundation, a US-based organization founded in 2004, is dedicated to ensuring that students in India's rural public high schools have equal access to India's rapidly growing economic opportunities. It directs its efforts towards its partner schools, helping students and especially women to achieve excellence, so that they are more likely to enrol in higher education and participate in India's new economy. By establishing strong partnerships with rural high schools and their committed principals, the foundation seeks to transform rural education from the inside out. Its unique fellows programme partners experienced educators with each school to mentor and inspire local teachers.

The Jain Network stands out among the migrant organizations we have described, in that its partnership work is largely directed towards university institutions: the network provides support to the Jain Academic and Research Centre, situated within Mumbai University, and also established the Department of Jain Studies at the Faculty of Comparative Religions, Antwerp, while supporting the International

School for Jain Studies in India. The network has also organized lectures and talks at community centres and interfaith gatherings.

Education for the Physically Disabled

As we have noted elsewhere in this volume, the burden of disability in India is very high, and some of the migrant organizations we have described direct their efforts towards alleviating this. However, action on disability is notably less common than initiatives for education or primary healthcare. Sewa UK is a charity of Indian origin that came to prominence in the 1990s when huge natural disasters affected India. Working in partnership with business leaders, politicians, civic society, and local communities, Sewa UK has raised substantial funds for various calamities internationally, and it remains committed to working in zones of humanitarian disaster, providing immediate relief and rehabilitation, mobilizing technical assistance to support relief operations, and investing in building infrastructure and services in the aftermath. Sewa also runs Gulmohar Special School, a residential school which provides education for children with mental and visual disabilities. Its efforts here remain modest, however, at present, the school operates from a small rented derelict building.

* * *

This chapter has reviewed the educational work undertaken by transnational migrant organizations. Based on our survey of organizations, which is admittedly incomplete, the broad trends in this field are as follows: transnational migrant organizations tend to partner with local organizations which can provide them with local contacts and insights, rather than attempting to manage major projects by 'remote control'. Moreover, the projects supported tend to be modest in scope, aiming at reinforcing or expanding existing services, rather than creating new institutions from nothing. That being said, there are several organizations are engaged in efforts that are so large and ambitious in scale as to qualify more as 'movements' than simply 'projects', with the Ekal Vidyalaya work to eradicate illiteracy standing out in this regard.

Appendix A5

Table A5.1 Transnational Organizations Engaging with the Education Sector

S. No.	Name	Year	Location	Coverage	Membership	Professional background of founder	Number of projects running in India	Number of partners in India	Beneficiaries (estimated)	Broad activities
1.	American Federation of Muslims of Indian Origin	1989	USA	Bihar, Uttar Pradesh, West Bengal, Gujarat, Maharashtra, and Tamil Nadu	Not specified	Medical professionals	33	Not specified	Not specified	Education and healthcare
2.	American India Foundation	2001	USA	Himachal Pradesh, Uttarakhand, Haryana, Delhi, Rajasthan, Uttar Pradesh, Bihar, Assam, West Bengal, Jharkhand, Madhya Pradesh, Gujarat,	Not specified	Business	449	227	Not specified	Education, livelihood, elementary education, women empowerment, HIV/AIDS awareness and public health

(Cont'd)

Table A5.1 (Cont'd)

S. No.	Name	Year	Location	Coverage	Membership	Professional background of founder	Number of projects running in India	Number of partners in India	Beneficiaries (estimated)	Broad activities
				Maharashtra, Andhra Pradesh, Odisha, Chhattisgarh, Goa, Karnataka, Tamil Nadu, and Andaman and Nicobar Islands						
3.	American Telugu Association	1990	USA	Andhra Pradesh	6,000	Business	6	6	100,000 people	Education, healthcare, and social empowerment
4.	Asha for Education	1991	USA	All states of India	Not specified	Engineers	400	200	291,708 children	Education and child care
5.	Asha Jyoti Community Welfare Society of Canada	1995	Canada	Bihar, Karnataka, Haryana, Gujarat, and Punjab	Not specified	Academician	7	Not specified	1,000 people	Scholarship and community service

6.	Asian Foundation for Help	1983	UK	Different parts of India	Not specified	Different sectors	539	105	Not specified	Healthcare, education, and community awareness
7.	Association for India's Development	1991	USA	West Bengal, Tamil Nadu, Andhra Pradesh, Delhi, Jharkhand, and Punjab	Not specified	Scientist	12	Not specified	Not specified	Education, healthcare, and community development
8.	Association of Indians in America	1967	USA	Gujarat	Not specified	Business	5	5	2000 people	Education, healthcare, and social empowerment
9.	Bichitra	1974	USA	West Bengal	Not specified	Different sectors	4	2	Not specified	Education, child care, hygiene, and vocational training

(*Cont'd*)

Table A5.1 (Cont'd)

S. No.	Name	Year	Location	Coverage	Membership	Professional background of founder	Number of projects running in India	Number of partners in India	Beneficiaries (estimated)	Broad activities
10.	Child Rights and You America	1979	USA	Bihar, Manipur, Odisha, West Bengal, Chhattisgarh, Gujarat, Maharashtra, Rajasthan, Uttar Pradesh, Haryana, Jharkhand, Telangana, Tamil Nadu, Andhra Pradesh, Madhya Pradesh, and Karnataka	Not specified	Different sectors	36	36	660,632 children/ 3,350 village/slums	Education, healthcare, and child care

No.	Name	Year	Country	Location		Sector				Focus
11.	Children's Hope (India)	1992	USA	Madhya Pradesh, Gujarat, Andhra Pradesh, Jammu and Kashmir, West Bengal, Maharashtra, and Delhi	Not specified	Business	25	24	50,000 children	Education, food, shelter, and health services
12.	Dr Ambedkar Memorial Educational and Welfare Trust	1984	UK	Odisha	Not specified	Different sectors	3	Not specified	400 students	Education
13.	Ekal Vidyalaya Foundation of USA	1989	USA	Different parts of India	Not specified	Scientist	35	52,000 schools	1,848,819 students	Education
14.	Guru Ravidass Educational Assistance Trust'	2005	UK	Different parts of India	Not specified	Different sectors	14	14	175 scholarships	Education

(*Contd*)

Table A5.1   (Cont'd)

S. No.	Name	Year	Location	Coverage	Membership	Professional background of founder	Number of projects running in India	Number of partners in India	Beneficiaries (estimated)	Broad activities
15.	India Development Service	1974	USA	Different parts of India	Not specified	Business	253	18	400,000 (approx.)	Education, healthcare, and skill development
16.	Jeevika Trust	1970	UK	Tamil Nadu and Odisha	Not specified	Different sectors	6	6	8,700 people	Education, skill development, employment training, nutrition, and public health
17.	Kashmiri Overseas Association	1983	USA	Jammu and Kashmir	662	Different sectors	17	2	5,000 people	Education, healthcare, and community development

No.	Name	Year	Country	Location		Type			Beneficiaries	Sector
18.	Lend-A-Hand India	2003	UK	Maharashtra, Gujarat, Telangana, Andhra Pradesh, Odisha, Delhi, Haryana, and Daman & Diu	Not specified	Different sectors	5	51	10,000 people/year	Education, community development, and skill development
19.	Lohana Community of United Kingdom (LCUK)	1978	UK	Rajasthan and Gujarat	Not specified	Different sectors	2	1	332 children	Education
20.	Manjari Sankurathri Memorial Foundation	1989	Canada	Andhra Pradesh	Not specified	Medical professionals	2	Not specified	250,000 people	EDUCATION AND HEALTHCARE
21.	Nanubhai Education Foundation	2004	USA	Delhi and Gujarat	Not specified	Academician	1	1	100 scholarships/year	Education
22.	SEWA UK	1989	UK	Maharashtra	Not specified	Different sectors	1	1	48 students	Education

(Cont'd)

Table A5.1 (Cont'd)

S. No.	Name	Year	Location	Coverage	Membership	Professional background of founder	Number of projects running in India	Number of partners in India	Beneficiaries (estimated)	Broad activities
23.	Toronto–Calcutta Foundation	1988	Canada	West Bengal	Not specified	Different sectors	11	10	1,000 students/year (approx.)	Healthcare, education, and employability
24.	Upkaar	1997	USA	Different parts of India	Not Specified	Academician	Not specified	Not specified	165 students	Education and scholarship
25.	Vibha	1991	USA	Delhi, Uttar Pradesh, Maharashtra, Andhra Pradesh, West Bengal, Rajasthan, Tamil Nadu, Gujarat, Madhya Pradesh, and Karnataka	2,200	Business	37	37	110,000 children	Healthcare and women empowerment

Source: Compiled by the authors from the organizational responses and/or respective websites of the organizations.

Conclusion

This book presented an overview of the engagement of overseas Indians in the development of education and healthcare provision in India. Our primary focus was to understand the modalities of the engagement process, and to this end we have carried out an extensive study of the development organizations established by Indians living abroad. As an underlying factor driving the development initiatives of Indians overseas, we consider that the homeland, whether real or imaginary, remains a key emotional reference point for migrants—it is the very fact of taking up residence overseas, whether temporary or permanent, that motivates individuals to take part in the processes aimed at the betterment of the home society. These engagements can take multiple forms, the most notable ones being remittances, entrepreneurship, and philanthropy.

Remittances and entrepreneurship may be considered as contributions which are restricted in scope: the recipients are often limited in number and the efforts thus serve minimal numbers of people. Remittances are intended to fulfil the requirements of a household, while entrepreneurship is primarily directed at individual gain. Our objective was thus to understand the truly philanthropic engagements of Indians living abroad, which, unlike the other two types of contributions, is directed to the benefit of India's very large numbers of poor and needy.

Through our research, we were able to identify a large number of organizations working towards the betterment of the Indian population, and particularly its deprived and tribal communities. Although we have not attempted to quantify the collective impact of these organizations in monetary terms—the exercise would present considerable methodological challenges, although indicative outcomes would nevertheless be of interest—it is clear that the impact is significant and helps a large number of people. In lieu of a quantitative assessment, this study attempts to enumerate the engagement of Indian immigrant organizations in the homeland, with special reference to engagement in the healthcare and education sectors.

Our research also comprised a review of the policies related to overseas Indian engagement put in place by the Government of India. We saw that the policies of India towards its overseas citizens have changed considerably in the post-independence era. The pre-1990s government policies towards Indians settled abroad were less than warm; however, the new millennium saw a significant shift in India's approach to its population abroad, expressed most clearly with the formation of the High-Level Committee on Indian Diaspora. Yet while the policies enacted by the Indian government represented a substantive attempt to engage greater numbers of the diaspora, the evidence suggests that the area of philanthropy was not greatly boosted by the new governmental policies, and only a few new philanthropic immigrant organizations were established: our survey of migrant organizations indicated that more than half were established before 2000, and about two-thirds before the landmark year of 2004, when the Ministry of Overseas Indian Affairs was established. In view of this, Indian government policy cannot be considered as a major catalyst of the engagement of Indian immigrant organizations in India.

Our research further looked into the socio-demographic characteristics of migrant organizations and of the NRIs who run them. This has not been a major area of concern for either academics or policymakers, and hardly any other studies exist on overseas Indians' organizational engagement in India. The book, thus, has spent significant time describing the formation, resource mobilization, outreach, functioning, and activities of these organizations. The organizations included in this book differ in terms of coverage and activities. While local organizations (immigrant organizations established and working in India) have relatively limited initiatives which are usually community focused, transnational organizations (immigrant organizations established outside India but working in India) have wider focus and work in many states. They also tend to work on multiple social issues, although their engagement tends to be expressed as helping local organizations through the provision of donor funds: thus, in general these organizations implement projects with the help of local NGOs. Yet there are also some very significant transnational organizations which maintain a direct engagement in India: as we saw, the AAPIO, one of the largest NRI medical professionals' associations, actually runs several hospitals in India, either directly or with a local partner organization.

Another significant subcategory of our sample of organizations comprised collective associations of people from the same geographical area or community, working together for benefit of a specific ethnic or geographical community. Thus the KOA runs several education and healthcare programmes for needy people from Jammu and Kashmir, while the NATS runs a scholarship programme for Telugu students, and the Capital District Malayali Association runs a number of programmes specifically for Malayali people.

Each organization selected for the study had its own particular story regarding its formation and history. While most of the local organizations were established by a single individual, the transnational organizations are mostly community initiatives and were established by a group. Although the organizations we have reviewed were selected for their focus on education, healthcare, and closely related areas, they differ in terms of orientation, objectives, and scale.

We have also documented the process of resource mobilization of the organizations. Local organizations with relatively lower capacity need correspondingly lower resourcing, and 17 out of 40 local organizations were established with the help of the personal savings of the founders, having no support from any funding agencies or donors. Ten organizations were established with the personal funds of the founders augmented by a few other key players, while eight were established with the help of contributions received from the membership. Other sources of start-up funding included NRI family funds and contributions by NRIs. In general, the process of resource mobilization can be divided into two categories: individual resources and collective resources. *Individual* resources largely concern the establishment of the organization with financial contributions by the founder himself/herself; *collective* resources broadly mean the establishment of the organization with the help of resources donated by two or more people.

The process of resource mobilization for transnational organizations largely depends on members' contributions and the availability of funds from different donor agencies. The transnational migrant organizations have a larger coverage area and objectives, and their financial requirements are correspondingly higher. Fundraising activities are a primary source of capital for many of these organizations. All the organizations organize a regular convention, conference, gala, or similar event to solicit funds. Donations and contributions by individuals as well as institutions are an important source of funds, and most of the transnational organizations tend to rely on donations. The organizations give their members the option to contribute funds directly through a payment gateway available on the website, and many also accept payment using credit cards.

We identified five distinct themes of resource mobilization from our overview of migrant development organizations:

1. Direct donations, according to which one donates a pre-specified amount or other amount as desired. The donation can be general purpose or for a specific programme.
2. Event-based mobilization, which is common in large organizations with a bigger reach. These organizations engage in fundraising activities to request donor funding that is either for specific programmes or unrestricted. Some small organizations also use small events such as picnics, cultural festivals, or community and religious events to collect funds for their programmes.
3. Grants from governments.
4. Sponsorship of specific activities and chapters, where many organizations also promote sponsorship of their entire regional chapter.
5. Collection of gifts and unnamed donations, from which many organizations receive a significant amount.

The analysis of immigrant engagement in the Indian healthcare sector shows that the medical facilities provided by migrant organizations can be considered as a major support to the sector. As we have seen, medical facilities in India have long been an area of concern, with India having a worryingly low doctor–patient ratio. Being well aware of these deficiencies, the migrant community, both local and transnational, has treated healthcare as an important area of engagement. All the local immigrant organizations working in India have a greater or lesser engagement in healthcare development for poor people and communities, ranging from establishment of medical institutes to the provision of medical camps, as well various special programmes for needy patients such as regular check-ups and vaccinations in slums. Since these organizations largely cover the vulnerable population with the most urgent requirements for basic healthcare and education, their activities are a lifeline for many people.

The most ambitious projects undertaken by migrant organizations, lying at the intersection of healthcare and education, were the establishment of medical colleges. Among all studied organizations, three had as a principal objective to run or plan to establish full-fledged medical educational institutions. Among these, one has already established a medical school. Considering the expense of medical facilities in India, these institutions' primary goal is to enable needy patients to access quality healthcare facilities.

Alongside the establishment of medical education centres, which is a goal to which only a few organizations are able to aspire, the establishment of hospitals and clinics is also a key concern. Many of the organizations have established clinics in different parts of India. Often linked to these clinics, many organizations also facilitate the exchange of medical professionals from overseas to India. These are important initiatives for medical professionals, although other forms of skill enhancement can also be considered, one of which is online leaning for medical students—a concept which is rather new and has not yet been properly examined, but may well prove to be crucial in the global knowledge society. Unlike transnational organizations, which have higher financial capabilities, local organizations have fewer resources to facilitate exchanges. Nevertheless, many local organizations do invite medical professionals to visit them and engage in their healthcare activities.

We found that the local organizations tend to focus their healthcare engagement in underdeveloped areas, where there are plenty of small-scale organizations handling many critical needs of ordinary people. And while hospitals and medical schools are standout initiatives, we must also note the many special programmes run by Indian diaspora organizations—for example, the establishment of a medicine bank by a Delhi-based organization, and the medical camps also often organized to address the health problems of the population in remote areas of the country. Polio and hepatitis vaccination camps and blood donation camps are also organized frequently. Such camps serve significant numbers of needy people, and are an effective means of healthcare development for deprived rural communities. Local immigrant organizations understand this, and organize camps in different parts of India, especially tribal regions.

In this volume, we also looked at proactive engagement in healthcare needs by immigrant organizations in India. One such engagement concerned elderly parents, for which we found three organizations that had been established specifically to address the health and psychological difficulties faced by parents of migrants. It was observed that many parents cannot go abroad to live with their NRI children, due to issues which include host country legislation, the inability to adapt to an alien culture, nostalgia, and others. For this reason, many parents choose to stay in the homeland. Concern for the wellbeing of the parents of migrants could thus be considered a cause of the emergence of local migrant organizations, since this is an issue which affects their founders most acutely. Some organizations hold regular meetings to connect the stay-behind parents with other parents, and also organize regular medical camps for parents—this being an interesting synergy between healthcare strategies designed to meet the needs of deprived rural communities, and the need to care for parents left behind. Such gatherings act as a platform to provide mutual emotional support and a sense of fellowship, especially through recreational, intellectual, and cultural activities, sharing of personal experiences, including problems and possible solutions. Further, the organizations can assist with common issues such as medical facilities, insurance, property, financial matters, travel, immigration, inheritance, transfer of funds abroad, and many others, all on an ongoing basis. These organizations also act as a support system for parents visiting their children, furnishing them with information about overseas medical insurance, foreign travel and related matters, and assisting with passports, visas, and travel planning, as well as counselling, assistance, and orientation for travel abroad, especially for 'first-time' travellers. Considering that in a number of cases elderly parents of migrants have died and lain undiscovered for months, such forums provide a vital defence against this kind of tragedy.

The research found that transnational immigrant organizations are engaged with the healthcare sector in India in broadly two ways: setting up healthcare institutions, mainly through FDI (although we also saw, above, that some larger organizations have directly set up institutions themselves), or supporting and funding local organizations. Indians living overseas have extended their interaction with homeland via remittances, knowledge exchanges mediated by professional networks, and permanent return to help the local community through their skills and expertise. We also found that many organizations working in India support local healthcare institutions through the donation of modern equipment, ranging from a new ambulance to specialized diagnostic machines.

Skill mobility has been an important phenomenon in recent decades, and the facilitation and promotion of exchange programme is an important initiative of Indian immigrant organizations. Under these programmes, hosts provide free lodging, boarding, and professional interactions to their guests. These programmes connect young professionals with NGOs and social enterprises in India in order to accelerate impact and create effective projects that are replicable, scalable, and sustainable.

Indian migrant organizations also undertake crucial engagement in areas that call for particularly urgent intervention, notably maternal and child health. Considering the importance of this area, many organizations have established maternal and child health clinics to provide essential medical services to those who would otherwise not have access due to the remoteness of their location. Another healthcare programme is related to HIV/AIDS awareness, ensuring equal opportunities for children living with HIV/AIDS by developing a high standard of care and reducing stigma and social barriers faced by these orphaned and vulnerable children. Through a comprehensive assessment of the standards and practices of childcare institutions in high HIV/AIDS prevalence states, migrant organizations work to build the capacities of childcare institutions and families and strengthen the links between institutions and existing services—to ensure that children get the care, support, and treatment they need while enjoying a stigma-free childhood.

Considering the huge demand for quality education in India, many of the organizations we reviewed have also engaged in education initiatives, and some have even built educational institutions for poor and needy people, both in cities as well as rural areas. The schools established by these organizations not only provide education but also serve unique and specific purposes: for example, one school in Bihar sought to provide education using modern technology. Despite being located in an extremely rural area where electricity is in short supply, the school provides opportunities such as eLearning, audio-video-conferencing-based classes, and other modern educational facilities, all to needy children. Another school, in Assam, was established to provide education specifically in order to reduce child labour. In general, all the academic institutions established by Indian immigrants serve a specific purpose, over and above providing quality education to poor and needy people.

As is evident from these examples, modern education methods are highly prized by the transnational organizations, and their activities include providing equipment to schools including computers and other advanced technical facilities. Many organizations have also installed the technical infrastructure to connect schools to digital libraries, these libraries being provided by national institutions like the National Council for Technical Education and others.

Our research has also identified that the scholarships and training provided by local migrant organizations have been crucial for significant numbers of people. There are examples of school-based scholarships, where the founder pays a minimum amount to students to encourage them to come to school and stop them drifting into child labour. There are also organizations providing training for the GRE/GMAT/TOEFL examination, including forums for debating groups, group discussions, and regular seminars and daily lectures on preparation for these exams. There is also an organization which takes zakat and distributes it to needy people as a scholarship.

In addition to basic education, many organizations also provide vocational education to enhance the employability of underprivileged communities. These training programmes cover a wide range of issues:

some organizations offer training for engineering and management students in the field of renewable energy, carbon credits, and energy management technology; another organization provides market-aligned skills training, targeting slum dwellers and school dropouts. Social workers employed by the organization are sent to nearby colonies to spread information about the programme and encourage the parents and kids to join the course. Under another programme, adult women are taught skills that would make them economically self-reliant.

Given their understanding of the difficulties faced in the process of migration, many organizations also provide awareness-raising and orientation activities to putative migrants. The aim of pre-departure migration training programmes is to familiarize people with the requirements that need to be fulfilled prior to migration. Pre-departure orientation is an important concern for many people in migrant-sending countries, since workers can face life-threatening problems at the host land due to lack of information about rules and regulations.

Another important area of engagement by Indian immigrant organizations concerns women's empowerment. Many of the migrant organizations run educational programmes intended to make women economically self-sufficient and independent. The education of slum children is also an important area of engagement for migrant organizations, as well as the education of street children, who face very similar issues.

The organizations established by migrants also work on sudden needs in areas where significant gaps suddenly become apparent. There are organizations working in forested areas with small amounts of funding and solely under the direction of their founders. We also found organizations working in rural India which had not received any funds at all, and were completely sustained by the savings and salary of the founder. Each organization, thus, has its own level of engagement and fulfils different urgent areas of need.

A constant theme identified in this study is that organizations operating at transnational level rely crucially on local partners in the homeland in the fulfilment of their programmes of work. Some of the organizations have astonishing numbers of local partners—one organization had over 200, working on over 500 projects. More common is for transnational migrant organizations to have just one or two local partners.

Other than the numerous cases of individual-level engagement, the study also looked into community-level initiatives. Many organizations discussed in this book work towards community awareness and empowerment, their programmes providing education that is aimed at raising awareness on various issues and creating an informed society, and generating an impetus for social change. These programmes are located both in rural communities (including tribal) and in cities, covering a broad range of issues including agriculture, general health, women's education, and community rights.

To conclude, it is evident that through their philanthropic orientation the organizations reviewed in this research have significantly benefited individuals and families. We thus consider that this book gives a much-needed insight into an important aspect of Indian development, which has not been sufficiently appreciated thus far. Perhaps because they fall between public and private provision, the organizations we have discussed have not yet been the proper focus of any significant programme of research. Although the work we have done here cannot claim to be exhaustive, we hope to have brought to the attention of the academic community a significant stratum of development activity, one that is richly deserving of closer investigation.

Bibliography

Abraham, I. 2014. *How India Became Territorial: Foreign Policy, Diaspora, Geopolitics.* Stanford: Stanford University Press.

Agarwala, R. 2015. 'Tapping the Indian Diaspora for Indian Development'. In *The State and the Grassroots: Immigrant Transnational Organizations in Four Continents,* edited by A. Portes and P. Fernández-Kelly, pp. 84–110. New York: Berghahn Books.

Aggarwal, S., A. Rai, K.S. Bath, H. Singh, V. Sharma. 2014. 'Migratory Trends of Medical Graduates in India', *J Pioneer Med Sci.* 4(4): 155–8.

Akcapar, Sebnem K. 2009. 'Turkish Associations in the United States: Towards Building a Transnational Identity', *Turkish Studies* 10(2):165–93.

Anand, G. 2011. 'India Graduates Millions, but Too Few Are Fit to Hire', 5 April. Available at https://www.wsj.com/articles/SB100014240527487 03515504576142092863219826, accessed on 12 January 2019.

ASER (Annual Status of Education Report). n.d. *India Rural: Analysis Based on Data from Households.* 589 out of 619 Districts. Available at http://img. asercentre.org/docs/Publications/ASER%20Reports/ASER%202016/ State%20pages%20English/allindia_english.pdf, accessed on 31 July 2018.

Arnold, F., P. Nangia, and U. Kapila. 2004. 'Indicators of Nutrition for Women and Children in India: Current Status and Programme Recommendations'. In *Demographic Change, Health Inequality and Human Development in India,* edited by S. Irudaya Rajan and K.S. James, pp. 141–164. Hyderabad, India: Centre for Economic and Social Studies.

Arnold Fred, Sulabha Parasuraman, P. Arokiasamy, and Monica Kothari. 2009. 'Nutrition in India', *National Family Health Survey (NFHS-3)*, India, 2005–06. Mumbai: International Institute for Population Sciences; Calverton, Maryland, USA: ICF Macro.

Arora, G.K. and A. Gumber. 2005. 'Globalisation and Healthcare Financing in India: Some Emerging Issues', *Public Finance & Management* 5(4): 567–96.

Avant, D.D. 2005. *The Market for Force: The Consequences of Privatizing Security*. Cambridge: Cambridge University Press.

Babis, D. 2016. 'The Paradox of Integration and Isolation within Immigrant Organisations: The Case of a Latin American Association in Israel', *Journal of Ethnic and Migration Studies* 42(13): 2226–43.

Bakewell, O. 2008. 'Keeping Them in their Place: The Ambivalent Relationship between Development and Migration in Africa', *Third World Quarterly* 29(7): 1341–58.

Bandyopadhyay, G. 2018. 'Determinants of Psychological Well-being and Its Impact on Mental Health'. In *Issues on Health and Healthcare in India*, edited by U.K. De, M. Pal, and P. Bharati, pp. 53–95. Singapore: Springer.

Basch, C.E. 1987. 'Focus Group Interview: An Underutilized Research Technique for Improving Theory and Practice in Health Education', *Health Education Wuarterly* 14(4): 411–48.

Bediang, G., B. Stoll, A. Geissbuhler, A.M. Klohn, A. Stuckelberger, S. Nko'o, and P. Chastonay. 2013. 'Computer Literacy and E-learning Perception in Cameroon: The Case of Yaounde Faculty of Medicine and Biomedical Sciences', *BMC Medical Education* 13(1): 57.

Beneditti, C. 2006. 'Islamic and Christian Inspired Relief NGOs', *Journal of International Development* 18(6): 849–59.

Bhagwati, Jagdish N. and Hamada Koichi. 1974. 'The Brain Drain, International Integration of Markets for Professionals and Unemployment: A Theoretical Analysis', *Journal of Development Economics* 1(1): 19–42.

Bharte, Umesh L. 2014. 'The Role of Highly Skilled Diaspora and Returnees in India's Development: Data Collection Strategies and Survey Methods'. In *Indian Skilled Migration and Development: To Europe and Back*, edited by Gabriela Tejada, Uttam Bhattacharya, Binod Khadria, and Christine Kuptsch, pp. 115–60. New Delhi: Springer.

Bharte, Umesh L. and Rashmi Sharma. 2014. 'Diasporic Paths to Development: And Indian Perspective'. In *Indian Skilled Migration and Development: To Europe and Back*, edited by Gabriela Tejada, Uttam Bhattacharya, Binod Khadria, and Christine Kuptsch, pp. 161–84. New Delhi: Springer.

Bhatt, S.C. and Ghopal K. Barghava (eds). 2006. *Land and People of Indian States and Territories.* New Delhi: Gyan Publishing House.

Bhattacharjya, A. and B. Corvino. 2014. 'Balancing Access and Innovation in Developing Countries'. In *India's Healthcare Industry: Innovation in Delivery, Financing, and Manufacturing,* edited by L. Burns, pp. 538–60. Cambridge: Cambridge University Press. doi:10.1017/CBO9781107360242.017.

Bhaumik, S. and T. Biswas. 2012. 'Free Medicine For All in India', *Canadian Medical Association Journal,* 184(15): 783–4.

Billaiya, R., A. Jain, R. Agarwal, and P. Jain. 2017. 'Introduction about Child Health Status in India', *International Journal of Health Sciences* 1(1): 12–22.

Binnendijk, E., R. Koren, and D.M. Dror. 2012. 'Hardship Financing of Healthcare Among Rural Poor in Orissa, India', *BMC Health Services Research* 12(1): 23.

Boeri, Tito, Herbert Brucker, Frederick Docquier, and Hillel Rapoport (eds). 2012. *Brain Drain and Brain Gain: The Global Competition to Attract Highly Skilled Migrants.* Oxford: Oxford University Press.

Berman, P., R. Ahuja, and L. Bhandari. 2010. 'The Impoverishing Effect of Healthcare Payments in India: New Methodology and Findings', *Economic and Political Weekly* 45(1): 65–71.

Breton, Raymond. 1964. 'Institutional Completeness of Ethnic Communities and the Personal Relations of Immigrants', *American Journal of Sociology* 70: 193–205.

Brij V. Lal, Peter Reeves, and Rajesh Rai (eds). 2007. *The Encyclopedia of the Indian Diaspora.* Honolulu. Hawaii: University of Hawaii Press.

Brown, Judith M. 2006. *Global South Asians: Introducing the Modern Diaspora.* Cambridge: Cambridge University Press.

Burki, S.J. 2015. 'International Migration and Economic Changes in South Asia: The Emergence of the Middle Class'. In *International Migration and Development in South Asia,* edited by M.M. Rahman and Tan T.Y., pp. 176–92. New York: Routledge.

Capolongo, S. 2018. 'A New Challenge in Healthcare for India'. In *Healthcare Facilities in Emerging Countries,* edited by S. Capolongo, M. Gola, and A. Rebecchi, pp. 1–11. New Delhi: Springer.

Castles, Stephen and Delgado-Wise, Raul (eds). 2008. *Migration and Development: Perspectives from the South.* Geneva: International Organization for Migration.

CBHI (Central Bureau of Health Intelligence). 2018. National Health Profile 2018. Ministry of Health and Family Welfare. Available at http://www.cbhidghs.nic.in/index1.php?lang=1&level=2&sublinkid=88&lid=1138, accessed on 22 November 2019.

Census of India (2011). *State of Literacy, Provision Population Tables- India*. pp. 98–136. Available at http://censusindia.gov.in/2011-prov-results/data_files/india/Final_PPT_2011_chapter6.pdf, accessed on 31 July 2018.

Chacko, E. 2007. 'From Brain Drain to Brain Gain: Reverse Migration to Bangalore and Hyderabad, India's Globalizing High Tech Cities', *GeoJournal* 68(2–3): 131–40.

Chakravarthi, I. 2008. 'Role of the World Health Organisation', *Economic and Political Weekly* 43(47): 41–6.

Chakravarthi, I., B. Roy, I. Mukhopadhyay, and S. Barria. 2017. 'Investing in Health: Healthcare Industry in India', *Economic & Political Weekly* 52(45): 51.

Chanda, Rupa. 2008. *Trade in IT and IT-Enabled Services: Issues and Concerns in an India-EU Trade and Investment*. New Delhi: Indian Council for Research on International Economic Relations.

———. 2010. 'Constraints to Foreign Direct Investment in Indian Hospitals', *Journal of International Commerce, Economics and Policy* 1(1): 121–43.

Chanda, Rupa and Deeparghya Mukharjee. 2014. 'Investment and Skilled Mobility Linkages Between India and the EU'. In *Indian Skilled Migration and Development: To Europe and Back*, edited by Gabriela Tejada, Uttam Bhattacharya, Binod Khadria, and Christine Kuptsch, pp. 47–70. New Delhi: Springer.

Chowdhury, M. and S. Irudaya Rajan. 2018. *South Asian Migration in the Gulf*. New Delhi: Palgrave Macmillan.

Clark, G.L. and D. Wójcik (eds). 2018. *The New Oxford Handbook of Economic Geography*. Oxford: Oxford University Press.

Coffey, D., A. Gupta, P. Hathi, N. Khurana, D. Spears, N. Srivastav, and S. Vyas. 2014. 'Revealed Preference for Open Defecation', *Economic & Political Weekly* 49(38): 43–55.

Collier, P. 2003. *Breaking the Conflict Trap: Civil War and Development Policy*. Washington, DC: World Bank Publications.

De Witte, J. 1969. *Indian Workers' Association in Britain*. Oxford: Oxford University Press.

Dhesi, A.S. 2010. 'Diaspora, Social Entrepreneurs and Community Development', *International Journal of Social Economics* 37(9): 703–16.

Diehl, C. and R. Schnell. 2006. '"Reactive ethnicity" or "assimilation"? Statements, Arguments, and First Empirical Evidence for Labor Migrants in Germany', *International Migration Review* 40(4): 786–816.

Dirk Halm, Patricia Pielage, Ludger Pries, Zeynep Sezgin, and Tulay Tun der-Zengingul. 2012. 'Polish and Turkish Migrant Organizations in Germany'. In *Cross Border Migrant Organizations in Comparative Perspective*, edited by Ludger Pries and Zeynep Sezgin, pp. 37–98. New York: Palgrave Macmillan.

Dubey, Ajay (ed.). 2003. *Indian Diaspora. Global Identity*. New Delhi: Kalinga Publications.

Dumont, A. 2008. 'Representing Voiceless Migrants: Moroccan Political Transnationalism and Moroccan Migrants' Organizations in France', *Ethnic and Racial Studies* 31(4): 792–811.

Espinosa, S.A. 2016. 'Diaspora Philanthropy: The Making of a New Development Aid?', *Migration and Development* 5(3): 361–77.

Faist, Thomas. 2008. 'Trans-State Space and Development: Some Critical Remarks'. In *Rethinking Transnationalism: The Meso-link of Organizations*, edited by Ludger Pries, pp. 63–80. New York: Routledge.

Faist, T., M. Fauser, and E. Reisenauer. 2013. 'Three Transnationals: Transnationalization, Transnational Spaces and Transnationality', *Transnational Migration*, by T. Faist, M. Fauser, and E. Reisenauer, pp. 1–17. Cambridge: Polity Press.

Faist, Thomas and Margit Fauser. 2011. 'The Migration–Development Nexus: Toward a Transnational Perspective'. In *The Migration-Development Nexus: A Transnational Perspective*, edited by Thomas Faist and Margit Fauser, pp. 1–28. Basingtoke: Palgrave Macmillan.

Faist, Thomas, Peter Kivisto, and Margit Fauser (eds). 2011. *The Migration-Development Nexus: A Transnational Perspective*. New York: Palgrave Macmillan.

Fan, V. and S. Anand. 2016. *The Health Workforce in India*. Available at http://www.who.int/hrh/resources/16058health_workforce_India.pdf, accessed on 12 January 2019.

Fauser, Margit. 2012. *Migrants and Cities: The Accommodation of Migrant Organizations in Europe*. London: Ashgate.

Fitzgerald, D. 2008. 'Colonies of the Little Motherland: Membership, Space, and Time in Mexican Migrant Hometown Associations', *Comparative Studies in Society and History* 50(1): 145–69.

Gabriela Tejada, Uttam Bhattacharya, Binod Khadria, and Christiane Kuptsch (eds). 2014. *Indian Skilled Migration and Development: To Europe and Back*. India: Springer.

Galatowitsch, D. 2009. *Co-development in Mali*. ISP collection. Paper 737. Available at http://digitalcollections.sit.edu/isp_collection/737, accessed on 12 January 2019.

Gamlen, Alan. 2011. 'Diasporas'. In *Global Migration Governance*, edited by Alexander Betts, pp. 266–86. Oxford: Oxford University Press.

Ganguly, D. 2003. *Return Migration and Diaspora Investments in the Indian Health Care Industry*. Bangalore: Indian Institute of Management.

Garg, C.C. and A.K. Karan. 2008. 'Reducing Out-of-Pocket Expenditures to Reduce Poverty: A Disaggregated Analysis at Rural-Urban and State Level in India', *Health Policy and Planning* 24(2): 116–28.

Gatrad, A.R., S. Gatrad, and A. Gatrad. 2007. 'Equipment Donation to Developing Countries', *Anaesthesia* 62(1): 90–5.

Ghatak, A. and N. Lalitha. 2018. 'Health in North-Eastern States of India: An Analysis of Economic Vulnerabilities', In *Issues on Health and Healthcare in India*, edited by U.K. De, M. Pal, and P. Bharati, pp. 127–61. Singapore: Springer.

Goldenberg, Suzanne. 1998. 'Boom Time in India as the Millennium Bug Bites', *The Guardian*, 30 December. Available at https://www.theguardian.com/world/1998/dec/30/millennium.uk, accessed on 17 January 2019.

Goldring, Luin. 2004. 'Family and Collective Remittances to Mexico: A Multi-Dimensional Typology', *Development and Change* 35(4): 799–840.

Govindasamy, P. and B.M. Ramesh. 1997. 'Maternal Education and the Utilization of Maternal and Child Health Services in India', *National Family Health Survey Subject Reports*. Available at http://hdl.handle.net/10125/3472, accessed on 12 January 2019.

Gupta, O.P., M.H. Joshi, and S.K. Dave. 1978. 'Prevalence of Diabetes in India', *Advances in Metabolic Disorders* 9: 147–65.

Halm, D. and Z. Sezgin, (eds). 2013. *Migration and Organized Civil Society: Rethinking National Policy*. New York: Routledge.

Halm, Dirk, Patricia Pielage, Ludger Pries, Zeynep Sezgin, and Tülay Tuncer-Zengingül, 2012. 'Polish and Turkish Migrant Organizations in Germany'. In *Cross Border Migrant Organizations in Comparative Perspective* edited by Ludger Pries and Zeynep Sezgin, pp. 37–98. London: Palgrave Macmillan.

Hammer, J., and D. Spears. 2016. 'Village Sanitation and Child Health: Effects and External Validity in a Randomized Field Experiment in Rural India', *Journal of Health Economics* 48(July): 135–48.

Hannan, Kevin. 2004. 'Indian and the Ambivalences of Diaspora Tourism'. In *Tourism, Diasporas and Space*, edited by Tim Coles and Dallen J. Timothy. New York: Routledge.

Hazarika, I., S. Bhattacharyya, and A. Srivastava. 2011. *India: Mobility of Health Professionals*. New Delhi: Public Health Foundation of India.

Hechter, Michael. 1978. 'Group Formation and the Cultural Division of Labor', *American Journal of Sociology* 84(2): 293–318.

Hercog, Metka and Melissa Siegel. 2011. *Engaging the Diaspora in India*. Maastricht: Maastricht Economic and Social Research Institute on Innovation and Technology.

Hermele, K. 1997. 'The Discourse on Migration and Development'. In *International Migration, Immobility and Development*, edited by T. Hammar, G. Brochmann, K. Tamas, and T. Faist, pp. 133–58. New York: Berg.

Hooda, S.K. 2017. 'Out-of-Pocket Payments for Healthcare in India: Who have Affected the Most and Why?' *Journal of Health Management* 19(1): 1–15.

Hooghe, Marc. 2005. 'Ethnic Organisations and Social Movement Theory: The Political Opportunity Structure for Ethnic Mobilisation in Flanders', *Journal of Ethnic and Migration Studies* 31(5): 975–90.

Hunger, Uwe. 2004. 'Indian IT-Entrepreneurs in the U.S. and India: An Illustration of the Brain Gain Hypothesis', *Journal of Comparative Policy-Analysis* 6(2): 99–109.

IDF (International Diabetes Foundation). 2019. IDF Atlas 9th Edition. International Diabetes Foundation. Available at https://www.diabetes-atlas.org/upload/resources/2019/IDF_Atlas_9th_Edition_2019.pdf, accessed on 22 November 2019.

Ireland, Patrick R. 1994. *The Policy Challenge of Ethnic Diversity: Immigrant Politics in France and Switzerland*. Cambridge: Harvard University Press.

Jāhāna, S. 2016. *Human Development Report 2016: Human Development for Everyone*. New York: United Nations Publications.

Jain, Amita. 2018. NEET 2018 Result Statistics, Careers360, 5 June. Available at https://medicine.careers360.com/articles/neet-2018-result-statistics, last accessed on 22 July 2018.

Jain, Prakash C. 2007. *Indian Diaspora in West Asia: A Reader*. New Delhi: Manohar.

Jamuna, D., and L.K. Reddy. 1997. 'The Impact of Age and Length of Widowhood on the Self Concept of Elderly Widows', *Indian J Gerontol*, 7(3–4): 91–5.

John, D., and V. Kumar. 2017. 'Exposure to Hardship Financing for Healthcare among Rural Poor in Chhattisgarh, India', *Journal of Health Management* 19(3): 387–400.

John, T.J. 2010. 'Is India Ready for an Overhaul in Healthcare?', *Economic and Political Weekly* 45(20): 14–17.

Johnson, Paula D. 2007. *Diaspora Philanthropy: Influences, Initiatives and Issues*. Boston: Harvard University.

Joint Monitoring Programme for Water Supply and Sanitation. 2012. *Progress on Drinking Water and Sanitation: 2012 Update*. New York: WHO and UNICEF.

Joseph, N., M. Nelliyanil, S.R. Nayak, V. Agarwal, A. Kumar, H. Yadav, G. Ramuka, et al. 2015. 'Assessment of Morbidity Pattern, Quality of Life and Awareness of Government Facilities among Elderly Population in South India', *Journal of Family Medicine and Primary Care* 4(3): 405.

Kabra, S.G. and R. Narayanan. 1990. 'Sterilisation Camps in India', *Lancet* 335(8683): 224–5.

Kadekar, Laxmi N., Ajaya Kumar Sahoo, and Gauri Bhattacharya. 2009. *The Indian Diaspora: Historical and Contemporary Context*. New Delhi: Rawat Publications.

Kapur, D. 2002. 'The Causes and Consequences of India's IT Boom', *India Review* 1(2): 91–110.

Kapur, Devesh. 2001. 'Diasporas and Technology Transfer', *Journal of Human Development* 2(2): 265–86.

———. 2010. *Diaspora, Development and Democracy: The Domestic Impact of International Migration from India*. Princeton: Princeton University Press.

Kapur, Devesh, Ajay S. Mehta, and R. Moon Dutt. 2004. 'Indian Diaspora Philanthropy'. In *Diaspora Philanthropy and Equitable Development in China and India*, edited by Peter F. Geithner, Paula D. Johnson, and Lincoln C. Chen, pp. 177–213. Massachusetts: Harvard University: Global Equity Initiative Asia Centre.

Karayil, Sajitha B. 2007. 'Does Migration Matter in Trade: A Study of India's Exports to the GCC Countries', *South Asia Economic Journal* 8(1): 1–20.

Ketkar, Suhas L. and Dilip Ratha. 2010. 'Diaspora Bonds: Tapping the Diaspora During Difficult Times', *Journal of International Commerce and Policy* 1(2): 251–63.

Khadria, Binod. 2000. *The Migration of Knowledge Workers: Second-generation Effects of India's Brain Drain*. New Delhi: SAGE.

———. 2004. 'Migration of Highly Skilled Indians: Case Studies of IT and the Health Professionals', *OECD Science, Technology and Industry Working Papers*, 2004/06, OECD Publishing. doi:10.1787/381236020703.

———. 2007. 'India: Skilled Migration to Developed Countries, Labour Migration to the Gulf'. In *Migration and Development: Perspectives from the South*, edited by Castles, Stephen and Raul Delgado Wise, pp. 79–112. Geneva: International Organization for Migration.

———. 2009. 'Bridging the Binaries of Skilled and Unskilled Migration from India', *IMDS Working Paper*, No. 14, International Migration and Diaspora Studies Project, Jawaharlal Nehru University, New Delhi.

———. 2010a. 'The Future of South Asian Migration: A Look at India, Pakistan and Bangladesh', *OECD Journal: General Papers* 2009/4. doi:10.1787/1995283x.

———. 2010b. 'Adversary Analysis and the Quest for Global Development: Optimizing the Dynamic Conflict of Interest in Transnational Migration'. In *Migration, Development and Transnationalization: A Critical Stance, Critical Interventions – A Forum for Social Analysis*, Vol 12, edited by Nina Glick Schiller and Thomas Faist, pp. 176–203. New York: Berghahn Books.

————. 2012. 'Migration of Health Workers and Health of International Migrants: Framework for Bridging Some Knowledge Disjoints between Brain Drain and Brawn Drain', *International Journal of Public Policy* 8(4/5/6): 266–80.

Koopmans, Ruud and Paul Statham. 2000. 'Migration and Ethnic Relations as a Field of Political Contention: An Opportunity Structure Approach'. In *Challenging Immigration and Ethnic Relation Politics: Comparative European Perspectives*, edited by R. Koopmans and P. Statham, pp. 13–56. Oxford: Oxford University Press.

Koopmans, Ruud, Paul Statham, Marco Giugni, and Florence Passy. 2005. *Contested Citizenship: Immigration and Cultural Diversity in Europe*. Minneapolis: University of Minnesota Press.

Kortmann, Matthias and Kerstin Rosenow-Williams. 2013. 'Commonalities and Differences of Islamic Organizations in Europe and the USA. In the United Kingdom and Spain' Practices'. In *Islamic Organizations in Europe and the USA: A Multidisciplinary Perspective*, edited by Matthias Kortmann and Kerstin Rosenow-Williams, pp. 242–52. London: Palgrave Macmillan.

Koshy, Susan and Rajagopalan Radhakrishnan. 2008. *Transnational South Asians: The Making of a Neo-Diaspora*. Oxford: Oxford University Press.

Kulkarni, V.S. 2014. 'Globalization of Remittances in India: Towards a Sociological Perspective'. In *Migrant Remittances in South Asia*, edited by M. Rahman, T. Yong, and A.K.M.A. Ullah, pp. 192–217. London: Palgrave Macmillan.

Kumar, Praveen, Uttam Bhattacharya, and Jayanta Kr. Nayek. 2014. 'Return Migration and Development: Evidence from India's Skilled Professionals'. In *Indian Skilled Migration and Development: To Europe and Back*, edited by Gabriela Tejada, Uttam Bhattacharya, Binod Khadria, and Christine Kuptsch, pp. 263–84. New Delhi: Springer.

Lacroix, Thomas. 2012. 'Indian and Polish Migrant Organizations in the UK'. In *Cross Border Migrant Organizations in Comparative Perspective*, edited by Ludger Pries and Zeynep Sezgin, pp. 152–209. London: Palgrave Macmillan.

Lall, Marie. 2003. 'Mother India's Forgotten Children'. In *International Migration and Sending Countries: Perceptions, Policies and Transnational Relations*, edited by E. Østergaard-Nielsen, pp. 121–39. Houndmills: Palgrave Macmillan.

Lal, Brij V., P. Reeves, and R. Rai. 2007. *The Encyclopedia of the Indian Diaspora*. Hawaii: University of Hawaii Press.

Landolt, P. and L. Goldring. 2010. 'Political Cultures and Transnational Social Fields: Chileans, Colombians and Canadian Activists in Toronto', *Global Networks* 10(4): 443–66.

Laubenthal, B. 2007. 'The Emergence of Pro-regulation Movements in Western Europe', *International Migration* 45(3): 101–33.

Layton-Henry, Zig. 1990. 'Immigrant Associations', In *The Political Rights of Migrant Workers in Western Europe*, edited by Z. Layton-Henry, pp. 94–112. London: SAGE.

Levi, Scott C. 2002. *The Indian Diaspora in Central Asia and Its Trade. 1550–1900.* Boston: Brill.

Levitt, P. 1998. 'Social Remittances: Migration Driven Local-Level Forms of Cultural Diffusion', *International Migration Review* 32(4): 926–48.

Levitt, P. and D. Lamba-Nieves. 2011. 'Social Remittances Revisited', *Journal of Ethnic and Migration Studies* 37(1): 1–22.

Levitt, Peggy and N. Rajaram. 2013. 'Moving Toward Reform? Mobility, Health, and Development in the Context of Neoliberalism', *Migration Studies* 1(3): 338–62.

Mahapatro, S.R., P. Singh, and Y. Singh. 2018. 'How Effective Health Insurance Schemes are in Tackling Economic Burden of Healthcare in India', *Clinical Epidemiology and Global Health* 6(2): 75–82.

Mercer, Claire, Ben Page, and Martin Evans. 2009. 'Unsettling Connections: Transnational Networks, Development and African Home Associations', *Global Networks* 9(2): 141–61.

Merz Barbara, Lincoln C. Chen, and Peter F. Geithner (eds). 2007. *Diasporas and Development.* Cambridge: Harvard University Press.

Ministry of Finance. 2018. 'Chapter 10: Social Infrastructure, Employment and Human Development', *Economic Survey 2017–18*. New Delhi: Government of India. Available at http://mofapp.nic.in:8080/economicsurvey/pdf/167-185_Chapter_10_Economic_Survey_2017-18.pdf, accessed on 31 July 2018.

Mishra, A., R.M. Pandey, J.R. Devi, R. Sharma, N.K. Vikram, and N. Khanna. 2001. 'High Prevalence of Diabetes, Obesity and Dyslipidaemia in Urban Slum Population in Northern India'. *International Journal of Obesity* 25(11): 1722.

MOIA (Ministry of Overseas Indian Affairs). 2015. *Annual Report 2014–15*. Available at https://www.mea.gov.in/images/pdf/annual-report-2014-15.pdf, accessed on 5 October 2019.

MOSPI (Ministry of Statistics and Programme Implementation). 2016. *Elderly in India*. New Delhi: Government of India. Available at http://mospi.nic.in/sites/default/files/publication_reports/ElderlyinIndia_2016.pdf, accessed on 12 January 2019.

Moya, Jose C. 2005. 'Immigrants and Associations: A Global and Historical Perspective', *Journal of Ethnic and Migration Studies* 31(5): 833–64.

Mukhopadhyay, I., S. Sharma, P. Datta, and S. Selvaraj. 2015. 'Changing Landscape of Private Healthcare Providers in India: Implications for National Level Health Policy' Paper presented at International Conference of Public Policy, Milan, Italy, 1–4 July.

Najam, Adil. 2007. 'Diaspora Philanthropy to Asia'. In *Diasporas and Development: Global Equity Initiative*, edited by B.J. Merz, L.C. Chen, and P.F. Geithner, pp. 119–51. Cambridge: Harvard University Press.

Nayyar, Deepak. 1994. *Migration, Remittances and Capital Flows: The Indian Experience*. Delhi: Oxford University Press.

Newland, Kathleen (ed.). 2010. *Diasporas: New Partners in Global Development Policy*. Washington, DC: Migration Policy Institute.

Newland, Kathleen and Hiroyuki Tanaka. 2010. *Mobilizing Diaspora Entrepreneurship for Development*. Washington, DC: Migration Policy Institute.

Newland, Kathleen, Aaron Terrazas, and Roberto Munster. 2010. *Diaspora Philanthropy: Private Giving and Public Policy*. Washington, DC: Migration Policy Institute.

NSSO (National Sample Survey Organization). 2004. *Health and Morbidity: Schedule No. 25.0*. New Delhi: Ministry of Statistics and Programme Implementation, Government of India.

O'Doherty, D., M. Dromey, J. Lougheed, A. Hannigan, J. Last, and D. McGrath. 2018. 'Barriers and Solutions to Online Learning in Medical Education–An Integrative Review', *BMC Medical Education* 18(1): 130.

Olzak, S. and E. West. 1991. 'Ethnic Conflict and the Rise and Fall of Ethnic Newspapers', *American Sociological Review* 56(4): 458–74.

Omelaniuk, I. 2016. 'The Global Forum on Migration and Development and Diaspora Engagement'. In *Diasporas, Development and Governance*, edited by A. Chikanda, J. Crush, and M. Walton-Roberts, pp. 19–32. Switzerland: Springer.

Osella, F. 2018. 'Charity and Philanthropy in South Asia: An Introduction', *Modern Asian Studies* 52(1): 4–34.

Osella, Filippo and Katy Gardner (eds). 2003. *Migration, Modernity and Social Transformation in South Asia*. New Delhi: SAGE.

Østergaard-Nielsen, E. (ed.). 2003. *International Migration and Sending Countries: Perceptions, Policies and Transnational Relations*. New York: Springer.

Outreville, J.F. 2007. 'Foreign Direct Investment in the Health Care Sector and Most-Favoured Locations in Developing Countries', *The European Journal of Health Economics* 8(4): 305–12.

Panchapakesan Padma, Prakash Sai Lokachari, and Rajendran Chandrasekharan. 2014. 'Strategic Action Grids: A Study in Indian Hospitals', *International Journal of Health Care Quality Assurance* 27(5): 360–72. doi:10.1108/IJHCQA-11-2012-0108.

Pandey, A., A. Aggarwal, R. Devane, and Y. Kuznetsov. 2004. *India's Transformation to Knowledge-Based Economy–Evolving Role of the Indian Diaspora*. Washington, DC: World Bank.

Pandey, Abhishek, Alok Aggarwal, Richard Devane, and Yevgeny Kuznetsov. 2006. 'The Indian Diaspora: A Unique Case?'. In *Diaspora Networks and the International Migration of Skills: How Countries can draw on Their Talent Abroad*, edited by Yevgeny Kuznetsov, pp. 73–97. Washington, DC: The World Bank.

Papademetriou, D.G. and P.L. Martin (eds). 1991. *The Unsettled Relationship: Labor Migration and Economic Development* (No. 33). New York: Greenwood Publishing Group.

Paralikar, S. and C. Shah. 2015. 'Medical Education Faculty Perceptions of the Strengths, Weaknesses and Future Prospects of the Current Medical Undergraduate Experimental Physiology Curriculum in Gujarat, India', *Indian J Physiol Pharmacol* 59(1): 109–16.

Parekh, Bhiku, Gurharpal Singh, and Steven Vertovec. 2003. *Culture and Economy in the Indian Diaspora*. New York: Routledge.

Park, R.E. and H.A. Miller. 1921. *Old World Traits Transplanted*. New York: Harper.

Perry, L. and R. Malkin. 2011. 'Effectiveness of Medical Equipment Donations to Improve Health Systems: How Much Medical Equipment is Broken in the Developing World?', *Medical and Biological Engineering and Computing* 49(7): 719–22.

Piper, Nicola. 2009. 'Temporary Migration and Political Remittances: The Role of Organizational Networks in the Transnationalisation of Human Rights', *European Journal of East Asian Studies* 8(2): 215–43.

Pirkkalainen, Paivi, Petra Mezzetti, and Matteo Guglielmo. 2013. 'Somali Associations' Trajectories in Italy and in Finland: Leaders Building Trust and Finding Legitimisation', *Journal of Ethnic and Migration Studies* 39(8): 1261–79.

Portes, A. and M. Zhou. 2011. 'The Eagle and the Dragon: Immigrant Transnationalism and Development in Mexico and China'. Working Paper 1387, Princeton University, Woodrow Wilson School of Public and International Affairs, Center for Migration and Development, Princeton, New Jersey.

———. 2012. 'Transnationalism and Development: Mexican and Chinese Immigrant Organizations in the United States', *Population and Development Review* 38(2):191–220.

Portes, Alejandro, Christina Escobar, and Alexandria Walton Radford. 2007. 'Immigrant Transnational Organizations and Development: A Comparative Study', *International Migration Review* 41(1): 242–81.

Portes, Alejandro, Cristina Escobar, and Renelinda Arana. 2008. 'Bridging the Gap: Transnational and Ethnic Organizations in Political Incorporation of Immigrants in the United States', *Ethnic and Racial Studies* 31(6): 1025–90.

Pratham. 2018. *Annual Status of Education Report (Rural) 2017.* http://img. asercentre.org/docs/Publications/ASER%20Reports/ASER%202017/ aser2017fullreportfinal.pdf, accessed on 17 August 2018.

Pries, Ludger. 2008a. 'European Works Councils as Transnational Interest Organizations?', In *Rethinking Transnationalism: The Meso-link of organizations*, edited by Ludger Pries, pp. 154–74. New York: Routledge.

———. 2008b. 'Transnational Societal Spaces: Which Units of Analysis, Reference, and Measurement?', In *Rethinking Transnationalism: The Meso-link of organizations*, edited by Ludger Pries, pp. 1–20. New York: Routledge.

Pries, L. and Z. Sezgin. 2010. *Beyond 'Identity or Integration': Cross-Border Migrant Organizations.* Wiesbaden: Springer.

———. 2012a. 'Migration, Organizations and Transnational Ties'. In *Cross Border Migrant Organizations in Comparative Perspective*, edited by Ludger Pries and Zeynep Sezgin, pp. 1–36. London: Palgrave Macmillan.

———. 2012b. *Cross Border Migrant Organizations in Comparative Perspective.* New York: Palgrave Macmillan.

Putnam, R.D. 1995. 'Tuning in, Tuning Out: The Strange Disappearance of Social Capital in America', *PS: Political Science & Politics* 28(4): 664–83.

Raghuram, Parvati, Ajaya Kumar Sahoo, Brij Maharaj, and Dave Sangha. 2008. *Tracing an Indian Diaspora.* New Delhi: SAGE.

Rahman, M.M. and T.T. Yong (eds). 2015. *International Migration and Development in South Asia.* New York: Routledge.

Rahman, M.M., T.T. Yong, and A.A. Ullah. 2014. 'Migrant Remittances in South Asia: An Introduction'. In *Migrant Remittances in South Asia: Social, Economic and Political Implications*, edited by M.M. Rahman, T.T. Yong, and A.A. Ullah, pp. 1–30. Palgrave Macmillan, London.

Rai, Rajesh and Peter Reeves. 2009. 'Introduction'. In *The South Asian Diaspora Transnational Netwroks and Changing Identities*, edited by Rajesh Rai and Peter Reeves, pp. 1–11. New York: Routledge.

Rai, Rajesh. 2014. *Indians in Singapore 1819–1945: Diaspora in the Colonial Port-City.* New Delhi: Oxford University Press.

Raina, S., R. Kumar, D. Kumar, R. Chauhan, S. Raina, V. Chander, R. Gupta, et al. 2018. 'Game Change in Indian Health Care System through Reforms in Medical Education Curriculum Focusing on Primary Care— Recommendations of a Joint Working Group', *Journal of Family Medicine & Primary Care* 7(3):489–94. doi:10.4103/jfmpc.jfmpc_92_18.

Rajan, S.I. (ed.). 2012. *India Migration Report 2011: Migration, Identity and Conflict*. New Delhi: Routledge.

———. 2013. *Internal Migration and Youth in India: Main Features, Trends, and Emerging Challenges*. London: United Nations Educational, Scientific and Cultural Organization.

———. 2015. *India Migration Report 2014: Diaspora and Development*. New Delhi: Routledge.

———. 2016. 'Politics of Conflict and Migration'. In *India Migrations Reader*, edited by S.I. Rajan, pp. 151–7. New Delhi: Routledge.

Rajan, S.I. and S.K. Kumar. 2015. *Emigration in 21st-century India: Governance, Legislation, Institutions*. New Delhi: Routledge.

Rana, P. and J. Sugden. 2013. 'India's Record since Independence', *The Wall Street Journal*, 15 August. Available at https://blogs.wsj.com/indiarealtime/2013/08/15/indias-record-since-independence/, accessed on 31 July 2018.

Rex John, Daniele Joly, and Czarina Wilpert (eds). 1987. *Immigrant Associations in Europe*. Hants: Gower Publishing.

Rex, John and Robert Moore. 1967. *Race, Community, and Conflict: A Study of Sperkbrook*. Oxford: Oxford University Press.

Roberts, Margaret W. 2009. 'Diaspora Philanthropy in Punjab's Health Sector: A Transnational Perspective'. In *Sikh Diaspora Philanthropy in Punjab Global Giving for Local Good* (1st ed.), edited by V.A Dusenbery. and D.S. Tatla, pp. 184–204. New Delhi: Oxford University Press.

Rose-Ackerman, S. 1997. *The Political Economy of Corruption, 'Corruption and the Global Economy'*, edited by Elliott K.A. Washington, DC: Institute for International Economics.

Safran, William. 1991. 'Diasporas in Modern Societies: Myths of Homeland and Return', *Diaspora* 1(1): 83–99.

Sahoo, Ajaya Kumar, Micheal Baas, and Thomas Faist. 2012. *Indian Diaspora and Transnationalism*. New Delhi: Rawat Publications.

Sahoo, Sadananda and B.K. Pattanaik (eds). 2014. *Global Diasporas and Development: Socioeconomic, Cultural, and Policy Perspectives*. New Delhi: Springer.

Salamon, L.M. 1987. 'Of Market Failure, Voluntary Failure, and Third-Party Government: Toward a Theory of Government-Nonprofit Relations in the Modern Welfare State', *Journal of Voluntary Action Research* 16(1–2): 29–49.

———. 1995. *Partners in Public Service: Government-Nonprofit Relations in the Modern Welfare State*. Maryland: JHU Press.

Salamon, L.M. and H.K. Anheier. 1992. 'In Search of the Non-Profit Sector. I: The Question of Definitions', *Voluntas: International Journal of Voluntary and Nonprofit Organizations* 3(2): 125–51.

Sandhu, K.S. 1969. *Indians in Malaya*. New Delhi: Cambridge University Press.

Santilli, J. and F.R. Vogenberg. 2015. 'Key Strategic Trends that Impact Healthcare Decision-Making and Stakeholder Roles in the New Marketplace', *American Health & Drug Benefits* 8(1): 15–20.

Saxenian, Anna Lee. 2005. 'From Brain Drain to Brain Circulation: Transnational Communities and Regional Upgrading in India and China', *Studies in Comparative International Development* 40: 35–61.

Schervish, P.G. 2005. 'Major Donors, Major Motives: The People and Purposes behind Major Gifts', *New Directions for Philanthropic Fundraising* 2005(47): 59–87.

Schrover, Marlou and Floris Vermeulen. 2005. 'Immigrant Organizations', *Journal of Ethnic and Migration Studies* 31: 823–32.

Sen, A. 1999a. *Development as Freedom*. New Delhi: Oxford University Press.

———. 1999b. *Health in Development. Bulletin of the World Health Organization* 77(8): 619. Available at http://www.who.int/bulletin/archives/77(8)619. pdf, accessed on 31 July 2018.

Seybolt, T.B. 2007. *Humanitarian Military Intervention: The Conditions for Success and Failure*. Oxford: SIPRI.

Sezgin, Z. and D. Dijkzeul. 2014. 'Migrant Organisations in Humanitarian Action', *Journal of International Migration and Integration* 15(2): 159–77.

Sezgin, Zeynep. 2008. 'Turkish Migrants' Organizations: Promoting Tolerance towards the Diversity of Turkish Migrants in Germany', *International Journal of Sociology* 38(2): 80–97.

Sidel, Mark. 2004. 'Diaspora Philanthropy to India: A Perspective from the United States', In *Diaspora Philanthropy and Equitable Development in China and India*, edited by Peter F. Geithner, Paula D. Johnson, and Lincoln C. Chen, pp. 215–48. Massachusetts: Harvard University, Global Equity Initiative Asia Centre.

Sidel, Mark. 2007. 'Focusing on the State: Government Responses to Diaspora Giving and Implications for Equity'. In *Diasporas and Development*, edited by Barbara Merz, Lincoln C. Chen, and Peter F. Geithner, pp. 25–54. Cambridge: Harvard University Press.

Singh, A.J., P. Garner, and K. Floyd. 2000. 'Cost-Effectiveness of Public-Funded Options for Cataract Surgery in Mysore, India', *The Lancet* 355(9199): 180–4.

Singh, G. and S. Singh. 2007. 'Diaspora Philanthropy in Action: An Evaluation of Modernization in Punjab Villages', *JPS* 14(2): 226.

Singh, Jaspal K. and Rajendra Chetty. 2010. *Indian Writers: Transnationalisms and Diasporas*. New York: Peter Lang.

Singh, Supriya. 2013. *Globalization and Money: A Global South Perspective*, London: Rowman and Littlefield.

Singh, Supriya. 2016. *Money, Migration and Family: India to Australia*, New York: Palgrave Macmillan.

Sökefeld, M. 2008. *Struggling for Recognition: The Alevi Movement in Germany and in Transnational Space*. New York: Berghahn Books.

Soni, J.D. and S.D. Soni. 2006. The Strategic Framework for Engaging India with Indian Diaspora. In *Sociological Perspectives on Globalisation*, edited by Ajaya K. Sahoo, pp. 271–84. Delhi: Kalpaz.

Stark, Oded. 1991. *The Migration of Labour*. Cambridge, UK: Basil Blackwell.

Stoddard, A. 2002. *Trends in US Humanitarian Policy*. London: Overseas Development Institute.

Supe, A. and W.P. Burdick. 2006. 'Challenges and Issues in Medical Education in India', *Academic Medicine* 81(12): 1076–80.

Tan, Tai Yong, and Md. Mizanur Rahman. 2013. *Diaspora Engagement and Development in South Asia*. New York: Palgrave Macmillan.

Tavecchi, G. and A. Rebecchi. 2018. 'The Current Indian Healthcare System and West Bengal's Health Status'. In *Healthcare Facilities in Emerging Countries*, edited by S. Capolongo, M. Gola, and A. Rebecchi, pp. 13–31. New Delhi: Springer.

Tejada, Gabriela, Uttam Bhattacharya, Binod Khadria, and Christiane Kuptsch. 2014. *Indian Skilled Migration and Development: To Europe and Back*. New Delhi: Springer.

Tejada, G., M. Hercog, C. Kuptsch, and J.C. Bolay. 2014. 'The Link with a Home Country'. In *Global Diasporas and Development: Socioeconomic, Cultural, and Policy Perspectives*, edited by S. Sahoo and B.K. Pattanaik, pp. 39–68. New Delhi: Springer.

Terrazas, Aaron. 2010. *Diaspora Investment in Developing and Emerging Country Capital Markets: Patterns and Prospects*. Washington, DC: Migration Policy Institute.

Thomas, K., S.P. Thyagarajan, L. Jeyaseelan, J.C. Varghese, P. Krishnamurthy, L.A. Bai, S.U. Hira, et al. 2002. 'Community Prevalence of Sexually Trasmitted Diseases and Human Immunodeficiency Virus Infection in Tamil Nadu, India: A Probability Proportional to Size Cluster Survey', *National Medical Journal of India* 15(3): 135–9.

The Times of India. 2003. 'UP-born NRI Doctors Moot Health Schemes', 23 December. Available at https://timesofindia.indiatimes.com/UP-born-NRI-doctors-moot-health-schemes/articleshow/376151.cms, accessed on 17 August 2018.

van der Veer, Peter. 1995. *Nation and Migration: The Politics of Space in the South Asian Diaspora*. Philadelphia: The University of Pennsylvania Press.

Vermeulen, G. 2007. 'Mutual Instrumentalisation of Criminal and Migration Law from an EU Perspective', *European Journal of Migration and Law* 9(3): 347.

Walton-Roberts, M., V. Runnels, S.I. Rajan, A. Sood, S. Nair, P. Thomas, C. Packer, et al. 2017. 'Causes, Consequences, and Policy Responses to the Migration of Health Workers: Key Findings from India', *Human Resources for Health* 15(1): 28.

Weisbrod, B.A. 1988. *Nonprofit Economy*, Massachusetts: Harvard University Press.

Wilson, J. 2000. 'Volunteering', *Annual Review of Sociology* 26(1): 215–40.

World Bank. 2019. 'Migration and Remittances: Recent Developments and Outlook: Transit Migration'. *Migration and Development Brief 31*. Washington, DC: World Bank, April.

World Bank. n.d. Education Expenditure, Education Statistics. Available at http://datatopics.worldbank.org/education/wDashboard/dqexpenditures, accessed on 18 June 2019.

WHO (World Health Organization). 2001. *Mental Health: New Understanding, New Hope*. Geneva: World Health Report, WHO.

———. 2011. *Medical Device Donations: Considerations for Solicitation and Provision*. Available at http://apps.who.int/iris/bitstream/handle/10665/44568/?sequence=1, accessed on 12 January 2019.

———. 2014. 'Global Status Report on Noncommunicable Diseases 2014', Report No. WHO/NMH/NVI/15.1. Geneva: WHO.

———. n.d. Tuberculosis Profile: India. World Health Organization. Available at https://extranet.who.int/sree/Reports?op=Replet&name=%2FWHO_HQ_Reports%2FG2%2FPROD%2FEXT%2FTBCountryProfile&ISO2=IN&LAN=EN&outtype=html, accessed on 22 November 2019.

Zachariah, K.C., J. Conde, and N. Nair. 1980. *Demographic Aspects of Migration in West Africa*. Washington DC: The World Bank.

Zachariah, K.C., E.T. Mathew, and S.I. Rajan. 2001. 'Social, Economic and Demographic Consequences of Migration on Kerala', *International Migration* 39(2): 43–71.

Zachariah, K.C., S.I. Rajan, and J. Jolin. 2014. 'Kerala Emigration to Saudi Arabia: Prospects Under the Nitaqat Law'. In *India Migration Report 2014: Diaspora and Development*, edited by S.I. Rajan, pp. 229–48. New Delhi: Routledge.

Zhou, Min and Rennie Lee. 2012. 'Traversing Ancestral and New Homelands: Chinese Immigrant Transnational Organizations in the United States'. In *Development at a Distance: The Role of Immigrant Organizations in the Development of Sending Nations*, edited by Alejandro Portes, pp. 27–50. New York: Russell Sage Foundation.

Zweig, D. 2006. 'Competing for Talent: China's Strategies to Reverse The Brain Drain', *International Labour Review* 145(1–2): 65–90.

Index

About the Authors

Md Mizanur Rahman

Md Mizanur Rahman is an associate professor at the Gulf Studies Center, College of Arts and Sciences, Qatar University, Qatar. Rahman's research interests include international migration of labor, South Asian diaspora, migrant remittances, immigrant businesses, migration and development, and migration policy. His research sites embrace countries in the Persian Gulf, Southeast and South Asia. His research articles have appeared in leading migration journals such as *International Migration, Journal of International Migration and Integration, Population, Space and Place, Journal of Ethnic and Migration Studies, Asian and Pacific Migration Journal, Canadian Journal of Development Studies,* and *Asian Population Studies.* He is editor of the Gulf Studies Book Series, Springer Nature.

Rakesh Ranjan

Rakesh Ranjan is an assistant professor at the Centre for Development Practice and Research, Tata Institute of Social Sciences (TISS), Patna, India. He is also an assistant editor of *Journal of Migration Affairs,* the organizational journal of the TISS Patna centre. Ranjan was a researcher at the India Centre for Migration, Ministry of External Affairs,

Government of India. His research interests include labour migration and development, migrant remittance, philanthropy, migration policy and immigrant entrepreneurship. His PhD dissertation examines Indian migrant entrepreneurs in Malaysia. He is currently working on Labour Migration from Bihar to Gulf Cooperation Council Countries.